C000173130

LONDON BUSES BEFORE THE WAR

First published 1995

ISBN 185414 182 1

Published by Capital Transport Publishing
38 Long Elmes, Harrow Weald, Middlesex

Printed by Bath Midway Press
Holt, Wiltshire

LONDON BUSES BEFORE THE WAR

Ken Glazier

Capital Transport

AUTHOR'S NOTE

This book continues the story of London's buses, trams and trolleybuses in the 1930s which was started in 'The Last Years of the General' and covers the first six years of Herbert Morrison's bold experiment with common ownership and management of London's transport. Outside London, too, the bus industry was being reformed radically, under the influence of Morrison's 1930 Road Traffic Act. By the autumn of 1939 the transformation was complete. The new LPTB had just finished the major part of its own fleet renewal and was taking a breather before launching on an entirely new phase, using the revolutionary RT; and the north London tram to trolleybus conversion scheme was all but complete. At this point the Second World War put a stop to any further development and the Board was never able to continue the work it had started, as it lost its independence for good when taken over by the government for the duration of the war.

Whatever one may think of the statutory changes which so changed the transport scene, they had some fascinating effects and it is without doubt an exciting period during which London grew rapidly and many wonderful new things were done. Despite this, the history of these years has not been covered previously in any great detail, with the one exception of Ken Blacker's comprehensive study of the STL. I have tried to repair the deficiency but no single volume can hope to cover everything in complete detail and I have therefore had to be selective, particularly in the chapters on service and general developments, where individual case histories of typical individual events must stand proxy for the rest, which are dealt with in summary.

Many of the decisions made and actions taken during these years were the basis of the London Transport fleet and operations which were an established fact when I began to be aware of the subject as a child, and it has therefore given me great personal pleasure to delve deeply into my own bit of pre-history. It has also been a poignant experience. Even as I was writing about these important public events and achievements, the organisation established by those two great men Lord Ashfield and Frank Pick was in the process of being dismantled, with the promise of deregulation to come and a return to a situation of free-for-all which had probably not existed in London since the middle of the nineteenth century, apart from those hectic years between 1922 and 1924. If I have done my job properly, the reader should be able to judge which of the two approaches has produced the best results.

Once again I must thank the same loyal band who had already given me so much help with the General book: B J Cross, Dr Andrew Gilks, Ken Blacker, Hugh Taylor, David Ruddom, Reg Westgate, Malcolm Papes, Brian Bunker, John Gent, George Robbins, the late Dick Turnbull, and Martin Elms. In addition, I am equally grateful to Alan Nightingale who has supplied much valuable material which throws considerable light on the background to many of the LPTB's decisions and also many rare photographs. Without the help of all these friends, this book would have been a much impoverished document.

London, May 1995 KEN GLAZIER

Facing page
Like many non-standard and open-top buses taken over from Independents, Charles H. Pickup's Dodson bodied Guy FCX, although only five years old, was withdrawn almost as soon as it was taken into stock. *D W K Jones*

CONTENTS

CHAPTER ONE THE BOARD TAKES CONTROL

At midnight on 1st July 1933 most of the buses and all of the trams and trolleybuses operating within the London Traffic Area and a sizeable proportion of those operating in the Home Counties passed into the ownership of the London Passenger Transport Board, many while still out on the road in service. The LPT Act which enabled this was a bulky piece of legislation running to 109 Sections and sixteen Schedules.

On vesting day, the Board assumed immediate ownership of all the operational companies owned by the Underground Electric Railway Company and thereby took control of the London General Omnibus Company and all its subsidiaries and associates: London General Country Services, Green Line Coaches, Acme Pullman Services, Bucks Expresses (Watford), Skylark Motor Coach Company, Overground, Tramways (MET) Omnibus Company, Watford Omnibus Company and the London operations of Tilling and BAT. The three 'Combine' tramways of the London and Suburban Traction Company were joined by all the municipal tramway undertakings, so that the Board was responsible for all trams and the small Kingston area trolleybus network from day one. The fifty-one London area Independents were named for takeover in Part V of the Act's Second Schedule and the London business of Thomas Tilling in Part IV but in their case the terms had to be negotiated and there was provision for arbitration, so none of these changed hands on vesting day but continued to operate as separate entities. Also named in Part V were Amersham & District, whose final acquisition by the LGOC had come too late to influence the wording of the Act and the three 'fringe' companies: Filkins and Ainsworth, Charles Russett & Son (St Albans & District) and F. Steer (The Colne Service). The non-operational businesses, such as the electrical generation side of South Met, the North Met Power Company and the Associated Equipment Company were specifically excluded from takeover and therefore started a separate and independent existence.

Outside the old London Traffic Area, the only companies specifically named, other than General associates, were (in the Eighth Schedule): Maidstone & District, who were required to hand over certain services in the Dartford and Gravesend area and the garages at Dartford and Northfleet; Aldershot and District, services in the Guildford area and the garage at Ewhurst; Eastern National, services in Grays; Redcar, the Tonbridge to Sevenoaks service; and Thames Valley, the Staines to Windsor route. By virtue of its special relationship with the Metropolitan Railway, the Lewis Omnibus Company had Part VI of the Second Schedule all to itself. So far as other operators in the monopoly area were concerned, Section 16 of the Act required them to seek consent from the Board and if consent was refused, the Board was required to negotiate terms for taking over the company. An arbitration procedure was laid down for any cases which were in dispute. The 'appointed day' for the completion of these procedures was set by the Act as 1st January 1934 and the deadline for applications was 1st October 1933.

Section 16, which established the new undertaking's monopoly powers, was perhaps the most important part of the Act, as it was to play a central rôle in the Board's activities for as long as it existed and in those of its successors right up to 1969. It laid down that no operator could run a bus service within the Board's special area without its express permission. It did not say that the Board should be the only operator but as things turned out, this was the way in which the Board and more particularly Frank Pick, generally chose to operate its powers. The only operators who did succeed in getting consent were those whose services were likely to be a serious drain on the Board's resources, either because they were exceptionally unremunerative, or because London Transport would find them uneconomically expensive to operate. The Board itself was not empowered to operate outside its defined area, except for limited 'outrunning' of half-a-mile (one mile in Berkshire) to reach nearby objectives. For private hire there was provision for them to run up to ten miles beyond the boundary but even this was reduced to five miles in Kent. No doubt these restrictions encouraged the regime at 55 Broadway to be particularly careful of its position within the area but it must be said that this protective (some might say 'dog-in-the-manger') attitude had some damaging results, particularly on the fringes.

Above **Congestion caused by road works was already a hazard in September 1933 as the new LPTB got to grips with its new job. All the buses in this scene originated with the LGOC, three of them LTs and three NSs.** John Aldridge collection

Facing page **LT 1427 in the new Country Bus Green and black colour scheme and carrying the fleetname 'GENERAL' initially adopted by the Board for all buses, at Wotton Hatch on the 425, a frequent route which linked a series of equally picturesque villages along the Tilling Bourne valley.** J B Gent collection

The decision to run the boundary through so many towns created route planning problems which were perhaps foreseen by Herbert Morrison whose original ideas would have avoided much of the splitting up of through services. The modified area and more restricted operating powers which emerged from the negotiations with the provincial companies prevented the Board from entering into cross-boundary joint running agreements and sharing the traffic inside its area in exchange for some outside. As the Board was required to earn enough revenue to cover its costs, it was left with little alternative but to fight for every penny's worth of business and therefore held on to the sections of through routes within its area at the expense of creating some absurd breaks. This was to be particularly damaging in Grays and Tilbury where direct bus services from home to work for many people disappeared and in Hertfordshire, where Buntingford became an unlikely southern terminus for Eastern National. Section 18 of the Act did allow the Board to enter into agreements with local authorities or other bus operators for the through running of stage services, under the same restrictions as applied to Private Hire but this seems to have been used as sparingly as possible. There was such an agreement with the Thames Valley company, allowing London Transport access to Slough Trading Estate and into the western area of High Wycombe, in exchange for the mileage operated by Ledbury Transport on the Reading – London service but there were no others of significance, perhaps because the ten mile limit put useful places out of bounds.

The Board started its life with a road services fleet of already impressive size, comprising 4,104 double-deck and 977 single-deck motor buses and coaches, 2,615 double-deck and 15 single-deck tramcars and sixty-one trolleybuses. A full breakdown is given in the appendices. To support these operations, the Board also took immediate possession of seventy-eight bus garages (twenty-six in the Country Area), and thirty-five tram depôts. Three of the garages were those from which Tilling's services were operated but which had been owned by the LGOC. LGOC's Chiswick Bus Overhaul Works, the Central Repair Depôt of the LCC at Charlton and the LCC's ticket printing works in Effra Road Brixton all passed to the Board along with the offices of the constituent companies, including the many local offices of the larger operators. There were also three closed garages at East Ham (the Invicta and Atlas premises) and Slough, Langley Road.

The Managing Director was Frank Pick. He and Ashfield were to stamp their personalities on the new undertaking with such force that the momentum was to continue long after they were both dead and gone. Pick in particular kept a firm grip on almost every aspect of the business and exercised a remarkable degree of central control through a series of committees covering every conceivable activity. The two of particular interest here were his Traffic Committee, which decided or endorsed all service changes, and his Engineering Committee, through which he directed the design, development and purchasing policy of the vehicle fleets. Some such control was probably made inevitable by the requirements of the Revenue Pool which made it necessary for almost every decision relating to expenditure, or which might affect the income of the undertaking, to be weighed against its effect on the Pool. Even so, it seems likely that Pick's natural disposition to keep his hands on every lever of power was the main driving force toward such extreme centralisation.

Operationally, the road services of the Board were put under the control of three departments. Central Omnibuses, with its headquarters at 55 Broadway, took control of the LGOC and associated services within the Metropolitan Police District and operated wholly within the Special Area. Country Omnibuses and Coaches, based at Bell Street Reigate, were intended to run local services outside the Metropolitan Police District and took responsibility for services operated by LGCS and Green Line Coaches Ltd. The Tram and Trolleybus department continued to be run for the time being from the old LCC offices in Belvedere Road. Not surprisingly the management of Central and Country Buses was unchanged from company days, the respective Operating Managers being A.W.C. Richardson and A.H. Hawkins. Equally unsurprising was the appointment of T.E. Thomas, the London County Council's Tramway Manager as the new Operating Manager for the Tramways department. It was as though the 'auld alliance' between the Underground Group and County Hall had been resurrected and was now set to eliminate all trace of the smaller fry in the London transport field, just as those minnows had feared.

The change to the new set-up took place smoothly and imperceptibly. Most travellers could have journeyed on 1st July without realising that anything had happened. The Independent buses were still there, in their varied liveries; the green solid-tyred British NSs were still trundling along route 24; south-east London was still heavily populated by buses loudly proclaiming their Thomas Tilling ownership; most LGCS buses looked the same, although a few recent overhauls had come out in a new green livery and carried the name 'GENERAL'; and the only hint that there had been any change on the municipal trams was that recent repaints lacked their coats of arms.

The exceptions were the users of coach services from Gravesend and Newmarket and of some cross-boundary bus services, where changes were made at short notice. At Gravesend the coach services operated by

Maidstone & District lost their local carriage rights and were re-routed via Watling Street. Their nearest picking-up point to the town was now at Tollgate and passengers were expected to make their way there by the Board's local services to Northumberland Bottom. Return tickets issued by the company before 15th June, when issue had ceased, were honoured on the Green Line routes, newly extended from Dartford, until 31st July.

The Newmarket changes were particularly damaging. The Acme coach service had to be curtailed at Bishops Stortford without ceremony because the Board had no powers to operate on the Newmarket Road and Varsity

Above **On the morning of 1st July, all trams and many buses appeared with new legal owner labels reading either 'LONDON PASSENGER TRANSPORT BOARD 55, BROADWAY, WESTMINSTER S.W.1.', or 'LONDON PASSENGER TRANSPORT BOARD, BELL STREET, REIGATE' and all had been so treated by 4th July. Two days after the LPTB took control, a former LGCS NS at Hatfield displays the Country Bus version of the new 'legal owner' panel with the Bell Street address.** D W K Jones

Left **A former British NS still operating from its old base at Rochester Mews, Camden Town, loudly proclaims its old status while it lays over at the 'William IV' Pimlico, twenty-three days after the takeover. Camden Town garage (AQ) closed on 1st October, on expiry of the lease, and its operations were transferred into Chalk Farm.** D W K Jones

Still in Maidstone & District colours and bearing its old fleet number, KP3057 has a new LPTB 'legal owner' label on the front skirt panel. This Short Bros bodied TD1, which was new in 1929, eventually became TD 148. J F Higham

Green Line route A was extended from Dartford to Denton on 1st July 1933, replacing the Maidstone & District service. KR6303 has been labelled for Green Line service but still has its old M&D fleet number just behind the sidelamp and is in Staines, far from its old territory. This thirty-one seat 1930 Short Bros bodied Leyland Tiger TS2 later became TR 13. J F Higham

Express's application for a licence to fill the gap had still not been granted by 30th June. The road was covered temporarily at virtually no notice and with questionable legality, by Eastern National running to the Acme times.

The LGCS routes and express services which went outside the Board's area were handed over to other companies. Route 405 (West Croydon – Handcross) was split at Crawley and the outer section taken over by Southdown, who extended route 23 to forge a Brighton – Crawley link. They also took the Uckfield end of the 409. In this case the Act provided powers for the Board to run out to Forest Row and an overlap was provided from East Grinstead by Southdown's new route 92 to Eastbourne. Route 24, which had been a joint Autocar/East Surrey operation, lost its East Grinstead – Hartfield – Tunbridge Wells section and the foreshortened Reigate – East Grinstead route was renumbered 424. The rest of the 24 and all but a small part of Autocar's network, went to Maidstone & District. The exception was the Tonbridge to Sevenoaks section, which became route 402A.

In the north-east, the two prongs of route 31 (Hertford to Royston) were split at Puckeridge and Buntingford and the outer ends went to Eastern National whose own route 2 (Epping – Chelmsford) was split at Ongar, the Board taking over the Epping end. Other route splitting resulted from the handover of Maidstone & District routes in the Gravesend and Dartford area to the Board. The Faversham to Dartford service was curtailed at Gravesend; the through route from Maidstone to Farningham was split at Wrotham, the Board supplying a replacement shuttle numbered 485; and the through Meopham – Cobham – Strood service disappeared. The latter provoked some complaints and London Transport offered to run a service on behalf of M&D but this did not materialise.

LGCS express services, excursions and tours operating outside the Board's area were generally handed over to one or other of the 'Area Agreement' companies but in the Watford area they were taken over by an independent, the Premier Omnibus Company's subsidiary West Herts Motor Services Ltd. The reason for this different arrangement arose from a deal between LGCS and Ernest George Hewitt, who owned Premier, under which the larger company acquired Premier's local services in the Watford area. As Hewitt was on the brink of going under, LGCS paid little for these services and were quite happy to hand over their local Excursions & Tours licences, which they considered of little value. In consequence the Premier and West Herts services were among those taken over by the Board on vesting day.

The ACME service from Charing Cross to Newmarket was brutally curtailed at Bishops Stortford on 1st July 1933, having passed into LGOC ownership the previous September. This 1929 Gilford 1680T, which had a Petty thirty-one seat body, became GF 41 in the Green Line numbering and GF 177 in the 1935 scheme. Malcolm E Papes collection

A judgement of the gods? In the summer of 1933 there was a series of heath fires on Hayes and Keston Commons and this one, on 16th September, is delaying Tilling 6063 (ST 887) on route 146A perhaps in symbolic support of the company's compensation fight with the LPTB.
John Aldridge collection

The Board was quick to show that it was no paper tiger. It went about its job of acquiring the scheduled Independent companies and handling the Section 16 consents with a relish and vigour rarely seen in public corporations. The process started on 14th July when the Metropolitan area companies were asked to supply details of their accounts, assets owned, numbers of staff, mileage operated and any liabilities. The companies were determined to fight their corner with equivalent vigour and most of them took the advice of the Association of London Omnibus Proprietors to refuse the Board's offer to acquire them all on a standard basis. Between them they negotiated hard and long and many cases were referred to the Arbitration Tribunal. To speed things up, where there was agreement as to the extent of the transfer, most companies who went to arbitration agreed to accept a payment on account so that the business could be transferred to the Board while the Arbitration Tribunal considered the case.

The first company to settle 'on account' was Thomas Tilling, whose London business was transferred on 1st October 1933. Given its close relationship with the LGOC (there were even seemingly well-founded rumours that they were about to join forces in some form of common management scheme when the Board was formed) Tillings might have been expected to have gone over on vesting day but its Directors had been so outraged by the compensation terms proposed that they were instead in the midst of a bitter dispute. This had the peculiar effect of making them temporarily more independent than they had been for a long time, as the Board's only legitimate interests were the 110 buses (eighty STL, eighteen TSM and twelve T) and the three operating garages formerly owned by LGOC which passed to them with that company. These were formally placed on loan to Tilling on 1st July 1933. Under the terms of the settlement, the LPTB took possession of the Bull Yard works in Peckham and the Obelisk Works in Lewisham as well as 191 STs and twenty-seven Tilling Stevens Petrol-electric double-deckers.

The same day was the day appointed by the Minister of Transport for the transfer of another scheduled company, the Lewis Omnibus Company of Watford. The twenty-five vehicles acquired with the Lewis business, included the six Regents and four Regals purchased between 1930 and 1932, and a mixed bag of Albions, Bristols, Lancias, a Karrier and a Morris. Lewis proved to be a thorn in the side of the LPTB as he displayed the same kind of independence in his dealings with them as had attracted the Metropolitan Railway to join forces with him. He shared the Metropolitan's distaste for the compulsory acquisition of their companies and he carried his fight over to his period of employment by the Board. He considered that the terms of his transfer under the Act gave him the right to go on managing the Lewis business but this would have vitiated the Board's attempts at integration, so he was appointed District Engineer. He seems to have had problems with meeting the standards set by the Board and after being offered a desk job at Reigate, which he refused, he was eventually dismissed for misconduct. He then sued for breach of contract and the matter was finally settled out of court.

Before this, the Guildford area operations of Aldershot & District scheduled in the Act, the routes to Dorking, Merrow and Ewhurst via Newlands Corner, were transferred on 1st August, together with one double-deck and five single-deck Dennises. On 1st September, the scheduled Grays area operations of Eastern National came into the Board's hands, together with four twenty-seat CP6 model Gilfords and a sixty-four seat Guy FCX double-decker. In addition to its share of route G40 there were three routes: between Tilbury and Purfleet via Grays; Grays to Romford via Aveley; and Grays to Rainham via Purfleet.

The ultimate insult, following the final takeover of Tillings by the Board, was the application of the 'General' fleetname to its vehicles, as on STL 66. John Aldridge collection

Aldershot & District's Ewhurst garage was one of the properties named in the LPT Act to be passed to the new Board. Although money was spent on providing it with the new owner's name, it was not used by them. The Duple bodied Morris Viceroy parked outside was less than a year old when taken over from the Grey Motor Coach service of Longfield, Kent, on 16th January 1934. It became MS 1B. Alan B Cross

At the end of August the first two acquisitions resulting from the Section 16 procedure took place, both in Watford. The applications from the Elite Omnibus Company for consent to continue running its St Albans Road to Cassio Bridge route and from Y S Coaches to continue running from Leggatts Rise to High Street were refused and the businesses passed to the Board on 30th and 31st August respectively. Both were typical of the majority of operators who were caught up in this procedure in being small concerns operating small buses. Elite had operated a fourteen-seat Chevrolet LQ and two twenty-four seat AJS Pilots, while the Y S fleet comprised one twenty-seat Reo Sprinter and a sixteen-seat Chevrolet LQ, hardly what one would expect to find working busy town services.

The first bus operator of any real substance to come under the Section 16 hammer was Gravesend & District Bus Services Ltd, which ran routes from that town to Dartford, Northfleet (Granby Place) and Northfleet (Waterdales), from Northfleet to Gravesend Aerodrome and local routes from Windmill Street to Poplar Avenue and Gloucester Road. It was a very mixed fleet with nine different models on six makes of chassis represented in its fourteen buses and six coaches. There were nine Dennises (Gs, 30cwts and a Lancet), six Manchesters, two Internationals and one each of Bedford (newly delivered), Minerva and Overland. These passed to London Transport on 1st October but the route to Gravesend Aerodrome, the Express services and the Excursions and Tours were handed on to Maidstone & District. Gravesend & District had two Dennis Aces on order at the time of its takeover and these were eventually delivered to London Transport, with whom they became DC 1 and 2.

The acquisition of operators in the Watford area was completed with the takeover of Biggerstaff's Bus Service of Sarratt on 8th November, opening the way for this town to be the first to have a co-ordination scheme, the details of which are covered in chapter six. Other companies acquired during November were: J. Kirby (Karriyu Coaches) of St Albans (9th); The Enterprise Motor Service of Gravesend (14th); and Peoples Motor Services of Ware (30th). Peoples was another substantial company, operating a network of eight routes radiating from Hertford with a fleet of twelve Thornycrofts, four Gilfords, two Lafflys and one Chevrolet. The garage at Ware also went to the Board, who continued to use it for the time being.

Also during November, the business of Charles Russett and Son passed to London Transport. Although the operations within the Metropolitan Traffic Area had been named in Part V of the Second Schedule of the Act, the four routes outside the area required London Transport's consent and the company duly applied. This was refused and the whole operation changed hands on 10th November. Fourteen buses of nine makes and two garages, a small one in St Peters Street and a larger one in Hatfield Road, became the property of the Board. The smaller premises were closed and eventually sold but the Hatfield Road site, which had been acquired by Russett as recently as 1932, became London Transport's base in the town until its own new garage could be built.

By the end of 1933, thirteen companies had been acquired through this procedure and by the end of its first year, the Board had taken over all or part of sixty-two such operators. At the end of 1933 it became clear that the process was going to be a lot slower than expected, partly because the companies themselves were slow to make their applications and some had failed to do so altogether. The fifty-six operators to whom consent had been refused but with whom negotiations were incomplete on 1st January 1934, were given special permits to continue operating until 31st March 1934. Further similar limited consents were granted case by case once this further deadline had been passed. The last operator to be acquired under the terms of Section 16 was A.E. Blane of Romford whose Imperial Bus service changed hands on 28th November 1934, bringing the total to sixty-eight. Nearly all were absorbed into the Country Bus department but the businesses of Romford and District, which was taken over on 11th July 1934, and A.E. Blane (Imperial) passed to Central Buses.

Top **Lewis's Cream Coaches of Brookmans Park had been taken over by the LGOC in May 1933 and retained its identity until 1st July. Three weeks later, at Portman Square, GF 51, a Duple bodied 1680T, still carries 'Cream Line' insignia, supplemented by a bulkhead label reading 'Green Line Service' and topped off with the new 'legal owner' lettering. This coach later became GF 190.** D W K Jones

Above **Sunset Pullman took delivery of this handsome Duple bodied Albion PV70 (AN 1C) in 1933, only months before being taken over by the LPTB. In this seemingly untroubled scene, it is about to set out from Brentwood on its regular run to Horse Guards Avenue.** J F Higham

Top **One that got away! The Walton on Thames Motor Company was allowed to continue to operate this Bedford on its local service between town and station, as the board could not run it economically.** D W K Jones

Above **One of the surprising survivals was the Imperial Airways coach service between Victoria and Croydon Airport, operated by Thomas Tilling to whom these two handsome Harrington bodied coaches belong. The complete absence of buses in Victoria forecourt is because the date is 24th May 1937 and the busmen are on strike.** D W K Jones

Another important group of companies taken over under Section 16 were the operators of local coach services. Many had already been acquired by the LGOC or Green Line before the formation of the Board and two, Lewis's Cream Coaches (Brookman's Park – Portman Square) and West Herts Motor Services Ltd (Hemel Hempstead – Marylebone) were taken over on vesting day. A third, Premier Line Ltd, came into the Board's hands with the Premier Omnibus business on 20th December 1933. Special provision had been made in Section 5 (2)(e)(ii) of the Act for Premier to require the Board to take the whole of its undertaking if it claimed that taking over the buses would seriously injure the rest of its business. Premier brought with it the routes to Windsor and Farnham Common, local bus routes in Slough and Maidenhead and no fewer than thirty-five modern buses and coaches on Leyland Titan (twenty-three) or Tiger TS3 chassis.

The first coach operator to be refused consent was J.H. Price (Super Coaches) who ran on the popular East Ham – Aveley route; the transfer took place on 1st December 1933. Battens' Tilbury route was acquired on 23rd December and then, on 10th January, the large and flourishing associated businesses of Edward Hillman's Saloon Coaches and Upminster Services Ltd. The routes to Brentwood and Upminster were retained by the Board but Hillman's longer distance operations into Essex were sold on to Eastern National. These were also modern fleets, although their special distinction was that they comprised almost exclusively Wycombe bodied Gilford 1680Ts. It was the loss of important customers such as this which led to the early disappearance of Gilford as a manufacturer of bus chassis. Five more companies were acquired between 17th January and 27th April 1934, the last being Beaumont-Safeway Coaches and their Dunstable route. The others were West London Coaches (Aylesbury via Amersham), Sunset Pullman Coaches (Brentwood), Strawhatter Motor Services (Luton via Barnet) and the night service between Aldgate and Romford operated by Fleet Transport Services Ltd. The latter was the only example of a former coach service being transferred to the Central Bus department when its runnings were absorbed into night route 617 on 13th June 1934.

Not all applications were refused, although the majority of those granted were not bus services. The principles adopted by the Board were that consent should be granted for operations to football, greyhound and horse racing, speedway and places of interest; for operations of an intermittent nature; and for general sightseeing tours. Consent would not be granted for regular stage services which both picked up and set down the same passenger within the Special Area, except in special cases where it would be impracticable or uneconomic for the Board to operate them. In its first year, of applications for special services which it received from 320 operators, the Board granted consent to 251, covering 1,404 different services. Another five operators were granted partial consents. This principle continued to be applied for the whole of the LPTB's existence, although as the years went by, Pick tightened up the rules so that excursions and tours wholly within the Special Area were operated as far as possible by the Board.

Examples of bus services which the Board found worthwhile but uneconomic to run themselves, were the Walton-on-Thames Motor Company's route from Walton station to the town, H.T. Lewis's Newgate Street to Hertford route and D. Hard's Thames Ditton to Esher service. Consent was also granted where the route was substantially outside the Board's area, such as the Beaconsfield to Maidenhead service of B&M, J. Henderson's Brentwood – Navestock – Hook End route and Renshaw and Leam's Woking circular. In many such cases consent was conditional on the operator harmonising its fares with those of the Board. Regular but special services wholly within the area were also sometimes given consent, the two most surprising being to Imperial Airways for the coach service operated on its behalf by Thomas Tilling between Victoria and Croydon Aerodrome and to Hillmans Airways for its Kings Cross to Romford Aerodrome operation.

Generally speaking, long distance services going well beyond the Special Area were either not covered by the provisions of the Act,

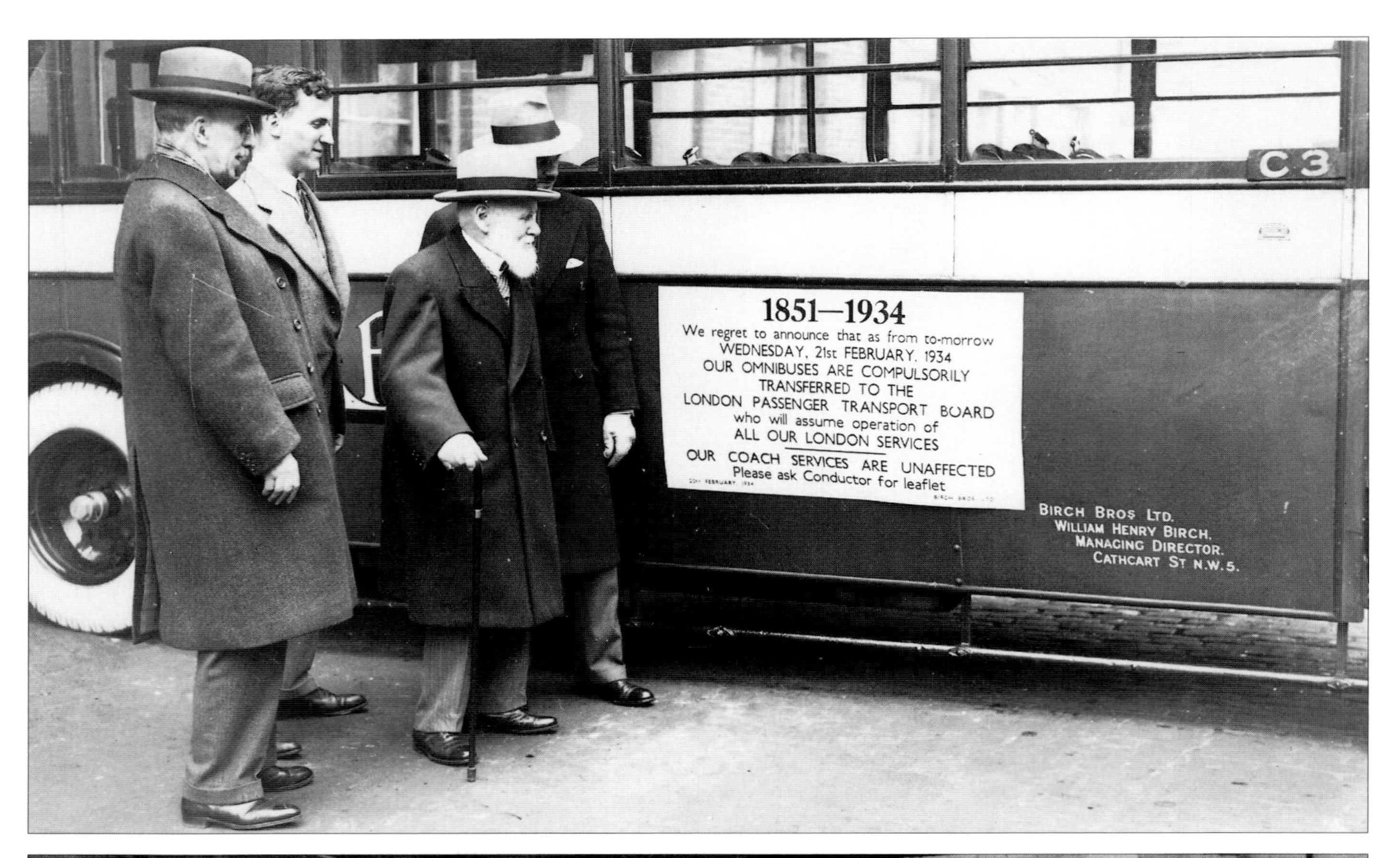
C3
1851—1934
We regret to announce that as from to-morrow
WEDNESDAY, 21st FEBRUARY, 1934
OUR OMNIBUSES ARE COMPULSORILY
TRANSFERRED TO THE
LONDON PASSENGER TRANSPORT BOARD
who will assume operation of
ALL OUR LONDON SERVICES
OUR COACH SERVICES ARE UNAFFECTED
Please ask Conductor for leaflet
BIRCH BROS LTD.
WILLIAM HENRY BIRCH,
MANAGING DIRECTOR.
CATHCART ST N.W.5.

BIRCH BROS. LTD.
LONDON KINGS +
HIGHGATE FINCHLEY BARNET POTTERS BAR HATFIELD
LONDON KINGS X BEDFORD KETTERING
SHEFFORD SHORTSTOWN CLAPHAM
BIRCH
UU 1464

Left **Management of Birch Brothers Ltd inspect the poster announcing the end of their London bus operations.** Arthur Ingram

Below left **Birch continued to operate between Kings Cross and Kettering, enjoying some local carriage rights in the LPTB area. Birch had bought nine of these Gilford 1680Ts in 1929/1930 and fitted them with its own coach bodies.**
D W K Jones

Right **TD 85, which carried one of the modern looking final version of the Birch body, was acquired from Birch Bros in February 1931 and being an oiler was allocated to Hanwell garage. On 4th May 1935 it helps carry traffic to the Rugby League Cup Final at Wembley.** D W K Jones

Below right **A substantial 'GREEN LINE' label has been pasted on the side of GK445, in alien territory outside Windsor garage, but the name 'Premier' still stubbornly peeps through on the front roof display panel. London Lorries supplied the twenty-six seat body for this 1930 TS3 model**

because they did not both pick up and set down the same passenger within the area, or were subject to limitations which the Board found acceptable for the grant of consent. One service which was to be a constant source of irritation to the Board and its successors was the Kentish Town/Wood Green to Southend route run jointly by Westcliff-on-Sea and New Empress Saloons Ltd. It had substantial sections outside the Board's area but the operators also had local carriage rights within the area. As the obvious solution of operating the service jointly was not open to the Board, it was more or less obliged to grant consent. The main problem was that workmen's rates were offered which were substantially cheaper than the Board's and attracted traffic to the service, causing inadequacy. City (who had become sole operator in 1935) therefore applied persistently for consent to increase its frequency. The arguments rumbled on until, as late as March 1939, the Board seriously considered putting on its own coach service between Slough and Brentwood, competing with City east of Wood Green. The opportunity would have arisen with the opening of the Central Line extension to Newbury Park, when the Eastern Avenue Green Line route X was to be withdrawn. This would have released the vehicles needed; but the war put a stop to that.

The first London area Independents to be acquired under Section 5 of the Act were Cardinal, Chariot, Glen, F.W. Hayes (The Adelaide), F.J.C. Kirk (Empire), Nelson, A.H. Raper, Ryan, Supreme and United, all of whom were taken over on 1st November 1933. Filkins and Ainsworth of Harefield were also acquired on the same day. In an attempt at some consolidation of effort, the Board asked the companies to continue operating from their own bases until 17th January 1934, when all companies taken over in the meantime would be absorbed into the Board's operations. Between the two dates a further twenty-six companies were acquired and all thirty-six were duly absorbed on the agreed date.

The Glen Omnibus Company was one of the earlier operators to fall to the LPTB and its runnings on route 73 were eventually consolidated into the main schedule. GJ8489 (TD 2) is seen at Hyde Park Corner.

Once these transfers had been completed, Pick ruled that the operations of the remaining companies should be transferred to an LPTB garage immediately on acquisition and that they should be absorbed or abandoned within fourteen days of the decision of his Traffic Committee. Five more companies were taken over on these terms the most important of whom was undoubtedly Birch Bros, who finally succumbed on 21st February 1934. Its principal weekday operations were immediately transferred into London Transport garages: route 214C to Hendon; 231 and 536 to Chalk Farm; and the 526 into Muswell Hill, where it was joined by the former LGOC Cricklewood allocation. The 231 took its fleet of Dennis single-deckers with it to Chalk Farm but the Birch double-deckers were redeployed, the Dennis Hs to Potters Bar and the Titans to Upton Park. In their place, London Transport allocated STLs to the 214C, LTs to the 526 and STs to the 536. The Sunday operations on the 27 group, 42 and 73 group were abandoned.

This left eleven companies with whom the Board had not been able to agree the 'extent of transfer'. In most cases this related to the ownership of garages but in the case of City and Westminster, there was also a dispute about the transferability of the Directors' contracts. There was a complicated interlocking series of hearings and appeals, culminating in City's request for 'Special Case' treatment, which was dismissed with costs. The eleven companies were taken over gradually, as their cases were settled, between 11th July and 5th December 1934. The very last company was the Prince Omnibus Company, whose takeover had been delayed because of complications over its coastal express coach services and a range of tours and excursions which it operated. These were taken over by the Board as part of the settlement but were immediately sold off, mainly to George Ewer, as the Board had no powers to operate them.

One other 'Section 5' undertaking needs to be mentioned, the Amersham & District Motor Bus and Haulage Company Ltd. This was another example of a company which might have been expected to transfer instantly to the Board, given that it not only had a close relationship with the LGOC but had in fact been bought almost outright by them in May 1933. A letter from the LPTB dated 28th June, asking for the company to be wound up as soon as possible does not seem to have inspired much activity on the part of the A&D Board and it was not until 24th November 1933 that the transfer of services took place; the company was formally wound up on 4th January 1934.

Of the 'provincial' companies mentioned in Section 17 of the Act, only one refused to go quietly, Redcar Services Ltd. The terms of purchase of its London – Tunbridge Wells service were unacceptable and it filed a claim with the Arbitration Tribunal for severance of its business. The Board's terms were based on the Eighth Schedule of the Act which had specified that it should take over three vehicles from Redcar, presumably because that was the number required to run the section of route within the Special Area. Redcar continued to operate but without local carriage within the LPTB area and the Board took the view that as the service still existed, no further compensation was due. The Tribunal took a different view and allowed compensation for severance.

When the St George Omnibus Company was taken over on 16th July 1934 its operations on route 70 were abandoned. Six weeks earlier Dennis 4-ton XX9806, which became D 197, starts out on the run from Clapham Common to Dorking, its red and white Dodson body gleaming.
D W K Jones

In the end Redcar elected to keep the three vehicles and the amount of the claim was adjusted accordingly. The Tunbridge Wells route eventually came into the LPTB's hands on 31st July 1935, when Maidstone & District acquired the company and handed over this and the Sevenoaks to Tonbridge bus service.

The fate of the vehicles taken over from the Independents was variable. Many of the older buses and those which were too non-standard for Chiswick or Reigate to stomach, were delicensed and stored either immediately or as soon as replacements could be found. The Central Bus petrol-engined Leyland Titans were all sent to Upton Park, starting with the first major batch on 17th January 1934 which replaced LTs and STs on routes 86, 126, 186 and 623. As more arrived, they went onto the 101. The Titan oilers and the three City Titanics joined the large fleet of oil-engined LTs at Hanwell and worked on the 18C. The ST-type Regents were all allocated to Camberwell, Redline's STL and DST to Harrow Weald and Pickup's open-top STLs went to Old Kent Road. The more modern Dennis double-deckers were sent to join their former Overground siblings at Potters Bar, while the elderly 4-ton model vehicles were withdrawn. The single-deckers operated by Birch on the 231 went to Chalk Farm, with the route. The remaining Leyland LBs, the Guy FCX six-wheelers, Allitt's two Karrier single-deckers and Gordon's Maudslay Mentor all bit the dust, often receiving LPTB fleet numbers after they had been withdrawn. The standard ex-LGOC types displaced by the new arrivals were used to cover former Independent workings. When City was taken over on 7th November 1934, Catford garage got a huge influx of thirty-seven STLs to work the former 536 (by then renumbered 137). Others were not necessarily so lucky, like Premier's customers on route 60, accustomed to travelling on that company's splendid Titans and who suddenly found them replaced by covered top NSs.

Looking rather sheepish in their unfamiliar new surroundings two TD1s on route 126, TD 77 ex-Birch Bros and TD 59 ex-Premier, are flanked by two Upton Park LTs on the 'White Horse' stand at East Ham.
Charles F Klapper Collection: Omnibus Society

Left **Pro Bono Publico's Dodson bodied Regent, an exact contemporary of the LGOC STs, is still in the company's colours at London Bridge station but has become ST 1030 and been allocated to Camberwell, whose code plate is carried on the newly fitted holders on the waistrail.** D W K Jones

Below **Cardinal's last new bus, this Dennis Lance of 1930, has had its identity thoroughly submerged under its LPTB colours and 'General' fleetname only three months after being acquired. It has a new country home at Potters Bar where Dennises are concentrated alongside the former Overground fleet, one of which is in the picture also with 'General' fleetname.** D W K Jones

Until 17th May 1934 this twenty seat Leyland LTB1 was working on the other side of the river, in Grays, under the Harris banner. It is now 18th February 1935 and it is running with the new 'LONDON TRANSPORT' fleetname from Northfleet. D W K Jones

The Country department was less well placed to weed out unwanted vehicles, as its starting fleet of ex-LGCS vehicles was much smaller and the number of extra buses proportionately much larger than in the Central area. Nevertheless many vehicles were withdrawn immediately on takeover. The acquired fleets contributed no fewer than thirty-one different makes of chassis, almost running the gamut of the alphabet from AEC to W&G, passing on the way such relative rarities as Brockway, Overland and Saurer. There were also many variations in models, of course. There were some makes which were particularly well represented. As well as the obvious presence of 116 Leylands (sixty-three Titans, forty-two Tigers, ten PLSC3s and a Cub), there was also the staggering total of two hundred and twenty Gilfords, seventy-six Dennises, thirty-one Chevrolets and twenty-seven Bedfords (mainly twenty-seaters). Apart from the condition or age of some of them, many were too small for the job and did not fit into the LPTB's statutory duty to run as efficiently as possible. In the case of Grays, where there had been an exceptional proliferation of proprietors running small vehicles on busy urban routes, some Titans were drafted in during 1934. Central Buses had helped out by transferring seven of its Titans to the Country area but the main programme for dealing with this had to await new vehicles.

The enormous variety of chassis makes must have been a headache for the beleaguered engineers, who also had to contend with a great number of 'stop' notices being put onto vehicles which did not meet the standards required by the Ministry of Transport vehicle examiners. Achieving these standards was not helped either by the lack of cover or proper facilities for many of the acquired vehicles, as in the example of Grays, where there were thirty-nine buses which had to be ferried to Romford for maintenance. Some help was given by attempting to concentrate certain makes in particular garages, such as Thornycrofts at Addlestone, Leylands at Northfleet, Commers at Hertford and Chevrolets, Fords and Morris Commercials at Windsor but most acquired vehicles stayed close to their original bases.

As the vehicles were taken over they were not necessarily repainted but did have the legal owner panel altered and a new fleetname pasted on the side. For reasons best known to itself, possibly because it was the cheapest way given that nearly all its buses came from the LGOC, the Board had made the incredibly insensitive decision to adopt the fleetname 'GENERAL' for all its buses, in apparent confirmation of the belief of many that the LPTB was merely the Underground Group in a new, protected guise. For the Country Area it had also decided to adopt a new colour scheme of predominantly green, with, on double-deckers, two black bands, one below the windows on each deck and on single-deckers a band below the saloon windows. Some LGCS vehicles had already appeared with this style before 1st July 1933. Acquired vehicles were repainted into this livery as they became due for overhaul.

This Metcalfe bodied Dennis Lancet was one of a pair which were the last new buses bought by A.E. Blane of Romford. At first numbered DL 35, it was renumbered DT 7B when transferred to Country Buses in February 1935. It was allocated to Amersham and is seen at Windsor on route 353. J F Higham

Most of the Central Area fleet already carried the GENERAL fleetname adopted at first by the LPTB. Shepherd's Bush LT 322 is seen in Whitehall.
Arthur Ingram

In the Central Area the established red, white and black of the LGOC was perpetuated and, again, former Independent buses were mostly repainted at overhaul; but there were some exceptions. When George Partridge's historic Express fleet was about to be taken over, it was decided to withdraw his runnings from route 11E as being superfluous. Mindful of the psychological effect on regular passengers of seeing their familiar and popular chocolate and primrose buses withdrawn without replacement, Frank Pick decreed that no runnings were to be taken off until all Partridge's buses had been repainted in the Board's colours. Another similar decree in the case of City's fleet caught Pick out. In preparation for the takeover, he had sent his engineers off to inspect the City fleet and come to an arrangement to start repainting them. Meanwhile, he had been wrestling with the problem of City's fares on route 536 being on a cheaper scale than those of the Board's bus services and in particular the fact that City issued workmen's tickets, which on the Board's road services were normally only available on trams and trolleybuses. Even the normally cheap tram fares were held at a lower level than standard because they would otherwise have been undercut by City. Pick's solution was that the buses should remain brown, to distinguish them from ordinary buses, while the matter of the fare scale was resolved with the London & Home Counties Traffic Advisory Committee. Unfortunately by then City had already started repainting work and the Board had to fall back on the idea of retaining the 'City' fleetname for the time being. The eventual solution was somewhat drastic; in 1937 the route, now numbered 137, was withdrawn completely south of Hyde Park Corner.

As the companies in the Central Bus area were taken over, the Traffic Committee reviewed their services. They were quite ruthless in their approach; by the end of 1934 over two million bus miles formerly operated annually by the London Area Independents (eighteen percent of their total) had been abandoned. The Main Line Railway members of the Revenue Pool became restless about the possible effect on receipts generally, which might lead to money being lost by the railways. Frank Pick therefore set an upper limit of just under five million (still very sizeable at forty-one percent) until the effect of the cuts could be analysed fully. The operations most vulnerable to being cut were those where independents supplied a small proportion of the service otherwise provided by the former 'Combine'.

In the Country Area, the complications and fragmentation of the operations was such that Arthur Hawkins's team had to adopt a different approach. For the most part, the services taken over continued to operate broadly as before until a series of major schemes could be put in place. These are described in chapter six.

The integration of services provided the opportunity to rid London of the excesses of the Bassom system of route numbering, no doubt to the great relief of passengers and staff alike. Pick had actually started the ball rolling at the last meeting of his LGOC committee on 28th June 1933 but it was not until March 1934 that any proposals were agreed. As modified by Pick these set out the basic principles, most of which were eventually adopted: each main route to have a distinguishing number; shortworkings to carry the same number, without a suffix letter, leaving the destination blind to convey the message; bifurcating routes to carry main service number with a suffix, unless the divergence was more than one-third of the route, in which case a separate number would be allotted; Central Buses to be in the series 1-299, outer routes being from 200 upwards and night and special services above 250; Country Buses to be 301-399 north of the river and 401-499 south. This was later amended so that single-deck routes would have been included in the series from 250 upwards.

In the final scheme, Central Bus single-deck routes were numbered 200 and above and night routes 299 downwards but there were some interesting ideas considered in the meantime. The possibility of numbering trolleybus routes in a series T1 upwards (possibly with the 'T' a permanent feature alongside the number blind) and Green Line coach routes G1 upwards were both ideas discussed at length. No such special arrangements were considered necessary for trams, although duplicated numbers were supposed to be eliminated. It was not until the summer of 1935 that the decision was made to use the 6XX series for trolleybus routes. The 5XX series had been considered and rejected, for reasons unknown.

The renumbering scheme was given the blessing of the Traffic Commissioner and was introduced with the Winter Programme on 3rd October 1934. There can be little doubt that the result was a good deal simpler for passengers and easier to operate than the cumbersome Bassom system; no doubt conductors were universally grateful for not having to remember to change umpteen numbers every time their bus went onto a different shortworking. Even so, the upheaval seems to have been greater than it need have been. There seems no particular reason for separating the single-deck routes, other than to satisfy an 'impeccable busman' (as Churchill once memorably called Pick). This caused some unnecessary renumberings (like 141 to 241) and was a nuisance in later years when routes were double-decked and had to be renumbered, quite unnecessarily (like 241 to 141!). Neither is it clear why a route like the 263 had to be renumbered (confusingly) to 236, unless this was a hangover from the earlier idea of keeping 250 and upwards for special services. Nor was there any good reason suddenly to change a well established number like 184 to 17, although this was its pre-1924 number and had been used for a virtually identical route (terminating at Norwood Road rather than Western Road, Southall) by some Independents and (unadvertised) by LGOC itself. It was presumably done to give an in-town route a low number, yet the 159 retained its number rather than taking a lower, or perhaps the obvious choice of 59A. The existence of the 159 was presumably the determining factor in the choice of the number 59, rather than the existing 58, for the Camden Town to Chipstead Valley route. Despite everything, once it had happened and settled down, the new system was a vast improvement.

Some tram routes were renumbered but the changes were sketchy and haphazard. It was understandable that routes due for early conversion to trolleybus operation were left unchanged but even leaving these aside, the numbers 7, 10, 55, 57, 60, 62, 63, 66, 67 and 68 were all duplicated, some of them running alongside routes which were renumbered. Clashes with bus routes were not eliminated either and there were many examples of bus and tram routes with the same number sharing sections of road. These were sometimes quite short, like the two 10s between Borough and Elephant & Castle, or the 21 bus and tram which ran alongside each other between Turnpike Lane and Manor House. Others were rather longer, perhaps the outstanding example being the 29s between Euston Road and Palmers Green.

The task of integration was immensely complicated and, apart from the services themselves, was not completed during the lifetime of the Board. The biggest problem was the differing fare scales and concession tickets which created a minefield through which the Board had to tread with circumspection. The problem was that the vast bulk of operations was tied to the fares and ticketing policies of the Underground Group which, on the whole, were more expensive than its competitors. Harmonisation meant either big losses of revenue on former Underground Group services if their fares were reduced, or big losses of passengers on the others if their fares were increased. The former was out of the question and the latter, which might have been right in a coldly commercial sense, was not easy because the Board was required by its Statute to consult with local authorities and it was in any case very sensitive to public opinion.

London Transport had been in business for five weeks when ST 289 was photographed on 8th August 1933 in Richmond Road Kingston, just about fitting into the roadway left by the contractors removing the former LUT tram track.

Local authority opinion was important because the municipal tramways in particular had a wide range of special concessionary fares, often protected by their enabling Acts. To complicate matters further, these were not consistent with one another, either in the rates charged or in the times when they could be used. The policy adopted by the Board was to eliminate workmen's and other special concession fares from buses where they were not parallel with tramways. This led to a great deal of discontent and the asking of many questions in Parliament. Some such concessions in the Country Area were retained where they were widely used and well established. The workmen's fares on routes taken over from M&D and Gravesend & District and those operating between Hertford and Ware were examples of this approach. An alternative method of dealing with the problem in the Northern Country Area was to offer weekly six-return journey tickets at a 33⅓% discount.

Less fuss seems to have been made about the withdrawal of another concession in West Ham, where it had been the practice of the corporation to allow the return halves of tickets to be used for any journey of equal fare value, although this was not formally stated on faretables. Passengers had got into the habit of buying a 3d return when making two consecutive 2d single trips and the Board cancelled the arrangement from 11th May 1936. Many of the tram concessions were either discontinued or brought into line with former LCC practice when trams were replaced by trolleybuses but the fares in East Ham and West Ham, which went up in halfpenny stages, remained unique until after the war and trams and trolleybuses continued to work on a different basis from buses right up to October 1950.

Green Line fares, as a general rule, had to be fixed in relation to the rates charged by the Main Line railway companies on parallel rail routes and were closely monitored by the Traffic Commissioners. A by no means unique example of the kind of problem which confronted the Board's commercial staff was the difference in rates on the Green Line and Strawhatter routes to Harpenden. Strawhatter had a standard rate for all destinations of 1s 6d Single, 2s 6d Day Return and 3s 0d Period Return, whereas Green Line had a graduated scale with, for example, a single fare of 1s 9d to St Albans and 2s 3d to Harpenden.

In the case of routes operated by Independents, the Board was often able to take a different line. The extreme example of route 536 (later 137) has already been mentioned in connection with the takeover of City. In another example, after wrestling with the problem of extremely low fares charged by Paterson on route 292 between Becontree Heath and Poplar, the Commercial Manager finally came to the conclusion that there was no satisfactory compromise and recommended that the route should be withdrawn. This took place on 18th July 1934, when additional buses were put onto routes 106 and 293.

The LPTB also had a major human relations task to perform in absorbing and integrating 77,500 staff (including railways) at all levels and with differing working experiences and different salaries, wages and conditions of service. The Board had started with 38,000 bus and coach and 19,600 tram and trolleybus staff. The number of bus and coach staff rose to 41,398 by 1936, with the acquisition of the many Independents and most of these were required to work for the wages and under the conditions of the department to which they were assigned. There was arbitration for hard cases and for the many managers or owners who were either not offered employment or did not wish to transfer to the new undertaking. Full integration of working conditions was never achieved by the Board, however. The Central Bus and Country Bus departments adopted the practices of the LGOC and LGCS respectively but in the case of the tramways it was impracticable to bring them into line with bus practice as they had a mixture of lower wages and better conditions which it would have been very expensive to eliminate. There were also different arrangements for retirement, for example; in the case of the LCC there was effectively no retirement age and staff taken over by the Board in 1933 retained this right and were to be found working to ripe old ages long after most people had forgotten that the LCC ever operated trams.

Indeed, integration of attitudes never really took place. Even twenty years after the event, staff were still commonly identified as 'an LCC man' or 'a General man' or 'an MET man' and resentments about their treatment also lingered on. Many of the LCC administrative staff were particularly put out that their careers in local government suddenly came to an end. Their takeover by the Board was to some extent happenchance, simply because at that particular stage in their working life they happened to be working in the Tramways department, rather than Education, Housing, Main Drainage, or whatever.

NS 1674 and another of the same class are flanked in Victoria bus station by the two extremes of LT class design: open staircase LT 95 and 'Bluebird' LT 1307, which had been one of the early conversions to oil engine in May 1934.
G H F Atkins

The public face of the organisation underwent a dramatic transformation in the early years of the LPTB. All buses were gradually repainted into either the red and white of the LGOC for Central Buses or the new Green and black chosen by the Board for its Country services; trams were repainted into red and cream. At first the fleetname adopted for buses was 'GENERAL' and for coaches 'GREEN LINE' but trams and trolleybuses did not settle down to anything, although some had a kind of electrical 'flash' symbol and others had a version of the Underground Group 'bullseye'. The first indication of future policy came on 5th October 1933 when the Board resolved to adopt, as an experiment for use in correspondence and publicity, the short title 'London Transport'. The experiment was apparently a success because on 5th April 1934 it resolved to use the fleetname 'LONDON TRANSPORT' on all its vehicles and trains, except that 'GREEN LINE' was still to be shown prominently on coaches. From then onwards the name began to appear until eventually the entire fleet was subsumed in the new corporate liveries.

It took the Board a while to settle on a corporate symbol too. In its early publicity, a kind of flying LPTB sign of two interlocking circles with wings was used but eventually the decision came down in favour of a modernised and cleaned up version of the Underground Group's bullseye. This was used everywhere: on stop signs; in publicity; on timetables; on direction signs; and of course throughout the Underground network.

London Transport continued the tradition of high quality maps and leaflets which it inherited from the Underground Group but went on to expand the range of material substantially. It adopted the style of bus map which the LGOC had introduced in 1931 and extended its use to separate publications for Trams and Trolleybuses and Green Line Coaches but not to Country Buses, which never had a map of its own in LPTB days. Given the Board's duty to co-ordinate services, it has always seemed a little odd that it assiduously kept its various activities separate in its range of maps. This was particularly unhelpful in the Central Area where large areas appeared to be unserved, depending on which map was used.

The London Passenger Transport Board has assumed control of most of the passenger transport undertakings which operate in an area within a radius of some 30 miles from Charing Cross. The services include the underground railways, tramways, omnibuses and coaches.

1. The Purpose

THE Board is a public authority appointed under Act of Parliament charged with responsibility for providing an adequate and properly co-ordinated system of passenger transport within the London Passenger Transport Area. It is required to take such steps as it considers necessary for avoiding wasteful, competitive services and for extending and improving London's passenger transport facilities, so as to meet the growing needs of the vast population working and dwelling within the area over which the Board's operations extend.

For all inquiries
LONDON PASSENGER TRANSPORT BOARD
55, Broadway, Westminster, S.W.1
Telephone: VICtoria 6800
Telegrams: Passengers Sowest London

This is No. 1 of a series of four announcements by the London Passenger Transport Board. Other announcements will be published at fortnightly intervals, as follows: 2. The Territory. 3. The Service. 4. The Staff.

The London Passenger Transport Board has assumed control of most of the passenger transport undertakings which operate in an area within a radius of some 30 miles from Charing Cross. The services include the underground railways, tramways, omnibuses and coaches.

2. The Territory

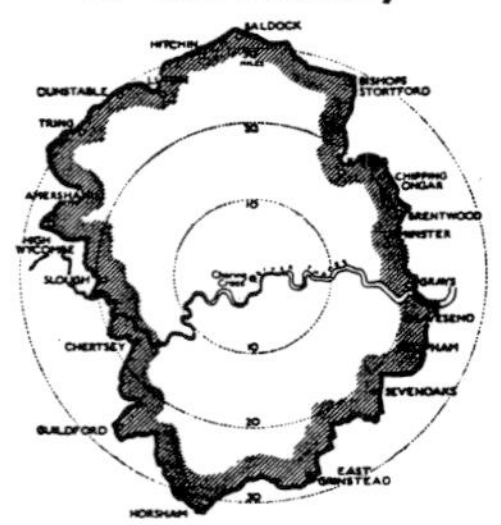

The area comprises 2,000 square miles, and the railway, tramway, omnibus and coach services which operate within its boundaries cater for a population of 9,000,000 people.

For all inquiries
LONDON PASSENGER TRANSPORT BOARD
55, Broadway, Westminster, S.W.1
Telephone: VICtoria 6800 Telegrams: Passengers Sowest London

This is No. 2 of a series of four announcements by the London Passenger Transport Board. Other announcements will be published at fortnightly intervals as follows: 3. The Service. 4. The Staff.

The original LPTB symbol was the one used on this leaflet describing the functions of the new undertaking. It is shown here with one of the four panels folded out. K W Glazier collection

The first attempt at a special fleetname for trams was this symbolic electrical flash design with the words 'LONDON TRANSPORT' arranged in an unharmonious shrinking and expanding style. The tram is former Leyton council E3 number 192. K W Glazier collection

The form of fleetname finally adopted for all purposes ultimately proved to be a classic of timeless quality. It is shown on Bluebird LT 1287 in Longbridge Road, Barking. J D P House

London Transport's greatest contribution to the improvement of information was in its timetables. A comprehensive range of monthly booklets was introduced in July 1934 which contained timetables for all bus, Green Line, Underground and Main Line railway services and summarised information for connecting bus services run by other operators to points outside the area. Six areas were covered by the new booklets: London, North-West, North-East, South-East, South-West and West.

In the summer of 1936 a fresh approach was tried with a series of local road and rail timetables covering smaller areas more comprehensively. These contained information about all bus, coach and rail services in the defined area of the booklet, irrespective of ownership and were also published monthly. The first six, covering Windsor, Beaconsfield, Gerrards Cross, Hayes, Uxbridge and High Wycombe, were published in July 1936. Although the range eventually covered the whole of the Country Area and the outer parts of the Central Area, they were inappropriate for the inner zone which was served instead by a new Central Area Guide (the 'Red Road Guide'), the first of which was issued in June 1936. Similar separate guides were introduced at the same time for the Underground and Green Line Coaches, which together with the Red Road Guide covered the information previously contained in the London area booklet. The other area guides were also withdrawn but, for a time, it was possible to buy a Northern or Southern Area timetable. The local road and rail timetables were a great success and were to endure for the whole time that London Transport was responsible for Country Buses (and beyond) but the Red Road Guide and the two larger area guides proved less successful and were withdrawn.

Above **At first, coaches also had the standard fleetname with a supplementary 'GREEN LINE' in underlined upper case placed above. T 366, a former Amersham & District Strachan bodied coach, is still on home ground outside Amersham garage but has now been drafted to Green Line service.** D W K Jones

Left **This C1 type car at Wood Green, which was number 208, is still in MET colours but its fleetname has been obliterated and a new fleet number, 2298, applied to the dash panel.** C Carter

Below **The series of new timetables introduced in 1936: the Central Area Red Road guide, one of the Country Area guides and the Green Line Coach Guide.** K W Glazier collection

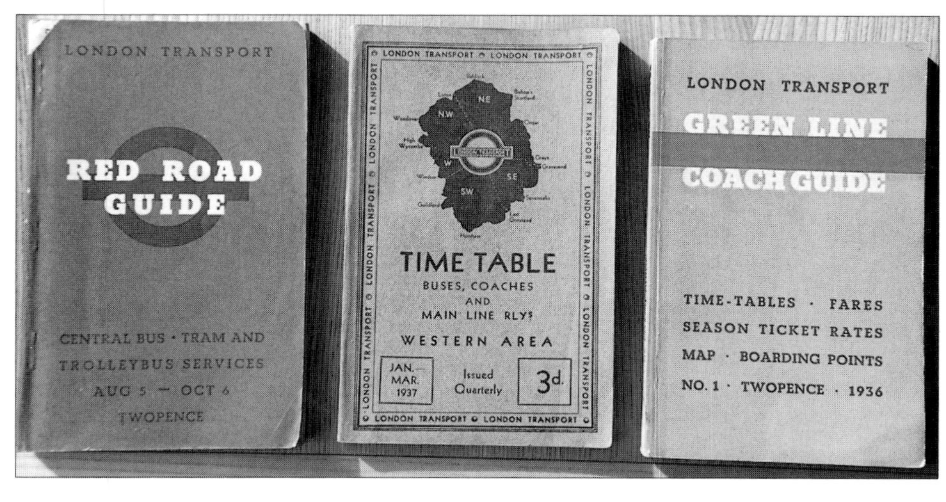

Stop signs went through a period of development, with early attempts at a variation of the bullseye idea looking rather crude by comparison with the final designs which appeared in 1938. For a time, the Board continued with the General 'domed' design of stop flag, with the top of the appropriate 'bullseye' running into the dome and the words 'BUSES (or 'ALL TRAMS' or 'COACHES') STOP HERE' in the rectangle below. The wording on the bar of the bullseye was 'LONDON TRANSPORT' (in white out of black) for both Country and Central buses, 'GREEN LINE' (white out of green) for coaches and 'TRAMWAYS' (white out of blue) for trams and trolleybuses. The background colour for the sign as a whole was green all over for Green Line coaches but cream for all others. It was the original intention to have separate flags for each form of transport, even where they shared a stopping place, but the local authorities asked for them to be consolidated into one sign. Combined designs were therefore developed in which the wording below the bullseye was shown on a series of strips using the appropriate background colour for the mode being described, such as 'BUSES AND (white out of red) COACHES STOP HERE' (white out of green).

Later designs adopted the rectangular shape with the words 'BUS STOP' (or whatever) across the bar of the device. Buses, whether country or central, used a red base colour, either on the circle of the bullseye or as background to a white circle in the case of Request stops. Green Line used green in the same way. In the early stages there was no new design for trams but a similar design, using blue, was eventually adopted. The choice of blue for trams was obviously a hangover from the 'Pullman' concept or perhaps a hankering after the unfulfilled promise of 'Bluebird' car number 1. The final design in 1938 settled down to the pure square which remained standard thereafter. An odd bit of independence was shown by Country Buses, whose Request Stops did not have the words 'By Request' on them, the distinction being left to the colour of the sign. This inevitably caused confusion and led to passengers missing buses through not understanding the rules but only came to the attention of the management at 55 Broadway when the Trade Union complained in 1939. A programme of adding 'Request' to these signs was then initiated.

In 1935 the Board embarked on a five-year programme of replacing old company (mainly General) signs with the new designs but in the case of the trams few new signs appeared as the future of the system was at best in doubt and at worst non-existent. By the outbreak of the Second World War the Board's identity was firmly stamped on London and, although there were still many old style tram stops still around, it was only the few brown and yellow LCC compulsory stops which really stood out as reminders of the old régime.

Top London Transport's earliest stop signs were based on the LGOC style of 'domed' sign but with the words 'London Transport' substituted.

Right Two photographs, taken at the Building Department's Parsons Green works, show various ideas which were tried and rejected, including an early example of the Holden designed 'TCP' bus stop post and some different thoughts on finials. L T Museum

The first standard design was this blank 'bullseye'. This one was designed as part of the shelter, an example of Frank Pick's desire to avoid clutter. This evolved into the design shown below left which subsequently changed only in detail. Below right The ultimate LPTB design: a flag which is a pure square; a neatly designed double frame to accommodate two flags on one post; and all attached to the elegant Holden post with red and/or green finials repeating the colours of the flags. L T Museum

Shelters went through fewer changes and a basic all-metal design soon evolved which could be modified for particular circumstances: a simple bench with enclosed ends and roof, as at 'The Travellers Friend, Bath Road (left)**; a similar style but with bullseye signs on the roof at moderately important points, like Hampstead Garden Suburb** (below)**; a more enclosed version, like a small waiting room, at important traffic points like Bounds Green station** (bottom)**; or extended to include a small office for Inspectors as at 'The Bell', Hendon** (right). L T Museum

Below left **Various concrete designs were tried, including this uncomfortable looking cantilever incorporated in the Bus Stop post at Kings Cross.**

Below right **Wooden structures were usually confined to the Country area but this one was built specially for the stand at Putney Common and includes a staff refreshment room at the far end.** L T Museum

CHAPTER TWO DOUBLE-DECK DEVELOPMENTS

When the Board assumed control on 1st July 1933, delivery of General's second batch of STL1s was still in progress and the last twenty-five went into service between 6th July and 4th August, when STL 161 was licensed at Elmers End. The balance of the order for one hundred (STLs 203-252) started to arrive immediately but differed markedly in appearance from their predecessors. The London General Omnibus Company had come to the conclusion that fifty-six seats was the optimum capacity for efficient operation in London conditions and that this capacity would give greater scope within the ten-ton weight limit for technical and design improvements. This gave the body designers the opportunity to move away from the severely angular lines of the STL1 body but, to most eyes, the result was far from being a design classic. Known variously as 'leaning-back' or 'sloping-body', the bodies had a backward sloping front from the top of the radiator to the roof and a curved dome at the back. The front was still rather angular and on these 50 its looks were marred by the arrangement of the front upper deck windows set in a slight 'V' shape. Internally a new, brighter colour scheme was used, with brown 'Rexine' panels and cream ceilings. The seats (thirty up and twenty-six down) were covered in a new design of green moquette which was particularly cheerful in appearance, a long overdue replacement for the dreary lozenge design.

Top **Old and new in Hendon garage. On the right STL 328 was a crash gearbox 6STL3 transferred from Tottenham in the summer of 1934. The NS on the left, which is having one of its pneumatic tyres renewed, shows the typical appearance of the rear end of this class when fitted with a covered top.** L T Museum U22099

Above **The Birch body of former Chariot ST 1031 did not look out of place on route 75 in Catford Hill, in the heart of territory dominated by Tilling's version.** J Bonell

The last of the STL1s still had to be delivered when the Board was formed and the very last were sent to Elmers End. This type had re-introduced the three piece indicator display to the rear and the side display was now supplemented by a route number stencil at the bottom of the rear saloon window. E G P Masterman

Mechanically, the batch was similar to STL 50 in having the D128 preselector gearbox made by Daimler and the A140 100mm petrol engine, and therefore took the same chassis classification, becoming 3STL2 or 1/3STL2. The latter applied to STLs 228-252, which had modified engines with experimental pistons. Other experiments on the 3STLs included a trial with three lighting systems, CAV/Bosch, Peto Radford and Simms. The purchase authority had included money for fluid flywheels but the engineers believed that they were not necessary and secured agreement to experimenting without them.

The first two chassis for the batch were delivered to Chiswick Works on 25th July and the first body was mounted on STL 203 on 3rd August. The first six were licensed on 31st August and the last on 1st December, all but one going to Clayhall where they replaced the 1STL1s. The obvious explanation for this surprising switch might have been a desire to try out the new specification on a central London route but, as many of the STL1s went to Willesden to work its share of route 8, the re-arrangement seems purposeless. The STs displaced from the 8 went to route 18, to which some STLs were also allocated, replacing covered top NSs which in turn replaced others with open tops, mainly at Old Kent Road. The rest of the STL1s went to Elmers End to work on route 169.

Having reviewed its vehicle needs over the following five years, the Board decided to enter into an agreement with AEC for the continuous supply of chassis so that the body shop at Chiswick could be fully occupied turning out completed vehicles at the rate of six or seven a week. At that time there were 1,100 life-expired NSs awaiting replacement and an urgent need for new vehicles in the Country Area. The vehicle purchases authorised at this time were an interesting mixture. The main order, for Central Buses, was for one hundred Regent chassis, without engines, to be bodied at Chiswick (STLs 253-352). The original authority was for all one hundred to have preselector gearboxes, seventy-five Wilson boxes and twenty-five of a new AEC design. In the event fifty had crash gearboxes and the rest D128 Daimler preselectors but there seems to be no record of the reason for this change of mind. Authority was given for all of them to have fluid flywheels and it is a mark of the stubbornness of Chiswick that even as late as October 1933 they were still saying that it might not be necessary to fit them.

The absence of engines arose because the Board had decided to adopt the oil engine as standard but the 8.8 litre A165 type currently available from AEC was not compatible with the standard STL body because it was too long and too heavy. It was therefore decided to buy separately one hundred A165-type engines and fit these to LT class buses, whose petrol engines would in turn be reconditioned and transferred into the new STLs. This was the subject of another change of mind and was later reduced to eighty-nine standard oil engines for LTs and eleven of a new experimental design, derived from one developed for the Q, for fitting into the last eleven STLs. This unit was compact enough to occupy no more space than the petrol engine.

Regents from STL 203 onwards had a less severe body style whose general appearance is displayed by this STL3 at Victoria, Tottenham's STL 257 which was a petrol engined preselector. K W Glazier collection

The STL2 design established the basic rear end which was to change only in detail during the production run of the class. STL 273 was an STL3 whose earlier examples had a small route number box and narrow destination which did not line up with the intermediate point display. Arthur Ingram

Later examples, like STL 277, had a neater arrangement with the indicator boxes matching in height and width and with the unused areas blacked out. Photomatic

The rest of the vehicle orders included the first for the new Country Bus department, twelve AEC Regents with lowbridge bodywork by Weymann for operation on route 410, which were to have oil engines and crash gearboxes, and two AEC Qs with Weymann bodywork, intended for experimental Green Line operation. The Qs were part of an order for four, the other two being for Central Buses, and were purchased primarily to experiment with different door layouts. The possibility of having two Qs as part of the order for route 410 was considered but the chassis was deemed unsuitable for lowbridge bodywork, even though Metro-Cammell had supplied just such a body to Birkenhead Corporation.

Three further Central Bus orders were placed for STLs in November and December 1933 (one hundred each) and March 1934 (200), bringing the total to five hundred, of which the first 350 were to have bodywork of basically similar design to STLs 203-252 but with minor improvements, and second hand 110mm petrol engines from LTs. A further 250 115mm bore oil engines for the LTs were included in the new orders, bringing the total to 339. Chassis specifications for the Regents were quite a mixture and included a surprising number of crash gearbox examples. STLs 253-291 and 403-405 had petrol engines and a D128 preselector gearbox (coded 4STL); STLs 292-341 and 353-402 were petrol with crash gearbox (6STL); STLs 342-352 were the experimental oilers with D128 Daimler preselector boxes and fluid flywheels (5STL); and STLs 406-552 and 559-608 were petrol with the new AEC D132 preselector gearbox (7STL). The D132 gearbox was introduced by AEC early in 1934 so that it could offer its own unit in what was becoming a market of some magnitude. It was similar in principle to the Daimler box, with only a slightly different sound to distinguish it from the earlier design.

The six missing numbers were allocated to five open top Regents acquired from Charles H. Pickup in November 1933 (STL 553-557, new between January and July 1932) and one from Redline (STL 558, March 1932) acquired in December 1933. The Pickups appear to have confused Chiswick who at first regarded them as STs, giving them the numbers ST 1032-1035, perhaps because they found it difficult to imagine an open top STL, but this was soon rectified and the vehicles themselves always carried the STL numbers. These had the same D124 crash gearbox as the 1STLs and 2STLs but their petrol engines were the larger A162-type 110mm unit. Braking was of the vacuum triple servo type, except that STLs 555 and 557 had Lockheed servo assisted hydraulics. The Redline bus also had the larger A162 engine and triple servo brakes but differed in having a preselector gearbox and fluid transmission. STLs 553-557 had their A162 engines replaced by A140-type 100mm units between January and May 1934, immediately after which they were fitted with enclosed top decks, as described later. Under the 1934 classification scheme STLs 553, 554 and 556 became 12STL8, STLs 555 and 557 1/12STL8 and STL 558 13STL9.

The decision not to have fluid flywheels on the earlier preselectors had soon been regretted as the buses were very jerky in operation and there was so much wear and tear that the gearboxes tended to have short lives.

Six (STLs 223, 224, 242, 243, 245 and 246) were therefore fitted experimentally with fluid flywheels in April and May 1934. Another, STL 252, was fitted with a Sinclair Traction Coupling, which was similar in principle to a fluid flywheel but had an additional reservoir which controlled the flow of oil to the working chamber in an effort to reduce drag at low speeds and slip at high speeds. In a more radical experiment, STL 221 was given a Leyland torque convertor instead of a preselector gearbox. The experiment with the fluid flywheels proved successful and the Board decided to adopt them as standard equipment. From the end of July, starting with chassis number 6612810 (STL 490), all new preselectors were delivered with fluid flywheels and the remainder (except STL 221) were converted during October and November 1934. STL 221 kept its torque convertor until August 1937, when it was replaced by a standard preselector gearbox and fluid flywheel. The Sinclair system was not abandoned immediately, but was used in a number of STLs in the 4xx series.

The first of the new STLs appeared at Tottenham on 30th November 1933 and most of the first hundred went there to replace LTs on the 73 and 76 groups of routes. (Tottenham also got the only one of the previous batch not allocated to Clay Hall, STL 226.) This gave Tottenham an unsatisfactory mixture of crash and preselective gearbox vehicles but, starting in July 1934, new preselectors were drafted in so that the crash box buses could be transferred to more suitable locations. LTs were also replaced at Athol Street, where route 106 got a batch of crash gearbox STLs, and at Sutton where the LTs only recently allocated to route 70 were ousted. The other routes to receive STLs at Sutton were the 157 and 165C and these were the first to have NSs replaced directly by STLs. The displaced LTs went to Hammersmith (displacing STs on routes 25A, 74B and 85 and NSs on route 88A) and Merton, in place of NSs on the 88 group. Between April and August 1934, Chalk Farm had a large delivery of STLs for routes 3, 63, 68/A, 169, 77/A and 177, yet again replacing large numbers of LTs except in the case of route 3, where it was NSs which were displaced. The earlier deliveries to Chalk Farm were crash gearbox buses but these were later taken out and transferred to Willesden, where they were used to eliminate NSs from route 6. The Hackney allocation on route 6 was covered by new preselectors, which went into service in August and September 1934.

STL 368, seen at Enfield Highway in 1937, was a 6STL3, with petrol engine and crash gearbox, and as such was a strange visitor to Enfield garage whose other vehicles were oilers. The conductor's signalling window was still an important feature and can be seen as a dark line at the back of the rearmost lower saloon window.
Malcolm E Papes collection

STL 420 was one of the petrol engined examples which had the new AEC D128 gearbox and was therefore a 7STL3. Turnpike Lane bus station has grown in size considerably by now and is used as the main terminal for Wood Green.
Malcolm E Papes collection

Right **One of the buses which interrupted the STL numbering flow was the former Red Line STL 558, which had the casing removed and reverted to open staircase in 1934. It was allocated to Catford and is seen on route 75 in Perry Hill.**
Malcolm E Papes collection

Above **Chalk Farm's standard STL was a petrol engined preselector, like STL 424 which must have been brand new when photographed at South End Green.** J F Higham

Left **Pickup STL 553 as rebuilt with a Chiswick designed top deck. The mismatch between lower and upper decks is particularly apparent in the marked overhang at the front, the different pillar spacing and the awkward join at the rear corner.** D W K Jones

The last allocation from this batch was to Catford to replace the former City vehicles on route 137. Some went initially to Cricklewood, for reasons unknown; it is possible but surely unlikely that a partial allocation of route 137 to Cricklewood was contemplated. Meanwhile, the eleven experimental oilers went to Hanwell to join earlier oil-engined LTs, between February and May. At first they worked on the 526 but in the summer programme starting on 16th May 1934, route 55 was extended to Greenford and acquired a Hanwell allocation of eleven buses, a handy number which neatly absorbed the new STLs. Route 526 reverted to LT.

The STLs again replaced LTs, some of them oil-engined, which went to Hammersmith. The other Renowns were despatched far and wide, ultimately replacing NSs. Examples of routes which took the LTs were the 3 at Norwood, completing the displacement of NSs, the 30 at Leyton and the 49, 70, 88 and 152 at Merton, replacing NSs. The STs deposed in the programme so far went to a variety of locations, replacing NSs at West Green on route 29 and Old Kent Road on route 67, single-deck LTs on route 602 (102) at Enfield and starting up new route 50 at Hounslow. Other LTs and STs were used to cover operations taken over from Independents, some of the LTs having been replaced at Upton Park by acquired Titans (TD class).

The Board had set out to withdraw all remaining open-toppers as quickly as possible and those which were acquired were more often than not delicensed immediately. One exception to this rule was of the five AEC Regents which were taken over from Pickup on 17th January 1934, as they were practically brand new and fitted well into the Board's standard fleet. After a brief spell at Old Kent Road they were found a useful role at Croydon where they replaced the four Tilling-Stevens O-type. These had hung on because they were needed for route 254, which went under a bridge in Croham Road which was too low for covered top buses. The Os ran for the last time on 28th January 1934, five days after the last six open-top Leylands had gone. As lowbridge buses were banned from the Metropolitan Police District under the standard specification set out on all Route Approvals, and as route 254 was too busy to be operated economically by single-deckers, it was diverted to avoid the low bridge in May 1934. The STLs were then taken to Chiswick, between May and September and fitted with new top decks, similar in shape to the STLs then being built but making an awkward combination with the mismatched lower deck. At the front, the upper deck projected some way ahead of the driver's cab and at the back the standard Chiswick profile had to be tapered sharply to follow the line of the Park Royal lower deck. The window pillars on the upper deck also failed to line up with those downstairs because the Park Royal bodies were of six bay construction, while the Chiswick top decks were based on the standard five bay layout. The seating capacity of the upper deck had to be reduced by three because the extra weight of the new top decks would otherwise have taken them over the ten-ton weight limit. They now became part of the normal petrol engined fleet. The last twenty-three Central Bus open top NSs, which had been running at Old Kent Road, were withdrawn and delicensed on 11th April 1934 but the very last Central Bus open-toppers were three Dennis Hs (DH 1-3), which were not delicensed until 3rd November 1934.

Above **The low bridge in Croham Road dictated the use of open toppers until route 254 was diverted in May 1934. To see out the last months, the Pickup STLs were allocated to the route.** Charles F Klapper Collection: Omnibus Society

Left **The Pickups were replaced on route 254 by Tilling STs. Although ST 1019 appears superficially to be in normal service at Selsdon, the presence of several important looking men and the unusual interest being shown by all, suggests that this is an official event, perhaps celebrating the new arrangements.** L T Museum U14764

The oil engines supplied by AEC for the LTs were the A165-type, AEC's standard since 1932, which had incorporated the Ricardo Comet type of indirect injection developed in 1931. It had proved a very reliable unit in service and was enjoying considerable commercial success. The buses chosen to receive the new engines were exclusively crash gearbox examples comprising the 171 Bluebirds with this specification, all dating from 1932, and 168 of the 1931 deliveries with numbers scattered through the series from LT 151 to LT 942. The Bluebirds were recoded from 5LT6 to 11LT6/4 and the 2LTs, which included vehicles with all three main types of body, were reclassified from 2LT3, 5 or 5/1 to 12LT3/3, 5/5 and 5/6 respectively. The only Bluebirds left with petrol engines at the end of this programme were the thirty preselectors which, together with the twenty-four earlier examples, were destined to remain in this condition for the rest of their lives. The decision to omit these from the conversion scheme seems strange in the light of the apparently trouble-free operation of the twenty which had been delivered new with the combination of oil engine and Wilson gearbox (LTs 1355-1374) and the fact that this was to be the standard combination on new buses after 1934.

The oilers were always easily distinguished from their petrol engined siblings because of their projecting radiators, which were set at a slight incline giving them a 'nose-in-air', perpetually disdainful look. Garages chosen for conversion to oil were Hammersmith, which received modified Renowns between October 1933 and March 1934, Dalston (March to May 1934), Seven Kings (May to August 1934) and Barking (August to October 1934).

One other Renown received an oil engine at about this time in a conversion which was unique in two respects. The vehicle chosen, LT 21, was the only open staircase LT ever to be fitted with an oil engine; and the A171 Comet Mk 1 engine, the same type as was then being fitted to new STLs, was the only 7.7 litre unit to be fitted to a Renown. The new engine was installed on 27th June 1935 and in its new guise LT 21 was reclassified from 1/2LT2 to 2/2LT2/2. The reason for this conversion is not known. It could be that the Board was considering replacing the remaining petrol engines in LTs and wanted to assess the suitability of the new, smaller oil engine. Alternatively, there may have been some idea of using the smaller engine in the open staircase vehicles. We may never know. Whatever the reason, the A171 must have proved itself in LT 21 as it remained with the bus until it was scrapped; but it was obviously not considered better than the 8.8 litre unit for the class as whole, as it was this size of engine which was eventually adopted for the remaining conversions of Renowns to oil at the end of the decade. LT 21 was allocated to Dalston on 29th June 1935 and also spent a few months at Hanwell before finally settling down in July 1936 at Mortlake; it was the only open staircase Renown to operate there. It was destined to stay at Mortlake for the rest of its life but had an enclosed staircase body after March 1940.

It is 10am on 24th November 1934 and an overhead fog has turned day to night in London, making traffic congestion at the Bank junction even worse than usual. LT 997 was one of those fitted with new oil engines in December 1933.

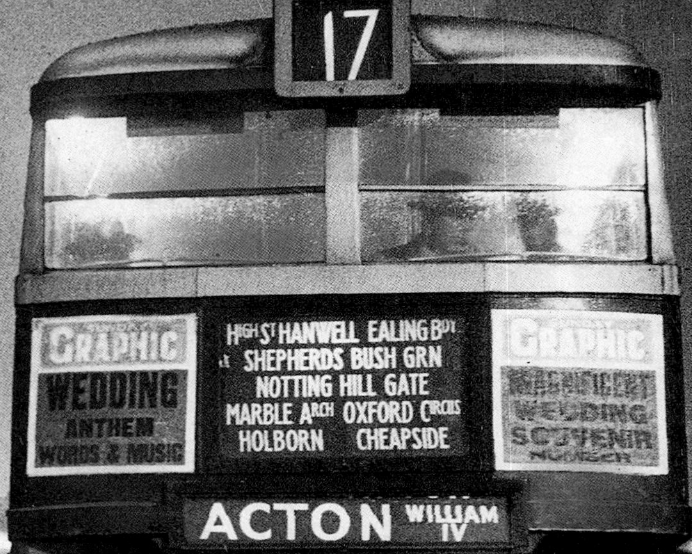

17
GRAPHIC
WEDDING
ANTHEM
WORDS & MUSIC
High St HANWELL EALING Bdy
SHEPHERDS BUSH GRN
NOTTING HILL GATE
MARBLE Arch OXFORD Circus
HOLBORN CHEAPSIDE
GRAPHIC
ACTON WILLIAM IV
GENERAL
GW 5835
AYO 268
Schweppes SODA WATER

Top **Reigate continued to show independence in specifying a standard product for its first new buses under LPTB management. The slender sidelamps, still in the traditional position above the canopy, were later replaced by a larger, more chunky design. As yet unnumbered BPF417 eventually became STL 1052.** L T Museum U15556

Above **The interior of the 'Godstone' STLs was quite unlike any standard LPTB product, with polished wood finishings, brightly patterned moquette, non-standard seats and moulded glass lampshades. The front entrance dictated a slightly awkward arrangement at the front of the upper deck but the problem has been solved neatly by Weymann by careful positioning of the stairwell.** L T Museum U15559

While all this had been going on, Country Buses had taken delivery of its first new buses under the new régime. In accordance with normal Country Bus practice at this time, they were not numbered but when fleet numbers were allocated in 1935, they became STLs 1044-1055. Always known as the 'Godstone' STLs these twelve, which were eventually coded 11STL7, showed little sign of Chiswick influence, their specification and design having been determined by the Reigate management. In this respect they were an interesting insight into what might have become the standard LGCS bus had the company remained in existence. Mechanically they were a considerable departure from contemporary London Transport standards. They were unusual among STLs in having 8.8 litre oil engines, the same A165 model as fitted to the LTs, and were also out of line in being equipped with AEC D124 crash gearboxes. Steering was the normal AEC worm and nut type and Lockheed brakes were fitted. When the buses were new they had three different rear axle ratios ($5\frac{3}{4}$:1, $6\frac{1}{4}$:1 and $6\frac{1}{2}$:1). This mechanical combination was ideal for the tough hilly terrain and indifferent road conditions in which these buses worked, the extra power of the engine being particularly useful for the exacting climbs over the North Downs, especially the long drag up Westerham Hill with its severe 1 in 7 gradient.

The MCW patented metal framed bodywork was to Weymann's standard design with only indicator displays, the Y-shaped rear upper-deck emergency window and the emergency door at the rear of the lower deck to mark them as LPTB owned. A full standard set of indicators was crammed into the limited available space between the decks, three apertures on the front and back and an intermediate point box above the door. A novel feature which reflected a particular preference of General Manager Arthur Hawkins, was the front entrance. Unlike later Country STLs, however, the 'Godstones' had vacuum operated 'Sunsaloon' platform doors supplied by G.D. Peters which had the desired effect of achieving a clean and draught-free atmosphere within the saloons. The interiors were luxuriously appointed with polished walnut mouldings on the windows and ceilings, brightly patterned green moquette on the cushions and seat backs, patterned green 'Rexine' on the side panelling and circular moulded lamp shades. The Ackles and Pollock lightweight tubular framed seats were of a more comfortable design than those on Chiswick products, with double curved high backs and deep cushions. There were forty-eight seats, twenty-six upstairs and twenty-two down. The upper saloon seats were arranged alongside the offside sunken gangway in alternate rows of three and four, well spaced to give room for passengers to get in and out comfortably.

The 'Godstone' STLs were only 13ft 1in high and this, allied to the dumpy looking design, the bulbous cab front and the protruding snout of the 8.8 litre engine, gave them a solidly workmanlike rather than gracious appearance. They were finished in the first version of the Country bus livery of light green with a broad black band below the lower deck windows, black mudguards, silver roof and green rear dome. They bore the fleetname 'GENERAL'. At first their side lamps were at cant rail level, a position which had a brief vogue at this time, but after a few years they were moved to a more conventional position below the lower deck waistrail. All twelve arrived in April and May 1934 and went onto route 410, nine from Godstone and three from Reigate, where they replaced the surviving open-top PS class ADC416As. For a time in 1936 and early 1937 two of the Godstone STLs were allocated to Watford (High Street) where they ran on route 336, otherwise normally served by the lowbridge STs. The only other garage to work the type before the war was Crawley, which received one to operate the local Horsham to Roffey Corner service on route 434 from July 1937.

Above **The brief visit to the 336 of two of the Godstone STLs in 1936/37 would have brought a bit of extra comfort to the route, normally served by lowbridge STs. Former Amersham & District Short Brothers bodied ST 1089B, its windows suffering badly with condensation, is seen close to home at Chesham Broadway.**

Left **Short Brothers bodywork is also carried by this ST, one of a number acquired from the Lewis Omnibus Company, which later in life received standard ST1/1 or ST2 bodies.** J F Higham

The two other buses which joined the fleet in May 1934 were quite different, being AEC 'Q' 761 double-deckers. Qs 4B and 5B (coded 3Q3) were more advanced in having fluid transmission and AEC preselector gearboxes but at this stage of development there was no diesel engine available for this chassis and these and the two for Central Buses had petrol engines. Weymann again supplied the bodywork to its own standard specification, including MCW patented metal framework. Although suitable for a larger capacity, they were fitted with only fifty-six seats (twenty-nine up, twenty-six down), then the London Transport standard. They had centre entrances and stairways as part of an experiment with doorway positions and the platform was enclosed by a pair of sliding power operated doors. The main modifications to the standard product for LPTB operation were the provision of a full set of indicator displays on the front, back and nearside (over the door) and of the standard STL design 'Y'-shaped upper deck emergency window.

The interior finishings were similar to those applied to the 'Godstone' STLs, including the moulded lamp shades, special moquette, patterned 'Rexine' and the non-standard design of seat. The twenty-eight seats on the upper deck were in forward facing pairs of two, except for one single and one double seat alongside the stairwell and a bench for five across the back. The intervention of the centre entrance and staircase and the presence of the side engine made the lower deck layout more complicated. Behind the entrance there were four forward facing pairs, the two rearmost rows at a higher level to clear the axle, and in the front section there were two longitudinal seats over the wheels and engine, with two nearside seats for two ahead of the front axle, one alongside the driver. Although the Green Line fleetname was carried when new, this was removed before they entered service and they were among the first buses to appear with the 'LONDON TRANSPORT' fleetname. They were never used as coaches but were sent instead to Leatherhead for use on route 406.

Above **Standard Weymann bodywork was also mounted on the two experimental 'Qs' for Country Buses and these too were licensed in Surrey. Q5B is seen in Reigate garage, after the Country Bus head office had moved to 55 Broadway and therefore displaying a new legal owner slip ahead of the front wheel.** H J Snook

Right **Another view of Q5B at Reigate, showing the stylish rear end treatment.** L T Museum U15539

The Central Bus version of the double-deck 'Q' had Metro-Cammell bodywork virtually identical to the Weymanns but with an undoored front entrance ahead of the front wheels and with fixed front windows on the upper deck. Qs 2 and 3 had their fleet number on each side of the front dash but this arrangement was not extended to the single-deck version. F Mussett/G H F Atkins

The two Central Buses, Qs 2 and 3 (coded 2Q2), were bodied by Metro-Cammell whose standard design for this model, based on an AEC registered design, was somewhat neater and more rounded than the Weymann products, with which they shared the patented MCW metal framework. These were the first London Qs to have entrances ahead of the front axle, the decision to adopt this no doubt being influenced by the Metropolitan Police requirement that there should be an open doorway. However this did allow full benefit to be derived from the engine position, although the capacity was held artificially low at the standard fifty-six (twenty-eight on each deck). Internally they had much more of a London look than the 3Q3s, with painted woodwork, wooden backed seats, lamp bulbs plugged straight into the ceiling panels and other standard fixtures and fittings. The colour scheme and moquette were the same as then being used on standard STLs. The seating layout on the upper deck was similar to that on the Weymann pair, except for the effect of the different position of the stairwell. The lower deck was much neater, with four forward facing pairs of double seats behind the engine compartment, three more doubles on the nearside opposite a bench seat for four over the engine; and a bench seat for two over the front nearside wheel. Qs 2 and 3 were also fitted with a full set of indicator displays, including a slightly awkward looking full size box over the platform even though this was so close to the front display. The use of standard STL components for the rear indicators and emergency window, gave a slightly ungainly appearance as both were too large to suit the Metro-Cammell body styling.

The first to be taken into stock was Q 3 on 25th May 1934, followed by Q 2 five days later. They went to Harrow Weald for training in June 1934 and were licensed for use on route 114 on 5th (Q 2) and 6th July but stayed only six months as they were transferred to Middle Row garage for route 52 in January 1935 to try out the concept on a busy in-town service. Interestingly, Pick refused to authorise their use on a service running through the City. The experiment was abandoned in July 1937 when both were repainted green and sent to work with the others at Leatherhead. There could have been at least one other type of double-deck Q, as Frank Pick was keen to develop a centre entrance version and issued instructions for designs to be prepared for both bus and trolleybus varieties. Neither project came to anything.

The last 150 of the March 1934 order for Central Buses (STLs 609-758; coded 9STL5) marked a watershed in London bus design and represented the first of a long run of over 2,000 of basically the same standard design which were built between the end of 1934 and September 1939. The petrol engine was finally discarded in favour of oil, using the new AEC A171 7.7 litre unit which had been tried out successfully on STLs 342-352. These engines had 106mm bore and 142mm stroke and produced a power output rated at 115 bhp at the governed speed of 2,000 rpm. The 9STLs were also the first oilers to have the AEC D132 preselector gearbox, which had been specified for the last hundred petrol Regents and was now the standard AEC model. AEC worm and nut steering, Lockheed servo assisted brakes and fluid transmission completed the mechanical specification.

The Chiswick-built composite bodywork was such a leap forward in design that it made the earlier STLs look old-fashioned when still only a few months old. The angularity of earlier designs was replaced by a handsome frontal profile, which ran in a clean, slightly curving line from bonnet to roof, with rather less slope overall than the STL 2 or STL 3, establishing a basic style which was to be much copied by other manufacturers and operators. The driver's cab was also made much neater and tidier. The dash comprised a single panel, flat in aspect on both front and side and running in a smooth curve around the offside front corner. The windscreen and the lower saloon bulkhead windows curved downwards, in harmony with the line of the radiator top and bonnet, to line up with the bottom of the side windows. These were set lower than on previous Chiswick bodies, improving both the outward view for passengers and the external balance of the design. The valance around the canopy was correspondingly deeper enabling it to continue in an uninterrupted line across the top of the windscreen. Two other details which gave further help in improving the finish at the front of the new vehicles were the removal of the Autovac tank from the front bulkhead to a position of decent obscurity under the bonnet and a new position for the sidelamps which were unobtrusively incorporated into the black beading above cantrail level. The latter arrangement proved somewhat impractical and within a few years the regulations were altered and they were replaced by conventional sidelamps below the waistrail, although the apertures could still be seen on many bodies.

The rest of the body design was similar to the STL3s but again changes in detail helped enhance the overall appearance. A seemingly minor change to the black beading around the roof, so that it swept down the back corner in an 'S' curve instead of continuing at the same level all round the bus, gave the rear end of the body a disproportionately more modern appearance. Downstairs, the window in the rearmost offside bay was reduced in size to a narrow signalling window for the conductor and the rest replaced by a metal panel. An oblong route number stencil was placed centrally in this panel and a similar stencil fitting was provided above the rear nearside window. These latter changes were subsequently incorporated in the bodies of earlier vehicles when they went for overhaul. A final touch of style was added by the mudguards which were swept back under the panelling immediately behind the wheel arches.

Above **The STL5 body introduced in 1934, allied to an oil engined preselector chassis (9STL), set the standard for the next five years. This picture of STL 877 at Victoria in September 1937 shows off well the smooth lines of the design.** G H F Atkins

The interior was brighter and neater too. This batch of STLs introduced the inspired idea of making a colour change half way up the windows. The lower part was brown, the upper pale green and the two halves were separated by a polished metal bracelet. The lower panels and seat backs were also green but in a darker shade. Extensive use was made of 'Rexine' as a cover for panelling but the lower section of the front bulkhead downstairs was finished in repp. The seat moquette was in the same brightly patterned green as used on the previous batch. The view that greeted passengers as they entered the saloon was breathtakingly modern, bright and cheerful, handicapped only by the old style wooden framed seats which continued to be specified for a while.

This design was continued in the further two hundred vehicles numbered STL 759-958, except STL 857 which had an experimental body. Because they had a modified lubrication system, the vehicles in this batch had the chassis code 1/9STL. For a time the bodies were officially coded 5/1, for the rather trivial reason that their seat cushions were trimmed with leathercloth, but this code was never carried on the buses and was later dropped altogether. A more important and enduring variation on the last fifteen bodies (coded STL5/2) was the introduction of a new style of chair, with a polished tubular aluminium frame, which put the final touch of modernity and style to the already excellent STL interior. The new design was so successful that it became the basis for the seats on all standard London buses from then until the present day.

Interior of an STL5 bodied vehicle, showing the newly introduced colour scheme around the windows of brown and pale green. L T Museum U16647

The STL ascendant, at Hyde Park Corner in April 1937. Four of the six buses in the foreground are STLs, including one Tilling on the 6. The one on the left, on route 14, has a modified livery, with red corner pillars. AEC

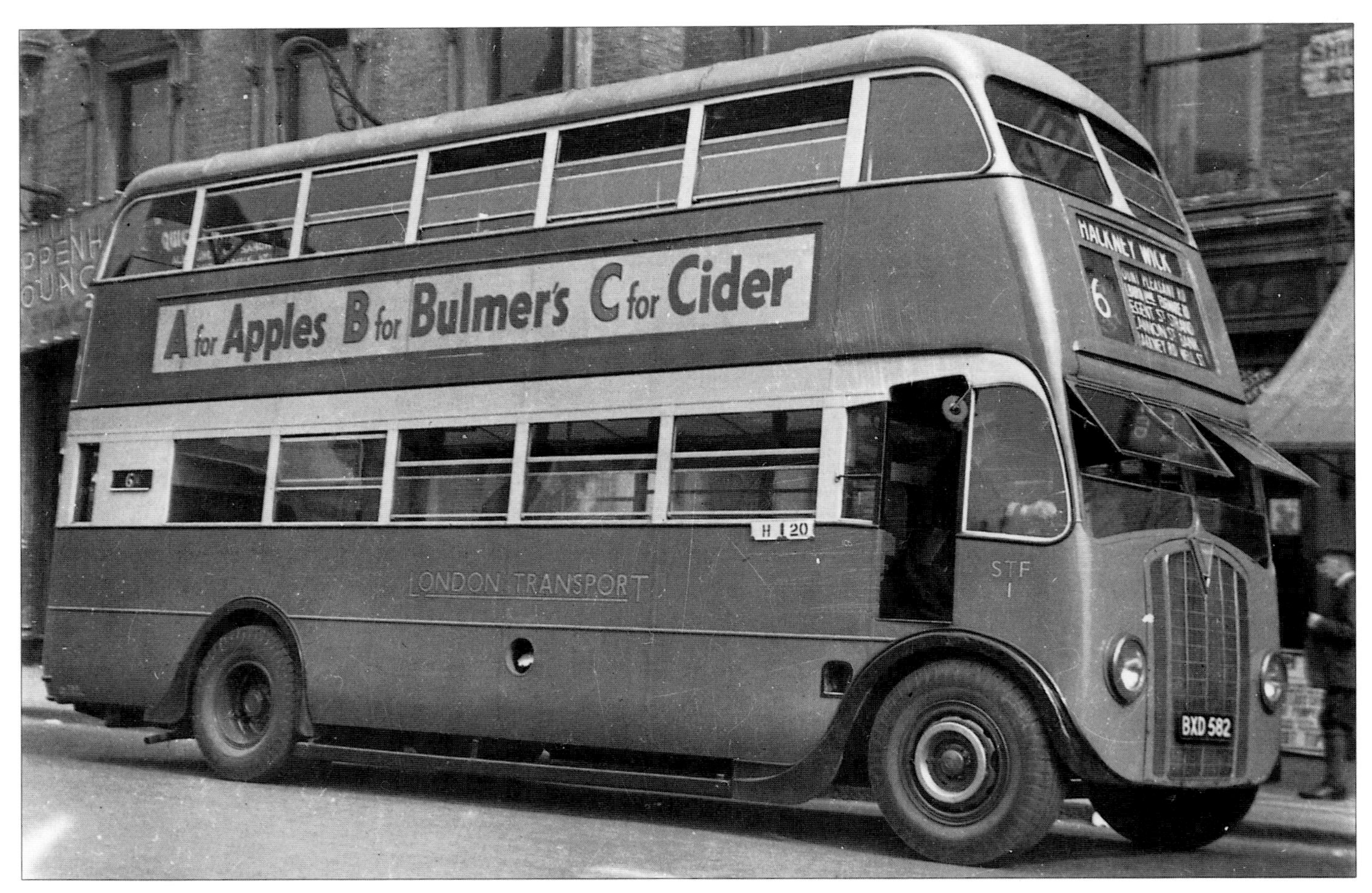

The experimental body on STL 857 was strikingly different from its contemporaries as it was London Transport's contribution to the attempts being made in various parts of the country to develop a truly streamlined bus. Frank Pick had been interested in the idea of a full-fronted design for some time, although his earlier interest had centred on the Q. This, and similar interest by AEC, may have been why the Board was prepared to try out something which was intrinsically less practical than the conventional half cab layout. Most of the innovation was at the front, the rest of the body being similar in general appearance to the standard STL but with differences of detail. The full width cab had much more sharply curved windscreens than usual, to line up with the curved top of an ornamental grille which replaced the aluminium radiator shell. The vertical curvature of the front was considerably more pronounced too, with rounded upper deck windows, and may well have represented Chiswick's early thoughts on the RT. The cab windows on both sides were also curved and the black beading above and below the windows on both decks ran round these curves to join up in a continuous sweep. As a result, the silver roof colour was carried down the front corner pillars and the whole of the front below the upper deck waist was red. The indicator layout was also changed with the destination box being placed above the number and intermediate point boxes, as was to become standard on later types of STL.

There were no fewer than five opening windows on each side of the upper deck and four on each side downstairs. At the back there was a deeper gutter over the upper deck emergency window and the rear dome was painted red, the overall effect being rather clumsy. This was also the first London bus to be fitted with a stop warning light, which was carried alongside the rear lamp above the registration plate. Internally, STL 857 was similar to the STL5/2s, except for the front end which, on the upper deck at least, looked rather like an RT. The complete vehicle was classified 1/9STL11/1, although there were a number of mechanical differences from standard and the body had little in common with the STL11 design, which had yet to appear. It went to Tottenham for route 73 for a while but was soon re-allocated to Hackney for route 6. It was later renumbered STF 1 and the body recoded STF1, at which time it was announced that if it were successful, production would start in June 1936. There was no production run. STF 1 was rebuilt with a half cab in May 1938, when it resumed the number STL 857 and its former body code, but was always instantly recognisable from its unique front end styling and its exceptionally generous supply of opening windows.

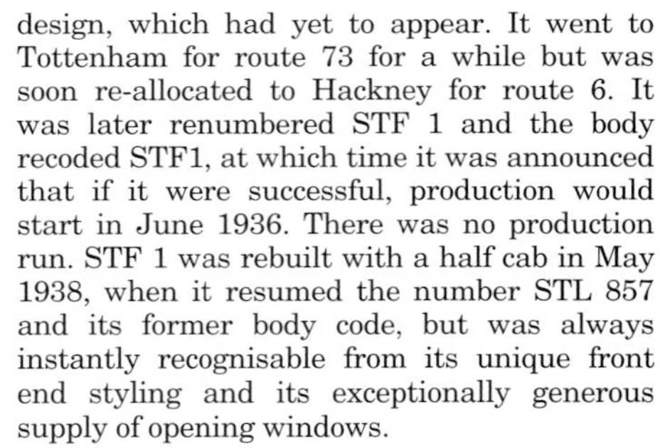

Above **One of many experiments by the energetic LPTB was this full fronted version of the STL, originally STL 857 but now STF 1. The heavy streamlining at the front end was a typical feature of many designs in the 1930s and foreshadowed the ultimate design of the decade, the RT.** J F Higham

Left **Upper deck of STL 857 showing the new style seat frames introduced on this and the STL5/2s.** L T Museum U19056

The evolution of the STL, illustrated at 'The Cricketers', Mitcham. STL 356 (centre) had a petrol engine and crash gearbox and the second style of 'sloping body'; STL 452 (left), a petrol engine and preselective gearbox with the later style of STL3 body without the deep moulding on the side panels; and STL 1295 was a standard oiler with preselective gearbox and an STL11 body. STL 1295 was one of ninety-one delivered in the spring of 1936 which were allocated a rag-bag of registrations when the LCC had a clear out. L T Museum U21246

Hanwell, home of so many 'firsts' was the first to receive the STL5s, in November and December 1934. They restored the class to route 26 and introduced it to the 97, in both cases once more taking over from LTs. Merton then began a marathon run of no fewer than 222, the largest single allocation of new STLs and surely of any type, eliminating its NSs from routes 32, 45 and 49 and ousting its complete stock of LTs running on routes 70, 77/A, 88, 133/A and 152. In June 1935, while Merton was still soaking up most of the deliveries, Dalston received its first STLs, first for its thirty-nine runnings on route 11, where they displaced LTs, then for routes 42 (NS), 47 (LT), 60 (LT) and 9 (NS). STLs also replaced the two LTs which had been covering the former Prince workings on route 38 since 5th December 1934. Hackney began to receive its first oilers in August, second-hand from Merton and then started to take some of the new ones in October. At first they took the place of petrol-engined ones which went to Catford and Tottenham but in November they started the modernisation of Hackney's share of route 42. Most of this batch were in service by the end of 1935 and had by then toppled the NS from its position as the largest Central Bus class. Since the formation of the Board, the licensed fleet of NSs had been reduced from 1,804 to 1,219, seven fewer than the double-decker LTs.

The LTs displaced in this programme went to four garages already operating LTs and to two which were new to the class. The existing garages were Cricklewood (60, 113), Forest Gate (66, 86 and 147), Leyton (10A and 30) and Palmers Green (new route 112). The more significant of the new locations was Sidcup, where its stock of STs on routes 21, 51, 61 and 132 was replaced. Outstandingly interesting but with less long-term significance was their allocation to Chiswick Tram Depôt which was then temporarily operating route 30 during the reconstruction of Chelverton Road garage. Other LTs and some of the displaced STs were again used to cover former Independent runnings, while a number of other routes were converted from NS to ST.

The new Road and Rail Traffic Act which became law during 1934 included a clause which allowed bridge authorities to designate bridges as weak and to limit the weight of vehicles crossing them. Among the many bridges in the London Transport area which were listed for this treatment was the bridge over the railway at Kilburn High Road station, which was to be limited to a maximum laden weight of twelve tons. The double-deck LSs, all of which were then operating on route 16 which crossed this bridge, exceeded this limit and it was decided to reduce their seating capacity. They were altered from sixty to fifty-six seats progressively, starting with LS 1 in July 1934 and finishing with LS 9 in September 1935.

This famous view of STL 989 turning from Market Street into High Street Watford bears repetition as it captures the atmosphere of a 1930s country town perfectly. On the right is one of the new 4Q4 single-deckers. AEC

The first major variant from the standard STL5 design was part of an authority from the Board on 4th October 1934 for the first stage in the Country Bus department's fleet renewal, the greater part of which was for 174 single-deckers. Interestingly, although the single-deck orders included one hundred AEC Qs, the model had been more or less abandoned in its double-deck form because of intractable problems with the internal layout, the seating arrangement and the variation in floor levels. The eighty-five STLs which were ordered became STLs 959B-1043B (10STL6) and in general appearance and mechanical specification were the same as the 9STL5s.

They were however fundamentally different in layout, as they had front entrances and staircases and only forty-eight seats. Unlike the 'Godstone' Regents there were no platform doors. Instead there was a wide open platform, reached by two steps, with its bulkhead to the saloon angled in what proved to be a somewhat futile attempt to prevent draughts. There were only nineteen lower deck seats, all facing forward, the space over the wheel arches being used as a parcel shelf; and twenty-nine upstairs. By the time the first of these buses was delivered in February 1935, the Country Bus department had adopted a new standard colour scheme using two shades of green with a black central relief and the STLs looked particularly fine in this livery. Unfortunately, it was not to prove very durable in service, as Frank Pick discovered to his dismay when he visited parts of the Country area in January 1938. He was particularly dissatisfied with the condition of buses at Northfleet, where the propensity for the green colour to fade was given added momentum by pollution from the industry along the River Thames, notably the abrasive deposits of cement dust from the factories in Greenhithe and Swanscombe. The engineers would have liked all buses to be painted in the standard red but this was overruled because of their use as reliefs on the Green Line, although Frank Pick did suggest retaining the green association in an otherwise red colour scheme, by having green lines across the body. The eventual solution was the famous Lincoln green and white livery, which was introduced at the end of 1939.

The first garage to receive the new Regents was Watford High Street, where they became the sole stock for trunk route 321, some of the later deliveries going to St Albans and Luton for the same route. The rest all went to southern area garages, the largest block to Northfleet for the busy Thames-side route 480 and Gravesend local services 487, 488, 495 and 496. The three other Kent garages all got allocations too, Dunton Green first, in April, for routes 401, 402 and 403 then Dartford for the 480's companion routes in north Kent, the 407 and 477, while Swanley's batch were used for the 423 and its share of routes 401 and 477. Meanwhile, Chelsham's allocation on route 403 was converted, along with a few runnings on route 408.

Above **The STL6s were born into a countryside still very rural in aspect and traditional in the pursuits followed by its inhabitants. It is Northfleet's STL 1030 that looks out of place here but the driver no doubt regards making his way around the horses and hounds of the Eynsford Hunt as all in a day's work. The elegant design of the front aspect of the standard STL body is well caught here, the gentle inward slope of the upper deck happily complementing the smooth backward curve of the front end. The inset sidelamps in the cantrail beading help to complete the smooth lines but this proved to be a transient feature of the design.** John Aldridge

Left **The wide open front entrance of Northfleet's STL 1002B leaves a clear run for wind and rain straight into the lower saloon, despite the carefully angled design.** Malcolm E Papes collection

A further four identical STLs were authorised in June 1935 (STL1056B-1059B) and delivered to Dunton Green and Swanley the following month. Vehicles withdrawn following the arrival of these eighty-nine buses included former LGCS NS-type and Dennis Hs acquired from Independents. The open-top TDs (143-151) were not withdrawn as might have been expected but instead, between April and December 1935, were fitted with enclosed top decks, reputedly from withdrawn NSs and certainly of that design.

Just before the STL6s were delivered, in February 1935, responsibility for the Country Bus fleet was transferred from Reigate to Chiswick, including overhauls and licensing. Chiswick soon put a stop to the peculiar arrangement under which the Country Bus department had operated without fleet numbers and these STLs became the first new vehicles delivered to the Country Bus department to have bonnet numbers. The rest of the fleet was then allotted numbers and this is how the 'Godstone' STLs came to have numbers between the main batch of STL6s and the four extra ones which did not arrive until June 1935 (1044B-1055B). Similar numbering peculiarities could be detected in other classes, particularly the Ts and STs, while the GF class received its third numbering plan. Some vehicles, notably NSs and STs, had their old LGOC numbers restored. The application of numbers did not occur overnight and there was a certain haphazardness about how this was done. The standard arrangement was for the number to be applied by gold transfers to the bonnet side and to the offside of the driver's cab but the offside number was often omitted by Country Buses and some garages used the old style of 'National' black letters and numbers for a time. Once all vehicles had been through Chiswick for overhaul, they conformed to the standard.

Top **Among the many vehicles sent on their way by the new STLs was the Maudslay Mentor from the Gordon fleet (MY 1B) which had been the 1931 Commercial Motor Show exhibit of the Dodson company. It was passed to Country Buses in February 1934 and is seen in its early days on route 408D at West Croydon.** Malcolm E Papes collection

Centre **Former Maidstone & District TD 143B at Slough station before being fitted with an enclosed top deck.** J F Higham

Right **TD 147B on route 444 in Slough, allocated to Slough garage, after being fitted with this NS style upper deck in 1936 in common with the other open-top TDs.** Alan B Cross

Once its experimental service as a coach was over, LT 1137 was modified for bus work by having its seating capacity increased to fifty-six, its staircase moved to the front, the platform door removed and a larger destination indicator box installed. It is in St Peters Street, operating from the new St Albans garage on route 330.
D W K Jones

Below **The modified lower deck of LT 1137, with the rather spartan wooden framed seats then in vogue. The revised position for the staircase has been arranged neatly and, unlike the STLs, there is a conventional half bulkhead on the nearside.**
D W K Jones

On the STL11 the destination blind was moved to the top of the display, presumably to make it easier for conductors to change, and the sidelamps returned to positions at lower deck waist level. STL 1132, one of those delivered new to the rebuilt Chelverton Road at the beginning of 1936, is at Putney Common in company with one of the fast diminishing NS class. J F Higham

Below **A new design of lightweight tubular seat was introduced with the STL11s and the use of a green moquette blended well with the brown and light green colour scheme. This is STL 1301.** L T Museum U20167

With the next order for 200 Central Bus STLs (1060-1259), authorised in May 1935, Chiswick took the design a stage further forward as the STL11. Altogether 500 vehicles were built to this improved design, a further order for 200 (STLs 1264-1463) authorised in December 1935 being followed in March 1936 by a huge order for 500, of which the first 100 were STL11s (STLs 1514-1613). The main differences on the body were the restoration of the sidelamps to the more conventional position below the waistline and the transfer of the destination blind box to the top of the display. These were also the first production London buses to be fitted with a stop light, which was positioned alongside the rear light above the registration plate. A few were equipped with disc trims on both front and rear wheels, adding further distinction to an already handsome design, but this idea was not adopted as standard on double-deckers for the time being. Internally, the most striking improvement was in the use of the new design of lightweight tubular framed seats which had been tried on fifteen of the STL5/2s.

The STL11s entered service over a period of ten months between December 1935 and October 1936 and a whole swathe of routes got STLs, either new or second-hand. The restocking of Dalston, including the replacement of its LTs on routes 47 and 60, and Hackney was continued with the first of the STL11s, after which Chelverton Road began to have its first taste of the new generation of buses, its fleet of NSs having remained unscathed so far. The garage had just been extensively rebuilt and route 30 had been housed temporarily at Chiswick Tram Depôt (CK) between 17th July 1935 and 4th March 1936, during which time it had been allocated LTs. To provide the Renowns, there was a complicated reshuffling of vehicles which ended up with the temporary reversion of route 45, at Merton, from STL to NS, which must have come as a bit of a shock to its passengers. When route 30 returned to Chelverton Road, it was allotted some of the new STLs, the others going to routes 39 and 72 (the latter on transfer from Turnham Green where it had been operated by NSs). Hanwell's apparently insatiable appetite for new buses was again indulged in February and March 1936, to continue the conversion of route 17 from LT, followed by more in May to satisfy the needs of a newly acquired allocation on route 83.

Another garage favoured with more than its fair share of new vehicles was Tottenham, which began to take in oil-engined STLs during the early summer of 1936, despatching all its petrol-engined examples to other garages while also replacing its NSs on routes 22 and 39. This tendency to restock routes by re-allocating second-hand, often quite new, vehicles which had been displaced by new ones, was particularly rife at this time so that, when Putney Bridge began to take STLs in May 1936, it was a mixture of new and second-hand vehicles that they were given. Routes 96 and 14 now lost their NS allocations, while the STs from route 74 went off to start another round of re-allocations. Petrol STLs, mainly displaced from Tottenham, were used to cover the withdrawal of Forest Gate's NSs from route 96, after which they continued to arrive in substantial numbers to replace the entire fleet of LTs on routes 25A, 25B, 66, 86, 147, 148 and 149. Two garages hitherto unacquainted with the LT class received Renowns from this released multitude: Holloway, to replace its NSs on route 27; and Elmers End, to replace STs on route 12, STLs on the 169 and NSs on the 194. Other displaced STs and LTs were used to start new routes 107, 110, 118, 122 and 123.

It was again mostly LTs which were displaced by the arrival of STLs at Cricklewood, although they were used also to start new route 119 in October. The routes which lost their Renowns were the 2 and 113 but most of this was achieved with the next batch of new Regents. During this run of deliveries another important milestone was passed when, at the end of May, the STL class overtook the LT to become the largest in the Central Area, with 1,231 licensed. By now the licensed NS fleet had shrunk to only 870 and the first two of the LS class had been withdrawn at Cricklewood.

The first of the two gaps in the numbering of the STL11s, STLs 1260-1263, was filled by a very odd quartet of vehicles, the cost of which must have been very difficult to justify. The four CH6 model Daimlers (DST 1-3/5) had been withdrawn in February 1936 but, although their chassis were not considered by Chiswick to be up to scratch, the bodies were only five years old and it was apparently considered extravagant to scrap them. Four special chassis were therefore ordered from AEC which had the same specification as the 3/9STLs, except that their wheelbase was shortened to 15ft 6½in. Having decided to distinguish between the short and long wheelbase Regents (unlike the LT class) it is odd that Chiswick did not classify these as STs. The ST-like bodies of DST 1-3 became STL 1260/1 and 1263, while STL 1262 had the Birch body from the former Redline DST 5. The first to be licensed was STL 1263, which was sent to Merton in April but it did not stay there long as it was re-allocated to Tottenham within a week and was joined there by the other three over the next six months.

Above **Once dominated by the LT class, Ilford Broadway is now the stamping ground of the STLs, three of which can be seen here. Just visible in the distance along the High Road is one of Ilford's new trolleybuses.**
E G P Masterman

Left **One of the hybrid short wheelbase STLs at Edmonton station, STL 1260. Apart from the registration and fleet numbers, these vehicles could be distinguished from STs by the thicker rear wheel centre.**
D A Ruddom collection

The second gap was filled by another batch of front entrance STLs for the Country Area (STLs 1464B-1513B). These fifty buses were ordered to enable the last of the NSs to be removed from the country fleet and, apart from the minor design changes already noted on the STL11, could be distinguished externally from the first batch only by the radiused tops to the front upper deck windows. The construction of their bodies was, however, radically different as they were built by Weymann of Addlestone, using the MCW patented form of all-metal construction. One internal difference which deserves mention was that the moquette used for the seats was the design then being used in coaches as there was at one time a possibility that the STLs might be used on the busy route Y1 from Romford. This is covered more fully in chapter six. The choice of Weymann was probably dictated by the statutory restriction on the number of bodies which Chiswick was allowed to build in a year, which was 527. This batch had the same mechanical specification as the 2/9STLs and were coded 1/10STL6/1.

They entered service between July and December 1936 and all but one again went to southern area garages. There were no doubt good operational or engineering reasons for this decision but it helped to reinforce a widely held belief, which never died during the whole time that Country Buses was part of London Transport, that Reigate, still embodying the spirit of East Surrey, tended to favour the south. The first three were licensed at Crawley and Reigate on 1st July 1936 for use on route 405. Reigate took the lion's share of the batch (sixteen) for operation on the 405, 406 and 414, while Leatherhead took enough for its share of route 406 and also to join Chelsham's earlier batch on the 408. Dorking's allocation was used mostly for route 70, still stolidly hanging on to its distinctive number and its unique quality as the only route worked jointly with Central Buses. The last of the batch were licensed in December 1936, when Guildford took four to complete the 408 and St Albans one for the 330, the sole allocation to the northern area. Apart from the NSs, the vehicles replaced included the lowbridge and former open-top TDs.

Top **The main feature which distinguished the STL6/1s from their Chiswick built predecessors was the radiused tops to the front upper deck windows. STL 1478, the only one of the batch to be allocated to a northern garage, makes an interesting contrast with Enfield's STL 2212, an STL14/1 six months its junior, in Cecil Road Enfield.** D A Ruddom collection

Centre **Just thirteen months after first entering service at Crawley, STL 1464 gets its feet wet in typical August floods in Brighton Road Purley.** J B Gent collection

Right **The last of the Country Bus NSs was withdrawn at the end of 1936, with the arrival of the second batch of standard STLs. NK6919, on route 303 at New Barnet in April 1935, was one of the class originally operated by the National Omnibus and Transport Co.** D W K Jones

Although it was clear by now that London Transport had nailed its colours to the STL mast for its double-deck requirements, in October 1935 it had given authority for another experimental vehicle, intended as a prototype for the Romford coach services. The model chosen was, surprisingly, the AEC Q; even more surprising was the choice of a three-axle layout (classified 763 by AEC), as this arrangement had been abandoned formally when the first volume orders for STLs were placed. The chassis was based on the single-deck design, whose dimensions it shared, and was fitted with the customary 7.7 litre oil engine and fluid flywheel. Some sources describe its gearbox as a Cotal electrically operated epicyclic unit of French design which as such would have been much in advance of the standard preselectors. However, official records do not support this.

Q 188, which was classified 7Q7 by London Transport, had a Park Royal fifty-one seat body combining some design ideas from the single-deck 6Q6 with an upper deck whose handsomely curved front end bore some resemblance to STF 1. Also striking was the arrangement of the upper deck windows as pairs in double length bays split by a slender pillar, which was painted black to give a sense of greater length. The arrangement of destination indicators was unusual too, with a large box placed centrally between two strip boxes, one of which was used to display the 'GREEN LINE' name. There were no side blinds as provision was made for a standard coach route board, as shown in official photographs of the completed vehicle, although this was destined never to be used in service.

Internally the vehicle was very modern looking, not to say somewhat ahead of its time in many ways. It foreshadowed the RT in having rounded window cappings with polished finishers and opening windows operated by a winding mechanism, although in this case it was operated by a handle placed centrally above the window, as on the single-deckers. The ceiling panels had an eggshell finish and other fittings and finishings also followed standard Green Line practice. The seat design was to Green Line standard with high backs and deep squabs and all were covered with moquette in the vertically striped cool greens and browns then standard on the Board's coaches. The twenty-eight upper deck seats were arranged in forward facing rows of doubles, with a gap alongside the stairwell where the door mechanism intruded. The ledge was used as a luggage rack. Downstairs a lot of space was wasted as there were only twenty-two seats, fourteen of them forward facing doubles and another three, ahead of the entrance area, longitudinal. For coach service, inward facing seats were apparently deemed undesirable at the rear of the saloon and there were therefore four single forward facing seats alongside the rear wheelarches.

Although Q 188 was taken into stock in February 1937, the plans for double-deck operation at Romford fell through and it languished until 1st June 1938, when it was at last licensed. Shortly afterwards it went to Hertford where it was used not as a coach but as a bus on route 310. It was joined there by the other four double-deckers, an indication that the Board had finally decided that it had no further interest in developing the Q.

Top **Official view of Q 188 when new. The entrance and staircase were situated slightly off-centre in the third bay and the arrangement was unusually neat and well proportioned because the single sliding door was the same width as the other window bays.** L T Museum
Centre **Q 188 interior, lower deck.** L T Museum
Above **Q 188 in its latter days, working as a bus from Hertford garage.** R S Turnbull

The large order for 500 STLs authorised in March 1936 was due for completion in June 1937, when there would be nearly six hundred NSs still in service. In January 1937, the Board decided to accelerate the replacement of the NSs and approved its biggest ever vehicle programme, involving the purchase of 672 double-deckers and 114 single-deckers. Of these, 572 were to be STLs but the balance of double-deckers was to come from Leyland who were to be entrusted with the supply of one hundred. Such a large programme took the number way above what Chiswick was allowed to build and it was therefore decided that the Leylands should be built complete by that manufacturer and that 175 of the STLs should have bodywork by Park Royal. In the event only 502 STLs were ordered and the number of single-deckers was increased by seventy. This change was tied up with another failed attempt to get double-deckers onto the Romford Green Line routes, for which these seventy vehicles were intended.

Not all of the 1937 orders were for fleet renewal. The development of the suburbs and the general increase in the population of the Board's area was establishing a need for additional resources and no fewer than 134 were intended for this expansion.

When the first of the remaining 400 STLs of the March 1936 order appeared they had bodywork which was widely acknowledged as being the best and most noble looking so far. The change which wrought this transformation was the re-introduction of the roof mounted route number box which, in this design, was tidily blended into the front dome. Ironically the main reason driving the change was a desire to improve the layout of advertisements on the front, which was probably as much commercial as aesthetic. The other important structural change was that these bodies were intended to have metal floor framing but there were production problems and only six were built in this form, which took the body code STL12.

Internally, they were similar to the STL11s, except that a slightly simpler, less attractive, moquette design was used and the light green above the windows was replaced by pale yellow. Twenty-five of the bodies had Widney Stewart PYP winding gear on their opening windows, instead of the usual pinch grip type, but the design was somewhat troublesome in operation and was not used on any other STLs. On the upper deck the front dome incorporated a lockable square flap, flush with the panelling, which contained the route number blind and winding gear, so that the number could be changed from within the saloon. This was a tidier and more convenient arrangement than on earlier roof-box vehicles in the LT and ST classes where the blind had to be changed using an external handle, reached through one of the front windows, with the help of someone down below to observe when the correct display had been reached. Of the STL 1614-2013 batch, 360 received this type of body, the bulk of them having the timber underframe and classified STL14.

The 327 Chiswick built bodies for the 1937 programme were numbered STL 2189-2515 and were again predominantly of the STL14 type (although inexplicably classified STL14/1), only ninety-four being of the intended STL12 type. One of the STL14/1 bodies in this batch, 17758 fitted to STL 2434, had an experimental front nearside wing mounting, designed to allow the use of a rubber mudguard, which incorporated a curved extension of the front bulkhead to meet the mudguard, so enclosing the usual gap behind the wing. This neat arrangement, which incidentally removed a dirt trap, was tried out as a production run on the 10T10 coaches and was eventually adopted as standard on the RT family.

The last three chassis in this block, STLs 2513-2515, were fitted with the uncommon A182 AEC direct injection oil engine which was a 115mm bore x 142mm stroke 8.8 litre unit, developing 130 bhp. This was an improved version of the A180 and was the basis of the new engine for the RT, which was then in the early stages of its development.

The Park Royal bodied buses were numbered STL 2014-2188 and classified 4/9STL15. Their design followed the Chiswick product very closely and the untrained eye would find it difficult to distinguish them from the STL14s. Structurally they were quite different as Park Royal used its own patented 'all-metal' construction, which was different from the MCW method and unfortunately, as time would tell, far less durable, at any rate on this application. Internally, the different origin was evident in the window cappings which were semi-circular in section and the side panels which were in one continuous piece with the window ledges and covered in brown instead of green Rexine.

The lower deck interior of Park Royal STL 2083, in which the rounded window cappings and the straight sided panels below waist level were the distinguishing features. A new colour scheme had now been adopted in which the pale green above the windows was replaced by cream and a new, slightly duller, moquette was used. L T Museum U23784

The roof route number box on the STL14s added an air of distinction to an already handsome body design, which in most other respects remained the same. STL 1833 was new at Twickenham garage in March 1937. J F Higham

The old station buildings on the Brighton side at London Bridge were doomed to be destroyed by bombing three years after the delivery of STL 2462, an STL12 identical in appearance to the STL14s. J D P House

The forty missing vehicles in the STL 1614-2013 batch had specially designed bodies for working through Blackwall Tunnel and were intended as replacements for the so-called 'clerestory' NSs. They were based on the STL11 design, without a roofbox, but with the upper deck tapered inwards and the rear end built narrower. Internally the important difference was that the profile of the roof required that the staircase had to turn through a full 180° to provide adequate headroom for passengers emerging onto the upper deck, which caused it to project into the lower deck and reduce the length of the offside longitudinal seat from three to two. Upstairs, the two single seats were placed one behind the other on the nearside. The chassis were standard 4/9STL type but were fitted with specially re-inforced tyres to prevent undue wear when rubbing against the kerbs in the narrow tunnel roadways. All forty entered service in March and April 1937 carrying fleet numbers scattered between 1809 and 1884 and were classified STL13. The first few were licensed on 17th March 1937, not for tunnel service but at Holloway, which eventually got ten, and later at Hackney, which got seven. The first three to go into service on route 108 did so on 24th March, after which Athol Street and Camberwell gradually received the whole batch. The NSs they replaced were the last solid tyred buses running in London, having been the first London buses to have enclosed staircases in 1927.

Above right **The inward curving roofs of the STL13s conspired to give a more curvaceous look to the front of the bus but otherwise they were standard. STL 1851, passing St George's Parade Catford Hill on 26th March 1937, two days after the first Athol Street ones started running, has a temporary small intermediate point blind and part of the indicator glass obscured.** Malcolm E Papes collection

Below **A different design solution had been used on the thirty-one vehicles replaced by the tunnel STLs. NS 2222 was one of the original batch built in 1927 for tunnel work, in which the upper deck seating was arranged down the centre, back to back and the side gangways sunken, which was how they came to be known as the 'clerestory' type. These buses also had enclosed staircases, the first in London.** J F Higham

The similarity of the Leyland body on the STDs to the Chiswick product was uncanny but only skin deep and, apart from the radiator and wheels, one external tell-tale was the small signalling window, which slightly spoilt the lines of the body. STD 88 is working a short to Burnt Oak and the driver seems to be getting agitated about the still seated passengers. Charles F Klapper collection: Omnibus Society

Below **STD 64 in its home town of Hendon in September 1937, four months after entering service.** G H F Atkins.

The Leylands, numbered STD 1-100, were nominally based on the standard TD4 and TD4c model Titan chassis but they were really a special design for London, using a combination of standard Leyland features and others specified by Chiswick. The steering on the TD4 was relatively highly geared, whereas London Transport normally specified low geared. AEC's standard product, no doubt developed primarily with London in mind, met this requirement and was therefore specified for the STDs. Another requirement was that the dumb irons should be suitable for towing and the towing arrangements should be interchangeable with the STL. A new design was therefore developed, which introduced the characteristic square-box-like arrangement which was subsequently introduced on the TD5 and remained a feature of all future front-engined Leylands. There were many other small variations. Ninety of the Titans were fitted with crash gearboxes (STD 1-90) and ten with torque convertors (STD 91-100). All 100 had the Leyland 8.6 litre oil engine which was rated at 98 bhp.

The bodywork was also the standard Leyland metal framed product modified to London Transport standards in many details, large and small. Externally they were modified in detail to resemble the latest style of roofbox STL, which they did with some success, although there were a number of features which marked them as different. The Leyland body had a slightly more bowed front than the Chiswick version and the use of the characteristic scrolled beading between the decks, rather like an inverted gutter, noticeably deepened the valance in front of the bulkhead and the panelling above the lower deck windows.

Internally they were equipped and decorated in the same style as the STL11s, except that Leyland made a distinct improvement by covering the pillars and window cappings in leathercloth, rather than painting the woodwork as was Chiswick's practice. There were two distinctive features which told passengers they were in an STD: the straight window line on the front lower deck bulkhead; and the downward slope of the floor at the front end of the lower deck, from which there was a shallow step up to the seats. STDs 91-100 also had one seat fewer than the rest, as the casing of the torque convertor projected into the lower saloon leaving room for only a single seat at the front nearside.

London Transport was strangely timid in deciding to have only ten torque convertor buses and it must have seemed odd to staff that, after standardising on the preselective gearbox, the Board suddenly took ninety new buses with crash gearboxes. This decision might have made more sense had the buses been allocated to the Country department, where their specification might have been more appropriate than the arguably over-engineered STL. Nevertheless, these buses were soon outperforming the STLs, to such an extent that Frank Pick was suspicious of the information he was getting in their early days, while the buses were being 'nursed' by Leyland engineers and insisted on further tests when they had gone. Experience with these fine buses was to influence Chiswick's thinking on the development of the RT, particularly in respect of the larger pot cavity engine. The torque convertors were not a success, however, or at any rate did not measure up to Chiswick's requirements and were replaced by crash boxes in 1938/39.

The first Titan to be received at Chiswick was torque convertor STD 91, which arrived for inspection on 18th March 1937. It went back to Leyland on 20th May, for modifications, returned to Chiswick on 28th June and eventually entered service on 6th July. The first to go into service were STDs 1 and 2, which were taken into stock on 5th April 1937 and licensed on 24th and 26th of that month. The first torque convertor into service was STD 92, which was licensed on 15th June, and the last Titan licensed was STD 100, which started work on 13th July at Hendon where all 100 were destined to spend most of their lives. The first Titans replaced the STLs on routes 52 and 113 and STs on routes 83, 121 and 183 but the remainder were direct replacements for NSs on the 13 and 28.

The roofbox STLs began to roll in October 1936 and the 687 vehicles spread themselves relentlessly around the fleet until the full programme was completed in June 1938 and the STL was the dominant bus in London. The first went to Cricklewood to complete the restocking started by the STL11s, then Holloway replaced the last three NSs on route 14, along with the LTs allocated to that route and the STs on the 27 and 111. When route 41 was extended from Crouch End to Archway in February 1937 part of its allocation was transferred to Holloway, for which some of the STLs were allotted; the rest of Tottenham's NSs on the route were also replaced by STLs. This arrangement lasted only a month. From 7th March 1937 an embargo was placed on the use of any type other than the LT on route 41 and the STLs were replaced by LTs on that date. The reason for this restriction is not known but was probably designed to reduce the axle loading over the railway bridge at Crouch End Station, on which there was a weight limit, by distributing the weight of the vehicle over three axles.

Twickenham was another garage which had so far resisted the blandishments of the Regent and Renown generation but it began to lose its NSs in December 1936, first from route 37, then from route 27A. More NSs were driven out by STLs from route 46 (Cricklewood and Camberwell garages), 37 (Chelverton Road), 93 (Putney Bridge), 56 and 57 (Athol Street) and 92 (Cricklewood). STLs turned out

Top **Belgravia saw its last NSs when route 24 received recycled STLs in 1937. A selection of other vintage vehicles completes the scene.** Lens of Sutton

Centre **The Battersea allocation on route 28 went over to STL in the summer of 1937 and sights like this, of NS 598 at Golders Green, became a thing of history.** Dennis Odd Collection

Above **NS 1770 at Wanstead Flats on 3rd July 1937, shortly before the class was eliminated from the route at both Camberwell and Forest Gate.** J D P House

Top **One of the last garages to have an allocation of NSs was Old Kent Road, who ran them on route 4. NS 1896 is at Finsbury Park in July 1937.** D W K Jones

Centre **A new role for the old warhorse; an NS, modified for use as a staff canteen, is parked outside the 'Archway Tavern' to serve the needs of staff on layover at Highgate Hill.** John Aldridge

Above **NS 289 in use as a staff canteen at Eccleston Bridge. In this case the body has been cut down, presumably to allow for low bridges.** Malcolm E Papes collection

of Hendon by the STDs were used for the Sutton allocation of route 93, while others displaced from Forest Gate by new oilers, went to Enfield to start the removal of NSs from the 69 and to Chalk Farm to modernise the 24 and 31. The 69 was completed with new buses at Enfield and re-allocated STs at Camberwell.

NS replacement at Holloway resumed with route 19 in June 1937, after which Battersea tackled its share of the 19, 28 and 31 and Cricklewood the mammoth task of re-equipping two of the last few remaining West End routes operated by the NS, the 13 and 16. Battersea, Cricklewood and Enfield were still receiving new buses when the first of the 1937 programme vehicles began to appear in July, after which Palmers Green started to receive them for route 29, replacing its large NS allocation, and later for the 34 and 112, replacing LTs. The allocation of STs to route 69 at Camberwell proved to be short lived as they were replaced by new and second-hand STLs, starting in August. Later arrivals at Camberwell joined with new deliveries to Forest Gate to oust NSs from route 40.

The STs displaced at various times during this programme were also used to help dispose of the NS class, notably at Camberwell, where they were allocated to routes 67 and 69, Holloway (4 and 44), Old Kent Road (4) and West Green, where the substantial allocations on routes 29 and 124 changed over. Other redundant STs were used to open up new routes 50, 72A, 115, 124 and 160. By this time the ST class was becoming well and truly scattered. Although there were still some garages with substantial allocations of the class, the neat arrangement of the early days had now been disrupted for good.

This flood of new buses made rapid inroads into the remnants of the once large NS fleet until on 30th November 1937 there were just four still running on peak hour route 166 from West Green garage. The very last service run of this trend-setting class took place just after 7pm that evening when NS 1974 left London Bridge for its last trip to Aldwych before returning home at 7.27pm via Bank. The ill-fated LS class six-wheelers had also disappeared by this time having dwindled away slowly since October 1936, until there were only three, which ran their last journeys on route 16 on 22nd March 1937.

Neither class disappeared completely. Twelve NSs were converted to staff canteens (29H-40H) for use at locations where the Board was unable to find adequate or economical permanent accommodation. In this form the class lasted for many years, although the original intention had been that most of them should provide only temporary cover until permanent facilities could be built and that no more than three or four should be retained for use at special events, such as Epsom Races. The last to be withdrawn was 30H (NS 250) in March 1954. Another eight were transformed into tower wagons (21H-28H), one became a trolley wire lubricator (41H) and three were rebuilt for tree lopping (42H-44H). Four of the six-wheelers (LSs 3, 6, 8 and 10) were found work as heavy breakdown lorries, for which they were fitted with new purpose-built bodies and were to be seen performing this rôle until 1951. LS 1 was used as a temporary waiting room at Sevenoaks bus station while the new brick building was being built.

Next for the chop were the Dennis Lances, the first of which was actually withdrawn on 29th November 1937, the day before the last NS, and the whole class had gone by the end of the year. The Lances had all been sent south from Potters Bar to Sutton to replace NSs as recently as November and December 1936, their place being taken by spare STs. They were only just over five years old and it seems likely that they were intended to have a rather longer career at Sutton, even though they were non-standard vehicles, otherwise the cost of re-allocation and of re-tooling Sutton garage would hardly have been worthwhile. They may well have been the first victims of the sudden reduction in vehicle requirements which followed the strike of busmen. They were replaced on routes 80 and 156 by petrol STLs dislodged from Camberwell by new oilers.

A couple of Upton Park's large fleet of TD class Leyland Titans had already been withdrawn when the DLs began to go but with the Dennises out of the way their replacement began in earnest. Thirteen were delicensed on

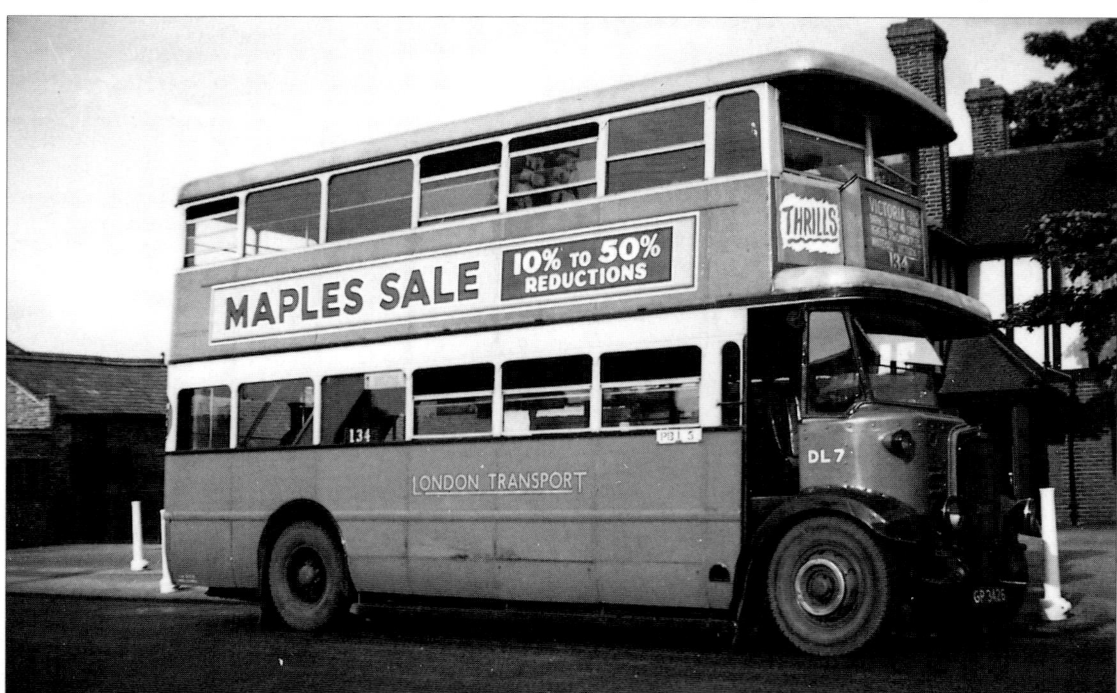

Above **Wanstead Flats at the end of 1937; E2 class trolleybus 628 has ousted the trams and STL 2005 has helped depose the NSs. Another STL can be seen approaching in the distance but a car and a cycle are the only other traffic.** Charles F Klapper Collection; Omnibus Society

Left **The Dennis Lances were withdrawn at the end of 1937, having been transferred from Potters Bar to Sutton a year earlier. In its last summer at its home base, DL 7 is on the time-honoured stand at Hadley Highstone 'Two Brewers', preparing to work a 'short' on route 134 to Victoria.** D W K Jones

30th December 1937 and by the beginning of February 1938, only seventeen petrol and nine oil engined machines were still running. However, nineteen were restored to service to meet the increased requirements of the new schedules on 1st June and the number then settled at between thirty and thirty-six for the next fifteen months, except that for a while in June seventy-five were licensed for Wimbledon Tennis and other special services. Also withdrawn at the end of December 1937 were the three former City Leyland Titanics (TC 1-3).

A minor element in the 1937 vehicle development programme was the fitting of oil engines to another twenty-four double-deck LTs. These released petrol engines which were reconditioned for use in the new LTC coaches (see chapter four). The A165 8.8 litre Comet Mk 1 was again the unit chosen for the conversion, which took place between May and July 1937. These conversions were all allocated to Mortlake garage where they joined the original thirty-two Ricardo conversions and LT 21, the unique one with a 7.7 litre engine.

Above **A mixed bag of withdrawn Lances in Chiswick Tram depot on 8th January 1938, including Birch and Dodson bodied examples formerly operated by Independents.** D W K Jones

Left **Also caught up in the mass disappearances of 1937 were the three Leyland Titanics which had come from City and latterly operated on route 18C at Hanwell.** D W K Jones

In October 1937, in the aftermath of the strike by busmen in May and June, the Board decided to slow down the rate of production from Chiswick because the need for new buses had diminished significantly. The severe loss of traffic had led to reductions in service levels and already 106 non-standard life-expired buses had been withdrawn without replacement. The programme for 1938/39 was therefore substantially smaller and was dominated by single-deckers and coaches. Only 115 double-deck buses were to be ordered and no provision was made for any service development. Another reduced programme totalling 355 vehicles was planned for 1939/40, after which an annual flow of 527, the maximum which Chiswick was allowed to build, was planned.

It had been hoped that the double-deckers would be of the new RT type, but AEC were not able to start volume production in time and the order that was finally placed was for another 115 STLs. This was supplemented in November 1938 by the addition of another seventeen, bringing the total to 132 (STLs 2516-2647; classified 15STL16). These seventeen were intended for Country Buses, who had also been allocated twenty-two of the Central Bus quota, in substitution for a planned order for a further fifty front-entrance STLs. They were the first new rear entrance buses taken by that department and probably intended as a temporary appropriation.

In these last pre-war examples, the class reached its pinnacle. After some earlier experiments on STLs and particularly the experience gained with the STDs, the chassis specification called for a direct-injection oil engine. London Transport had been slow to move away from indirect injection because it preferred the higher power output and smoother running which it delivered but the experience with the STDs had shown conclusively that direct injection gave substantially better fuel economy and this finally convinced the always cautious Chiswick engineers. The AEC A173 engine had a 105mm bore and 146mm stroke, the same as the A171 used on earlier STLs, but with a power output of 95 bhp at 1,800 rpm rather than 115 bhp at 2,000 rpm. To overcome the increase in diesel 'knock' fully flexible engine mountings were fitted and the effect was a very smooth running vehicle. Other novel features of the 15STL chassis were R.P. automatic brake adjusters, which eliminated manual shoe adjustment between liner renewals, and automatic chassis lubrication, which reduced the number of greasing points from fifty-six to twelve.

The bodywork was almost identical to the STL12 and 14 types but with some detailed improvements, presaging their introduction on the RT. Externally, the only noticeable design change was in the arrangement of the driver's windscreen on which the lower section, which had been fixed on earlier buses, could now be opened. The completed bus was made to look exceptionally handsome by the deeper radiator recently introduced by AEC, onto which the registration number plate was fixed, and the handsome disc trims fitted to the wheels. The platform handrails were partly covered in white Doverite plastic and the grabrail over the understair luggage compartment was of an unusual design, flat in section and much deeper than the usual tubular rail. A similar design was used on the first RTs. Internally, the appearance was much like other STLs but the top rails on the seats were thinner than usual, except at the gangway end where they widened out to the same size as the rest of the frame. This untidy arrangement spoilt the otherwise stylish appearance of the saloons.

Six of the batch, STLs 2621, 2642, 2643 and 2645-2647, which had the last six bodies, were the subject of an experiment with hand-built rubber mudguards. The purpose was to overcome the loss of resilience and tendency to warp in later life which were features of units moulded by machine. Rubber mudguards produced by hand were more bulbous and it was therefore necessary to eliminate the inward curve of the body, resulting in an unhappy marriage which created a messy bulge. It was also necessary to eliminate the rearward sweep of the mudguards which had added style to the earlier STL bodies. The official classification of these six buses was 1/15STL16/1.

The first 15STL chassis (for STL 2516) was received at Chiswick on 26th January 1939 and they continued to arrive at an average rate of about seven a week until 14th April, after which there was a gap in production until 16th May. The remainder came at a slightly slower pace and the last chassis (STL 2647) was not taken into stock until 23rd August. All thirty-one chassis received up to 22nd February and a further ten of those delivered between then and 3rd March went straight into store at Staines, Addlestone, Windsor and Reigate garages (in that order). The first to go for bodying was STL 2544 which was also the first to be delivered direct to Chiswick, on 21st February. It is not altogether clear why this hiatus occurred but a possible explanation might be connected with the fact that the chassis for the TF Green Line coaches had arrived from Leyland later than expected. The coincidence of deliveries would have increased the rate of construction in the body shop at Chiswick above the 6½ a week authorised by the Board and it may have been necessary to wait for the authority to be increased before work could start. Even so, by bodying only TFs during February, Chiswick was singularly under-utilised and there may have been some other reason.

The first seven STL16s were licensed on 25th March at Hanwell, where all but sixteen of the Central Bus examples were sent. The others went to Alperton, a brand new garage which had opened only in June, where the last eight were licensed on 1st and 4th September. Withdrawal of the TDs was resumed with the delicensing of Hanwell's oilers, while another type which now started to disappear was the Tilling ST, twenty-one of which were withdrawn on 1st August in an event of double significance, as the STLs which replaced them were the first oilers to be allocated to Catford garage.

The apogee of the STL design was reached with the STL16s, most of which were allocated to Hanwell. STL 2580 is joined in this picture with new suburban housing, the elegant bus shelter, the Holden bus stop sign and even the cyclist, to sum up the 1930s. L T Museum

The last of the Country Bus Titans was withdrawn in 1939. TD 136B which came from Maidstone & District is at the other extreme of the Board's area, Slough station, on route 353. D W K Jones

The Titans at Grays were replaced by displaced Qs and STs. TD 170B was a Dodson bodied example, originally owned by Aston. D W K Jones

Below **The double-deck Qs were withdrawn from Hertford in the summer of 1939 and transferred to Grays. Former Central Bus Q 3 is seen in Cecil Road, Enfield the previous summer.** H F C Adcock

The Country Area buses had three distinct body number blocks and were allocated fleet numbers scattered between 2517 and 2638. The first three (STLs 2539, 2553 and 2559) began work at Northfleet on 1st May. The entire batch was concentrated in this busy Thames-side industrial area, where their higher capacity was of great value, twenty-five going to Northfleet and fourteen to Dartford. The arrival of the STLs marked the withdrawal of the Country department's TDs which was completed on 1st August, those on Dartford's and Northfleet's works services directly by the new STLs and those at Windsor by front-entrance STLs transferred from Northfleet and Dartford. The Grays Titans were replaced by STs displaced from Dartford's route 492 and the five double-deck Qs, which were transferred in from Hertford. The Qs and some STs were replaced on routes 310, 310A, 395 and 395A at Hertford by front-entrance STLs culled either directly or indirectly from Dartford and Northfleet.

The arrival of fifty-six seaters in the Country Bus fleet coincided with the outcome of a review of the capacity of the STL6s, in the light of overcrowding which was occurring on some services. The report recommended that all eighty-nine of those built at Chiswick should have their seating increased to fifty-two by having longitudinal seats fitted over their rear wheel arches. Another benefit of this alteration was that the number allowed to stand was automatically increased, under the PSV Regulations, from four to five. The cost of each conversion was estimated at £25 10s, or £2 17s a year for each remaining year of their lives, plus the increase in Road Fund Tax of £10 a year. The extra cost was considered to be cheaper than buying and running additional buses and the conversion was authorised by the Board on 15th June 1939. Work started immediately and was finished by November.

A curious digression in 1939 was the remodelling of Tilling ST 839 with an STL cab and smooth side panels, just as the class was about to be withdrawn. On 21st May 1939 it is on a shortworking of route 12 at Addiscombe 'Black Horse'. Malcolm E Papes collection

The experimental 'CC' buses were withdrawn in May 1939, by which time they had been fitted with standard AEC petrol engines and re-allocated to Streatham who usually ran them on route 133. LT 1202, which had always carried a standard LT body, is on the 'Swan & Sugar Loaf' stand at South Croydon. J Bonell

Below **A sizeable queue boarding STL 1001 at Harpenden shows why it was decided to increase the seating capacity of these eighty-nine vehicles. The combined Bus and Coach Stop has one of the smaller flags generally adopted in the Country area.** AEC

In the meantime, on 19th May 1938, the LPTB had decided that the economic benefits of the diesel engine were sufficient to justify the conversion of 400 LTs and 386 STLs from petrol to oil. By this time, 467 Renowns had oil engines, including those originally delivered with them and the 339 which exchanged engines with the earlier STLs. Twenty-four were of quite recent origin having made a similar exchange with the new LTC coaches in 1937. In January 1939, the Board authorised the conversion of another 150 LTs, bringing the total in this programme to 550 and the final total to 1017. The 150 open staircase vehicles and the CCs were omitted, as they did not have a long enough life expectancy. Also omitted, ostensibly because they were non-standard, were the fifty-four preselectors at Plumstead, a happy decision for those who came to know the delightful mixture of a quiet running engine and a musical gearbox when they were still going strong a decade later. The opposite view was taken with the STLs, the oil engines being fitted to the preselectors (STLs 203-252, 254-262, 264-289, 291, 403-552 and 559-608).

The engine specified for the Renowns was again an 8.8 litre unit but of a radically different design from the A165. The smooth performance of the Leyland 8.6 litre engines in the STDs had so impressed London Transport that they had decided to adopt a larger engine and the direct-injection pot-cavity design for the new 10T10 coaches (see chapter three). The new 8.8 litre engine produced by AEC to this specification was coded A180 and it was this which was used for the LT conversions. The vehicles re-engined in this programme were therefore reclassified differently from the earlier examples, the 2LT3, 4, 5, 5/1 and 6 becoming 1/12LT3/3, 4, 5/8, 5/7 and 6/4 respectively. The work on the LTs was completed between August 1938 and January 1940 and the garages which changed over were, in sequence, Upton Park (between August and November 1938), Elmers End (September to November 1938), Nunhead (November 1938 to January 1939), Muswell Hill (December 1938 to February 1939), Sidcup (February/March 1939), Norwood (September/October 1939), Old Kent Road (October to December 1939) and Tottenham (October 1939 to January 1940). This left only Leyton, Loughton and Plumstead running petrol LTs.

The engine chosen for the Regents was the same A173 direct injection unit with flexible mountings as used in the 15STL16s and, as they were also fitted with automatic brake adjusters, these buses were now mechanically right up to date. After conversion, they took on the familiar uplifted front which earned them the 'sit-up-and-beg' nickname in some quarters and tended to accentuate the already old-fashioned look of their bodywork. The changes justified a complete recoding: the chassis from 3STL to 16STL, 4STL to 1/16STL and 7STL to 2/16STL; the bodies from STL3 and 3/2 to STL18 and from STL2 to STL18/1.

The jump in classification from STL16 to STL18 came about because the code STL17 was reserved for an important modification to the bodywork of these buses. The proposal was that the front and rear ends of the bodies should be rebuilt to the same profile as the STL16 bodies, including the provision of a front roof number box. Unfortunately, these changes were never carried out, perhaps because the cost was difficult to justify. The code was later applied to the twelve bodies built at Chiswick in 1941 to replace air raid losses.

The first to be modified was STL 493, which was done as a prototype in February 1939. The main programme was carried out between March and November 1939, although all but twelve were completed by July. Chalk Farm garage was the first to benefit, receiving its first three oilers (STLs 533 and 536 and prototype STL 493) on 28th March and by the end of the programme only Bromley, Catford, Croydon, Harrow Weald and Willesden had petrol STLs.

LT 429, on route 43 in the far bay at London Bridge, was included in the new programme of fitting oil engines and received one in January 1939. Bluebird LT 1250, in the foreground, was an earlier conversion, taking an STL engine in 1933. One of the new STL16s can also be seen behind the Bluebird.
Charles F Klapper Collection, Omnibus Society

On 3rd November 1938, the LPTB decided on its vehicle programme for 1939/40 of which the seventeen STLs have already been mentioned. Among the vehicles due for replacement in this programme were the eight lowbridge STs operating on route 336. No special provision was made for these as the Board had decided to splash out the £500 needed to alter the Black Horse Bridge between Amersham and Chalfont & Latimer to make it suitable for full height double-deckers. However, the war overtook this project and the bridge was still untouched when these vehicles were finally replaced in 1950. The balance of the 355 new buses planned for this programme comprised 338 RT type double-deckers, development of which had been going on for about three years. A model of the new bus was being studied by the Board at the beginning of 1938 and the prototype chassis was completed in the spring of that year and delivered to Chiswick on 23rd May. As its specially designed body was not ready, an open staircase Dodson body from withdrawn TD 111 was mounted on the chassis and in this form it ran, disguised as ST 1140, in experimental service on route 18C from Hanwell garage between mid-July and the end of 1938. At this stage its power unit was an experimental 8.8 litre model of the A182 type which had also been fitted to STLs 2513-2515 but, before the completed bus reappeared as RT 1, this was replaced by a 9.6 litre engine derived from the same basic design; it also owed much to the experience gained with the Leyland units on the STDs. Other novel features included air operation of both gearbox and brakes. Comfort for the driver took a great leap forward with the provision of a sliding cab door to give the first fully enclosed cab on a standard London Transport double-deck bus, an adjustable seat and a steering column-mounted gearchange lever. The compact design of the engine and chassis components enabled the bonnet to be lower and nearly as short as that on the STL, giving the driver excellent all-round vision and providing a more spacious environment for lower saloon passengers.

The new body was put on the chassis on 27th March 1939 and one of the most striking and enduring designs ever to roll off a production line appeared for the first time. Frontal curvature reached its zenith on this design, with a continuous even curve running from an almost flush radiator shell upwards and backwards to the roof. The combination of smooth contours, four bay construction and the low bonnet line produced an exceptionally handsome, yet practical, vehicle. The use of the roofbox also reached its ultimate, with identical arrangements at both front and back. Unfortunately, in striving for the ideal æsthetic the designers chose to reduce the width of the ultimate destination blind to be the same as the intermediate point box, reducing the display to an undesirably cramped layout.

Inside too, the details had been thoroughly rethought and a pleasantly handsome appearance was the result. Particularly notable was the use of curved window cappings, a feature which had been in use on single-deckers for three or four years but only now made its appearance on a standard double-decker. The success of the new brown, green and cream décor was perhaps vitiated by the continued use of the rather ordinary looking striped green moquette of the later STLs but the overall effect was strikingly fresh and airy.

RT 1 was shown to the Press and other guests on 13th July 1939 and finally entered service on Wednesday 9th August, on route 22 from Chelverton Road garage. Three and a half weeks later, the country was at war, further development was halted for seven years and only 150 of the planned 338 RTs were built.

Sparkling new and carrying a very important load of passengers, RT 1 set off from Aldwych on its press demonstration run on 13th July 1939. At 'The Spaniards Inn' Hampstead Heath these officials are probably seeking the driver's opinion of the new bus. Features which remained unique to RT 1 were the backsweep of the mudguards under the bodywork, the sloping top to the driver's cab window, the position of the offside route number, the vestigial 'signalling' window on the offside of the platform and the slight overlap of the front dome over the windows.
Charles F Klapper Collection, Omnibus Society.

CHAPTER THREE SINGLE-DECK DEVELOPMENTS

While the double-deck fleet was moving remorselessly towards greater and greater standardisation, London Transport's single-deck fleet became something of a cornucopia of types from 1934, although within a broadly standard specification. This was slightly ironic as one of the Board's desired aims was to rid itself of the wide variety of vehicle makes and types which it had acquired and to establish a stable and efficient fleet. This problem was particularly rife in the Country Area, where a very high proportion of the acquired vehicles came in penny numbers but profuse variety from an overabundance of small operators, as described in chapter one.

The most pressing need was for a new small bus to replace the multifarious vehicles of this type taken over from small operators. The first single-deck purchase authorised by the Board, on 1st February 1934, was therefore one KP3 model normal control Leyland Cub for the Central Bus department. In preparation for this decision, a Cub chassis (KP3 2257) had been inspected at Chiswick between 15th and 23rd January. This was a comparatively new model introduced only in 1931 and London Transport, knowing little of its capabilities, therefore wished to gain some service experience with it before committing itself to large scale orders. C 1 (AYV 717), whose composite body was completed at Chiswick Works in June 1934, had the then standard Leyland six-cylinder 4.4 litre side valve petrol engine and a crash gearbox. The body styling and interior furnishing and finishes followed the standard of the contemporary STLs and the sliding door was designed to be operated by the driver. Its wheelbase of 15ft 6ins was just over three feet greater than the Dennis Dart and the completed vehicle was correspondingly longer, with an overall length of 23ft 11⁵/₈ins. It was also four inches wider, at 7ft 6ins and this greater floorspace allowed all twenty seats to face forwards. It went into service on route 237 at Hounslow where it was licensed on 10th October 1934 and later operated at Merton and Barking. While at the latter, in June 1935, it was fitted with a Perkins four-cylinder oil engine. It was transferred to the Country Department in November 1935.

Almost at the same time as Chiswick was finishing off C 1, the fleet renewal programme for the Country Bus department was being put together with a long-term aim of achieving standardisation within six years. In the two years to 30th June 1936, the plan was to replace 296 buses and 120 coaches and after that to replace the remainder of the fleet at the rate of 200 vehicles a year until 1939. So far as single-deckers are concerned, the first two-year buying programme originally recommended was for 120 AEC coaches and 100 AEC single-deck buses, all 220 with bodies from an outside supplier, plus twelve Thornycroft one-man operated (omo) twenty-seaters, twelve omo Dennis Darts, fifty omo Leyland Cubs and the conversion of 37 Reliance coach bodies to buses. While approving the proposals, Frank Pick ruled that the order for fifty Cubs should be suspended pending the completion of the trials with C 1.

By the time the programme for 1935 was approved by the Board on 4th October, the Thornycrofts and Darts had disappeared and the omo requirement had been consolidated into an order for seventy-four Leyland Cubs. This decision may well have owed a lot to the fact that the Cub was now available with an oil engine (in which form it was known as the KPO3) and the Board had by now decided to standardise on oilers. The conversion of existing Reliance bodies from coach to bus was also dropped in favour of a proposal to buy forty-three new single-deck bodies instead. Renewal of the large saloon fleet was to be concentrated on the AEC 'Q', which must have come as a surprise to many as the model showed little sign of taking off outside London. The bodywork contract was also a surprise as it went to a manufacturer new to London Transport or its main predecessors, the Birmingham Railway Carriage and Wagon Company. Construction of the Cub bodies was assigned to Short Bros of Rochester. Both the Cub and Q orders were subsequently increased by two vehicles.

Above **The only Leyland Cub to be bodied by Chiswick was the experimental C 1, which went into service in October 1934 at Hounslow and ran on route 237.** Alan B Cross

Above left **This fourteen-seat Morris Z6 which Martin & King had run on services to Old Windsor and Virginia Water before being acquired in February 1934, was the sort of vehicle the Board was anxious to replace. It is in Slough in March 1935, carrying the 'WC' code originally allotted to Windsor garage.** D W K Jones

Above right **Although smartly painted in London Transport's new Country Bus livery, this five year old Chevrolet LQ was withdrawn within a few months of being acquired from Bell's Bus Service of Slough in 1934.** J F Higham

Left **Listed for replacement in the Board's first vehicle programme were the single-deck S class, whose relative antiquity is well shown in this rear view taken at Epping Forest in March 1936. Also to be withdrawn were the small Dennises, like DM 3, a Duple bodied GL which had come from Romford and District.** D W K Jones

In the Central Area, the immediate need was to replace the remaining thirteen S-class single-deckers, the LS, ten Dennis E (DE), seven Leyland Lions (LN) and fourteen assorted small single-deckers of Bean, Dennis and Guy manufacture. No fewer than another forty-nine full size single-deckers were claimed to be needed for expansion, even though there were thirty unwanted ones awaiting disposal. Also, theoretically, there were enough unused single-deck LTs in the fleet to cover the replacement of the Ss. However, the operating departments were having great difficulty in getting approval for the longer vehicles on any more routes and the Board had already decided not to order any more buses of this type. The one-man bus fleet was already at full stretch and six more vehicles were needed immediately.

Although C 1 had been operating for only three months when this review was taking place, the Board had been getting satisfactory results from a similar vehicle which they had acquired from St Albans and District in November 1933 (C 76B, JH2401) and the early performance of C1 was good enough for Pick to have the confidence to approve it as the standard one-man bus. Q 1 had been running longer and had also been giving a good account of itself and it was therefore this model which was chosen for Central Buses. The Board therefore authorised the purchase of eighty Park Royal bodied AEC Qs and twenty more Leyland Cubs with Weymann bodywork.

This former Hawkins Leyland Lion was one of seven earmarked for early replacement by London Transport. It was still running on route 202 from Old Kent Road garage when photographed at Surrey Docks in April 1936. D W K Jones

The Gordon Omnibus Company bought this Dodson bodied Dennis E in 1926 and it was one of many non-standard types which the Board disposed of in 1936. Originally numbered D 193 when acquired in December 1933, it was renumbered DE 28 in January 1934. It was allocated to Old Kent Road garage, near which it was photographed in July 1934, for use on route 202. L T Museum

The first new single-deckers taken into stock were the Country Bus KPO3 model Cubs numbered C 2B-75B and coded 2C2. They were registered in the series BXD627-700 but the first six were out of sequence. The chassis were the same as C 1 except that they had the new Leyland overhead valve pot cavity oil engine. This was a six-cylinder unit of 3½in bore and 5½in stroke giving a capacity of 4.4 litres and a power output of 55 bhp at 2,200 rpm. The twenty-seat bodywork, which was among the last to be supplied to any operator by Shorts, was also very similar in appearance to that on C 1 but was of metal-framed construction. Seating and interior décor were the same as on contemporary STLs but the special distinction of these buses was that they were the first to have rounded window cappings and polished metal finishers, features which were not adopted as standard on double-deckers for another four years. Other features which distinguished them from C 1 were an emergency exit in the second bay on the offside, a deeper and better proportioned radiator shell and a tapered rather than curved panel at the front, which gave rise to a running board under the emergency door.

The first five (Cs 2, 3, 4, 7 and 8) went into service at Northfleet garage on 17th April 1935, followed by Cs 5 and 6 the following day. The remainder were licensed at (in approximate sequence) Dunton Green, Hertford, St Albans, Chelsham, Guildford, Leatherhead, Addlestone, Windsor, Watford, Dorking and Amersham. The last to enter service was C 71, at Hertford, on 4th September. They replaced a polyglot band of small buses ranging from fourteen to twenty-seaters on chassis by Bean, Bedford, Commer, Dennis, Ford, Guy and Thornycroft.

The Short Bros bodies on the Country Bus Cubs were similar to C 1 but with an improved rear end and radiused window pans. C 44, one of six allocated to Guildford in June 1935, is at the 'Horse & Groom' terminus of route 448. J F Higham

There was a chromium plated trim in imitation of the front bumper bar and an outward sweeping skirt panel at the back of the Short Brothers Cubs, as can be seen in this maker's photograph probably taken in Rochester. A miniature version of the fleetname was used on these smaller vehicles. R S Turnbull collection

The interior finish of the Cubs was ahead of contemporary double-deckers in having curved cappings on the window frames but the whole was let down by the old fashioned looking timber framed seats. Arthur Ingram

A Commer Invader, acquired from Harris of Grays, at work in the Hertfordshire lanes in territory then typical of Country Bus operations. Alan B Cross

KX7164 was a Petty bodied Gilford AS6 which was one of the Chesham & District buses acquired by Amersham & District in November 1932. It was withdrawn soon after this photograph was taken in Slough on 16th March 1935. D W K Jones

Nine Leyland coaches were acquired from Maidstone & District in July 1935 when the former Redcar coach route was handed over to London Transport. KR1168 was one of the five Tiger TS2s with Beadle bodywork and became TR 39. It is seen here at Horse Guards Avenue soon after acquisition, still wearing M&D colours and its original side route board but with Green Line emblems and, as yet unused, garage and running number plate holders. The unusual cab front destination display did not survive long in London Transport service. D W K Jones

The pronounced slope of the roof on these BRCW bodies became their hallmark but note also the untidy arrangement of side windows dictated by the position of the emergency door behind the engine. Q 6 is operating on route 336, normally stocked by lowbridge STs, presumably covering a temporary shortage. D A Ruddom collection

The arrival of the 4Q4s had been anticipated by Q 1 which was transferred to the Country department in February 1934 and allocated to Reigate garage. At this time it was still virtually in original condition but its front end was later modified to look more like the later version. Alan B Cross

In July 1935, Country Buses started to take delivery of the new 0762 model Qs. The chassis specification differed from Q 1 in having an AEC A170 indirect-injection oil engine, fluid flywheel and preselective gearbox but broadly speaking the design was the same. The six cylinder indirect injection A170 engine had been designed for the Q, with anti-clockwise rotation and inclined cylinders. It had a bore of 106 mm and stroke of 146 mm, giving a swept volume of just under 7.7 litres. This design was the basis of the A171 engine used in contemporary STLs.

Numbered Q 6B-105B, 186B and 187B, and coded 4Q4, they were registered BXD527-576, CGJ161-219 and (Qs187/188) CLE127/128 but two in each of the main batches were out of sequence. Their BRCW thirty-seven seat bodies made them one of the most distinctive classes operated by London Transport. They were also stunningly modern for their day and would not have looked too out of place on a bus twenty years their junior. The feature which marked out the 4Q4 from all its siblings was the roof, which sloped from a neatly blended front destination indicator box, gently downwards to the rear. The sliding saloon door, which when opened was concealed in a slot between the external and internal panelling, was in the third bay, immediately behind the front wheels and there were five further bays behind it. The foremost bay was slightly longer than the rest and widened at both top and bottom to match the depth of windscreen. The front, showing influence from AEC's registered designs for bodywork on this model, was gently curved above waist level and the curve continued in the same arc into the dome. The windscreen was in two sections, both of which could be opened, and sloped gently downwards from the centre. The dash panels were handsomely uncluttered, with only a triangle badge immediately under the windscreen, headlamps about two-thirds of the way down, a registration plate immediately below these in the centre and a foglamp set into the nearside corner panel. The sidelamps were set into the front dome immediately above the windscreen in the same fashion as on contemporary STLs and trolleybuses. The presence of a driver's cab door, a centrally placed emergency exit and the ventilation grilles on the engine compartment cover, made the offside rather less well organised in appearance. The rear end styling was virtually identical to the Cubs, with a single window across the back of the saloon and a reverse curve in the lower panelling.

Internally, the finishings included rounded window cappings and polished metal finishers, the only jarring effect on an otherwise advanced design being the choice of the rather ugly wooden framed seats then still in vogue. The colour scheme was the same brown, pale yellow and white then favoured on the STLs and the seats also had the same attractive patterned green moquette. There was a longitudinal seat over the wheel arch and engine compartment on the offside and another, shorter one over the nearside front wheel but otherwise all seats faced forward, mainly in pairs of two seaters. As built, the Qs had a seat for two passengers alongside the driver but this arrangement interfered with the driver's sightlines and they were removed between March and October 1936, reducing the number of seats to thirty-five and undermining the value of the type in terms of capacity. In their place a full width bulkhead with a centre communicating door was installed.

Q 8B was licensed on 6th July 1935 and all but two, which went into service in July 1936, were in service by January 1936. The first and largest allocation (sixteen) was to Watford High Street where they became the sole large saloon type in the garage, working on routes 306, 311, 311A, 312, and 335. Six went to Dartford for the local route 499, four to Amersham for the 353/362 group, eleven to Hertford and three to Hatfield for the 303, 340 and 341 and six to Leatherhead for the 418. The other Watford garage, at Leavesden Road, then became the second largest operator of the type, with only one fewer than High Street and enough to cover all its large saloon requirements on routes 317 (group), 318 (group) and 385. Other garages to receive Qs in the second half of the delivery programme were: Swanley (five); Addlestone (five); Dunton Green (two); Godstone (two); Reigate (five); Dorking (four); Guildford (eight); Windsor (seven) and St Albans (three, including Qs 186 and 187). Most of the vehicles replaced were the elderly ADCs inherited from LGCS, as well as a few Thornycrofts from the same source and a number of Tilling Stevens B10A2s.

Top left **One of the miscellaneous types replaced by the 4Q4s was this former London Midland & Scottish Railway Leyland Lion with rare Derby built bodywork, which had been allocated to Northfleet as part of the Board's attempt at some vehicle standardisation at garages. Although the bus is in full London Transport regalia, the driver appears to be wearing rather casual clothing.** D W K Jones

Top right **R 43, formerly a Battens coach and now in use as a bus at Windsor in 1936 is fitted with a body similar to the T7 type coaches.** D W K Jones

Above **This rear view of R 2, before it was registered, shows the modern lines of the Weymann body, unhindered by antiquated fittings. The rear end in particular strongly resembles the Chiswick products of this period.**

Towards the end of the 4Q4 delivery programme, in September 1935, the first of the forty-three rebodied Reliances and Regals began to arrive. The body contract had been awarded to Weymann who produced an exceptionally handsome, nicely rounded design, following LPTB contemporary ideas on single-deckers in many respects with resemblances to the 4Q4 and Cub designs, in a front entrance, six bay layout. They had modern interiors similar to the Qs with curved 'Resistoid' window cappings and polished aluminium window frames and pillar sheaths. All forty-three bodies were twenty-six feet long, as this length was dictated by the wheelbase of the Reliances.

The first thirty-one were on AEC Reliance chassis which, with one exception, had previously carried canvas roof coach bodies (R 1-16, 19, 20, 22-24, 26-34, 44). These had thirty timber framed seats, whereas the twelve bodies fitted to the AEC Regals had only twenty-six seats of the new tubular metal framed variety. This was later increased to thirty. The Ts had also been coaches, numbered T 346-357, formerly owned by Blue Belle and Queen Line. They were given Green Line fleetnames and ran as such for a time, mainly as weekend extras, first at Reigate and Watford (Leavesden Road) and later at Luton, until they were replaced by the 6Q6s. They were classified 5T4.

The handsome new Weymann bodywork fitted to the Reliances in 1935 hardly matches the antique style of radiator carried by this marque. R 7B is at Castle Hill Windsor. D W K Jones

The new Weymann bodies made a better match with the Regal chassis and the complete vehicle could have passed as a new bus. T 354, in Green Line service at Golders Green, had previously carried a London Lorries coach body and had originally been owned by Queen Line Coaches. D W K Jones

The interior of the Weymann bodywork for the Reliances matched the outside in forward looking design in having 'Rexine' covered curved cappings on the window frames. As with the Cubs, the effect is spoilt by the old fashioned looking timber framed seats favoured by Chiswick. R S Turnbull collection

The Central Bus Qs, which began to go into service in March 1936, were numbered Q 106-185, coded 5Q5 and registered CLE129-208. After the faltering attempts with the Cs and the 4Q4s, these were the first London Transport buses to be registered fully in sequence. They had the same mechanical specification as the 4Q4s but were otherwise quite different. Their Park Royal bodies had a wider pillar spacing, which reduced the number of side windows from seven to five, a higher saloon floor, which increased the height by $7\frac{1}{2}$ inches and a less sloping roof line, a combination which gave them particularly distinguished looks. The appearance of the offside was also markedly improved by the removal of the emergency door to the centre of the rear, in what was becoming the characteristic Chiswick fashion. The most important operational difference was that Central Buses had specified a 16ft 6in wheelbase, so that the front wheels could be set back to allow for a passenger entrance beside the driver. This arrangement was practicable on Central Area buses because there was no need to accommodate a sliding platform door, as such refinements were still outlawed by the Metropolitan Police who believed they would slow down the speed of boarding.

The purpose was to enable the scope for high capacity to be exploited fully without interfering with the driver's view to the nearside. In this way it was possible to accommodate thirty-seven passengers in a two-axle vehicle, two more than in the two foot longer single-deck LTs. These were arranged mainly in forward facing two seaters either side of the gangway but there were longitudinal seats at the front of the saloon, one for six in two sections divided by an armrest on the offside over the engine and a shorter one for three on the nearside. The internal appearance was greatly enhanced, compared with the 4Q4s, by the use of the new lightweight tubular steel seat frames which, allied to the dual-tone rounded window cappings and generally cheerful décor, produced a sparkling overall effect which was to set the trend for two more generations of vehicle. Another novel feature was the use of a winding mechanism for the opening windows, the handles for which were placed centrally above each of the three centre bays on each side.

The position of the passenger door on the 5Q5s was to prove a safety hazard, more serious than with a conventional open platform because of the risk that anyone falling out could slip under the front wheels. The problem was sufficiently serious for Frank Pick to call for a special report, whose findings

The old LSWR Raynes Park station footbridge rises dramatically above the rear end of Q 110 which was one of the first Central Bus 5Q5s to go into service in March 1936, at Merton on routes 200 and 225. The Park Royal body benefited from having its emergency door in the rear wall, enabling a much tidier window arrangement to be adopted and there is a neater arrangement of the cabside window which is surmounted by a route number stencil behind glass. J F Higham

The 5Q5s were another step forward in single-deck design inside also, the tubular aluminium seats and winding mechanism for the opening windows setting standards for years to come. L T Museum

showed that passengers were more likely to lose their balance and to do so at a lower speed on a front-entrance Q than on a rear entrance vehicle. There were so many accidents on route 202 (a tortuous route), including some fatalities, that an experiment was carried out in which the conductor collected all fares at stops and returned to the platform before giving the starting signal. No lasting changes in operating practice emerged from this.

The operators had some problems in getting route approvals because of the longer wheel-base and front overhang of the Qs. Country Buses had also been having problems which were compounded by the Traffic Commissioner insisting on regarding the 4Q4 and 5Q5s as different types of vehicle for approval purposes. He was prepared, for example, to authorise 5Q5s on the 425 but not 4Q4s. Such were the problems that the Commissioner had asked that no further vehicles of the type should be ordered. Whilst Frank Pick insisted on maintaining the Board's right to do so if it wished, the difficulties were obviously regarded as intractable and these initial orders were to prove to be the last.

The first garages to get the 5Q5s were Dalston and Merton, where the first four (Qs 108, 110, 112 and 115) were licensed on 4th March 1936, followed by Chalk Farm, Old Kent Road and Kingston. At Dalston and Merton they replaced single-deck LTs on routes 208 and 200 which, in turn, were sent to Bromley to give some extra capacity on the hard pressed route 227, uprooting the former Tilling Ts once and for all from their ancestral home. They went to Kingston, where they remained. At Old Kent Road, the vehicles replaced on route 202 were the Dennis Es (DE), the last of which were delicensed on 29th April and the Leyland Lions (LN) which went on 29th May. A few DEs had been held at Chalk Farm for Saturday working but the bulk of them had been replaced by surplus Ts in August and October 1934, following complaints from passengers, surprisingly about the condition of the former Birch Bros vehicles. The Kingston Qs were used for new route 255, which started on 27th May 1936, and some of the Merton ones to upgrade route 225 from one-man operated Darts on 29th April. The Qs replaced S-types directly in only one case, the 230, as those at Croydon and Enfield on routes 235 and 242 were replaced by decanted Ts. The honour of being the last route operated by this venerable class went to the 230 at Harrow Weald, where the last eight were delicensed on 17th June 1936, two days after the last of the Qs had gone into service (Q 161).

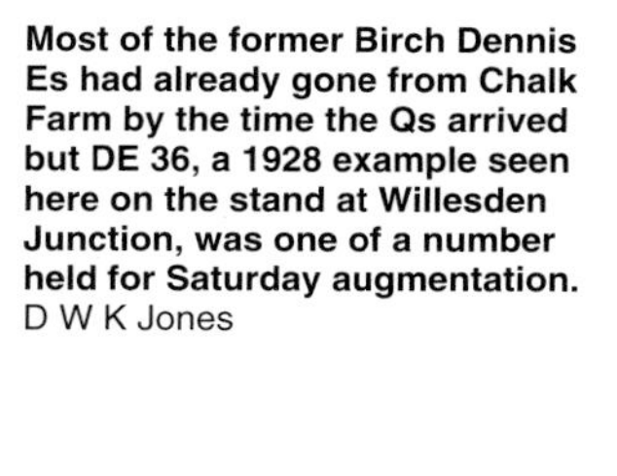
Most of the former Birch Dennis Es had already gone from Chalk Farm by the time the Qs arrived but DE 36, a 1928 example seen here on the stand at Willesden Junction, was one of a number held for Saturday augmentation.
D W K Jones

The last route to be operated by S class vehicles was Harrow Weald's 230, on which S 892 is seeing out its last days at Kenton.
J F Higham

Q 171, one of the twenty-seven 5Q5s sent to the Country department, is at Hertford car park working on route 341 from Hatfield garage. J F Higham

GF 94C was a Strawhatter coach, then Green Line but has been downgraded and is being used as a bus on route 313 at St Albans. D W K Jones

This accounted for fifty-three of the eighty 5Q5s. It is far from clear for what use the other twenty-seven were originally intended but the use to which they were eventually put was unexpected. The last twenty-seven to be bodied, not the last numerically, were delivered in Country Bus green and sent to Reigate (one), Amersham (five), Two Waters (three), Northfleet (six), Hatfield (four) and Hertford (eight) garages.

Among them was Q 152, which had been in use as a demonstration chassis for engineers' training between 4th March and 25th July and had therefore been bodied late. The complete consignment comprised Qs 151, 152, 155, 159, 162-164 and 166-185. They were licensed between 7th July and 19th August and their arrival released a like number of 4Q4s which were delicensed at the end of the summer augmentation season, on 1st October, and taken into works so that they could be modified for use as Green Line coaches. The reason for this was that the 1936 orders for coaches had not been sufficient to replace all the remaining Gilfords in Green Line service and the Country Bus department was impatient to be rid of them. The modifications were confined to the essentials of livery, fleetname, luggage racks, saloon heaters and external brackets for the Green Line route boards; the seats, rather spartan even by bus standards, were not changed. They were reclassified 1/4Q4/1, relicensed on 25th March 1937 and put into service at Northfleet and Staines (routes A1/A2), Amersham (partial conversion of Q and R) and Leatherhead (L).

Meanwhile, the hundred coaches for the 1936 programme were authorised by the Board on 6th February 1936. Although half of them were again to be Qs, the other fifty were to be AEC Regal 0662s, the first indication that the Board might be moving away from the side-engined vehicle for its standard single-decker. The Regals were the first of this model to be purchased new by London Transport and also the first production run with oil engines and preselective gearboxes. Their mechanical specification was virtually the same as the contemporary STLs, including the 7.7 litre engine. Their metal-framed bodywork was by Weymann and introduced a style which was, with refinements, to be used for most single-deckers delivered between then and 1939. They were quite handsome, with gently curving front and rear ends and indicator boxes neatly incorporated into the roof domes. At the front the nearside wing was embodied into the front bulkhead and built up to incorporate the headlamp. The wings were continued behind the wheels under the first bay and in a continuous sweep under the radiator, the whole effect being finished off with a bumper bar. There was a similar stylish back sweep on the rear mudguards, which tapered upwards to join a narrow chromium 'bumper' strip running across the back. Like the Qs, the Regals had an enclosed sliding door. One feature which spoilt this generally harmonious arrangement was the stepping up of the rearmost two window bays, in line with the seats, to clear the wheel arch.

The same five bay construction as adopted on the 5Q5s was repeated, as were most details of the finishings and décor but there were differences to give them a more luxurious style for coach operation. The thirty seats were of a larger tubular metal type with deeper cushions and upholstered in the green and light brown moquette then being adopted for coaches. The seat backs were covered in repp and each had an ashtray placed centrally. The floor and cove panels were covered in linoleum. They were also furnished with substantial looking luggage racks and Clayton Dewandre saloon heaters, whose characteristic large circular grille, set in a chromium frame, occupied a prominent position in the front bulkhead above the flywheel housing. A final touch of class was provided by a clock, which was placed in a central position at the top of the front bulkhead.

Ts 403C-452C (CLX551-575; CXX151-175) were classified 9T9 and were licensed for service between June and November 1936, the first being T 405B, on 8th June at Watford Leavesden Road. They were allocated to Amersham for route B (four); Watford (Leavesden Road) (thirteen), Crawley (four) and Reigate (fourteen) for routes I and J; and to Hatfield (two), Hitchin (seven), Leatherhead (four) and Dorking (one) for route K1. Some of the surplus vehicles at Reigate and an odd one initially allocated to Two Waters were later used to make up the deficiencies at Hatfield and Dorking. Those at Leatherhead replaced the 1/4Q4/1s which went to Watford for route T. Although sturdy and smooth running, the 9T9s were handicapped by their 7.7 litre engines and were soon to be overshadowed by improved members of the breed.

Newly modified for coach work, Q 102C is seen at Eccleston Bridge on route A1. A new 'Green Line' fleetname was introduced at about this time, incorporating the words 'London Transport' in a rectangle between the larger first and last letters. G H F Atkins

T 446C at Eccleston Bridge in September 1937. The attempts at smoothing out the bumps and projections around the bonnet on the 9T9s conspired to produce a rather bulky look. G H F Atkins

The coach Qs were mounted on the 18ft 6in wheelbase version of the chassis, with shorter overhangs at both ends, as a central entrance with platform door was required. They had Park Royal bodies of a slightly different design from the 5Q5s with a deeper roof, which did not slope towards the back, and a larger windscreen. On these the sidelamps were incorporated into the headlamp housing but the inclusion of a rather mundane looking ornamental radiator grille (which served no purpose) combined with the very substantial headlamps and the openable ventilation panels above the screen, gave the front an untidy and somewhat graceless look compared with its predecessors. The five bay layout was disturbed in this design by the entrance door, which was about half a bay in width, leaving a short window at the back of the saloon and giving a slightly less tidy effect. Because of the deeper windscreen, the side windows did not sweep down at the front and the effect was as though the cab area had been bolted on separately.

There was a full-width cab, separated from the saloon by a bulkhead, leaving room for just thirty-two seats, hardly much of a bonus compared with the Regals. The bulkhead was in three parts, the middle section containing a swing communicating door and the section behind the driver being slightly further back, with a short angled section linking it to the door. Finishings, fittings and décor followed the same pattern as the Ts, except that there was a longitudinal seat for four, with Underground-like armrests, over the engine and another for two over the nearside front wheel. An ash tray for each of these was attached to the front bulkhead for the use of passengers in the longitudinal seats.

Qs 189C-238C (CXX382-406; DGX220-244) were classified 6Q6. The first, Q 189C, was received at Chiswick from Park Royal on 25th September 1936 and after inspection was returned to the bodybuilders on 8th October, presumably for modifications to be made. It came back on 10th November, went to Hertford a fortnight later and was finally licensed for service on 1st December. Meanwhile, others had been going into service, the first to do so being Q 197, at Guildford, on 3rd November. They all entered service between then and 21st January 1937 at Hertford (eighteen), Guildford (twelve) and Addlestone (three) for routes M1, M2 and M3; Luton (eight) for route H3; and, for routes Q and R, Amersham (five, to run alongside the 1/4Q4/1s) and High Wycombe (four).

Top **The final version of the Q, for coach work, had the appearance of its Park Royal body further enhanced by the virtual elimination of any slope in the roof line. The effect is slightly marred by the introduction of a driver's cab door, a consequence of the decision to have a full width cab, which upsets the symmetry of the side windows. Q 228C is at Hertford.** J F Higham

Right **The inn sign for the Salisbury Arms, Hoddesdon frames a scene redolent of the 1930s. There is a complete absence of other traffic and it is second nature for the mother and child to travel on the Green Line, especially in the comfort of Q 205.** AEC

The vehicles ousted in this programme, with the help of the converted 4Q4s, were predominantly Gilfords which left the fleet in droves and brought to an end the dominance of a type which had found so much favour with some Independents. Other withdrawals included a number of Commer Invaders, including the six taken over from LGCS, and the Dennis EV acquired from Amersham & District.

The last of the 1936 orders to start appearing were the Central Bus KPO3 Cubs, Cs 77-98 (CLE105-126). (C 76B was the one taken over from St Albans and District and had a petrol engine.) They had Weymann metal-framed bodies of more or less identical design to their country cousins but had the new, slightly larger, 4.7 litre Leyland engine, which caused them to be classified 1/2C2/1. This engine was an indirect injection unit, with $3^1/_2$in bore and 5in stroke and a power output of 65 bhp which was apparently considered more appropriate for Central Bus service. It had first been tried out in November 1935 on Country Bus C 51, which was transferred to the Central Area in exchange for C 1 at the same time.

The Cubs were licensed between 3rd April and 5th May 1936 and were allocated to Mortlake, Hanwell, Enfield, Barking and Harrow Weald. They replaced the remnants of the Dennises taken over from Imperial and Romford & District, the DSs running for the last time on 5th April and the DMs two days later; and the Guys and the Beans all of which which ran for the last time on 28th April. Although the Monday-Friday schedule now required only twenty Darts, forty-four remained licensed, partly as spares but also to cover the much larger Saturday schedule which called for thirty-two. This disparity was a subject which exercised the mind of Frank Pick at this time but he had to accept that, apart from ensuring that the maximum use was made at weekends of vehicles held as engineering spares, there was little that could be done if the passenger demand was to be met. The arrangements therefore continued and the problem remained throughout the 1930s and well into the post-war era.

Top **The main loser from the influx of new coaches was the fleet of Gilfords which disappeared rapidly in 1936 and 1937. GF 166 is parked in the access roadway to the former Hillman garage in London Road, Romford on 21st November 1936, shortly before being replaced by decanted 7T7s. It was originally owned by Beaumont Safeway Coaches.** D W K Jones

Centre **It was the performance of former St Albans and District Leyland Cub, C 76, which persuaded Chiswick to standardise on the model for its one-man fleet. When this photograph was taken it was running in far distant Gravesend on local route 456A.**

Right **The Weymann version of the Cub for Central Buses looked much the same as that for Country Buses, except that the front bumper bar was omitted. A gleaming C 94 was one of these allocated to Enfield.** Alan Duke

One of the Inter-Station Cubs at Victoria on 20th July 1937, when there appear to be no trains. To simplify the internal layout, the sliding door on the Park Royal body opens towards the front of the vehicle, enabling passengers to have direct access to the short flight of stairs to the 'poop' deck. These buses had a unique fleetname, based on the style adopted for Green Line and a special blue, yellow and black livery. The black line visible on the front bulkhead pillar is a semaphore trafficator signal. D W K Jones

Another small group of vehicles taken into stock by Central Buses at the end of 1936, outside the main vehicle renewal programme and unique in many respects, were eight forward-control Leyland Cub SKPZ2s, powered by 4.7 litre petrol engines (C 106-113, registered CLX543-550 and classified 3C3). They were intended for operation on the inter-station service which was taken over from P. Hearn on 7th October 1936 and their Park Royal bodywork was therefore designed to take a large quantity of luggage in a 1½-deck layout. The internal décor and seating were finished to the coach standard of the day and they were painted in a special scheme of light blue and yellow, with a black roof. C 106 was delivered on 28th April and spent the next four months going back and forth between Chiswick and Park Royal before being licensed on 7th September. The rest were delivered between 7th and 21st May and licensed, at Old Kent Road, on 1st and 21st October.

The Private Hire fleet of Regals with sun-saloon roofs and swing doors introduced by LGOC and East Surrey in 1930 and 1931 and the two Lewis Regals of 1931 came under scrutiny at the beginning of 1937. The Board decided to retire them and, on 18th March 1937, authorised the purchase of a fleet of new coaches, specifying the use of six-wheeled chassis. The chosen chassis was the AEC Renown 663, the last of the model to be produced by AEC. The choice of the short wheelbase version meant that the vehicles were limited by the Construction & Use Regulations to a length of twenty-seven feet, which held their carrying capacity down to thirty. They were therefore actually shorter than the 9T9s and were presumably chosen because their single rear wheels reduced the amount of wheel arch protrusion into the saloon. Had the longer wheelbase version been chosen, that could have been built to the full length of thirty feet, with a useful increase in capacity, but this would have limited their scope of operation, even as Private Hire vehicles. Although oil engines were bought under the same authority, these were not used in the new coaches but were exchanged for reconditioned petrol units from double-deck LT buses, in the same way as had been done with the STLs in 1933-34. Combined with the fluid flywheels and preselective gearboxes these gave an exceptionally quiet and smooth ride, ideal for their intended purpose.

The external appearance of the Weymann bodywork was virtually identical to the 9T9s except that they lacked the built-up bonnet and front wings, had no rear indicator box and had a touch of extra flamboyance in the deep rear mudguards which had a downward sweep to the rear. The loss of the moulded wing arrangement was compensated visually by having the side panel of the front bulkhead curve out to meet the mudguard, partially hiding the box containing the autovac. As they were not intended for service use, the upsweep of the cantrail moulding to accommodate a Green Line side board was also omitted. They were not fitted with headlamps but had two foglamps, one on each side of the bottom of the radiator, just above the bumper bar. The LTCs did not have disc trims on either front or back wheels, perhaps because these were also the first Renowns to be fitted with fully floating rear axles, giving them a fatter hub centre than on the LTs, similar to those on contemporary AEC trolleybus chassis.

Internally, they differed from the Ts in having sliding panels in the roof and seats which were fully to coach standard with head-rolls and armrests. The seats were arranged in pairs but each seat was separated from its pair by being slightly staggered. Provision was also made for a radio to be installed in the saloon but Pick had yet to be convinced of the justification for this and he authorised an experiment with only five at first. They were given bonnet numbers LTC 1-24, registered EGO505-528 and classified 1LTC1. The first seven went into service at Brixton Private Hire garage in November 1937.

The Renowns had a very short spell at Brixton, as the responsibility for Private Hire in the Central area was transferred to Central Buses at this time and the whole fleet of coaches was moved to Old Kent Road on 22nd December 1937. This enabled Brixton to be closed and sold. Interestingly, 'ownership' of those vehicles which were delicensed for the winter, including eight LTCs and ex-Hillman LT 1429, was not officially transferred from Country to Central until they were relicensed in March 1938. The remaining LTCs went to Old Kent Road in January (seven) and March 1938 (ten). The coaches withdrawn were Ts 150-154, 319-324, 360, 363 and 399-402. Also withdrawn were London Transport's sole remaining Daimler, DST 6, and Albion AN 1C.

Above The body styling pioneered on the 9T9s was continued on the new Renown coaches but the fussy trimming of the front end was omitted and the shorter body length imposed a narrower rear saloon window. Unlike previous coaches, the LTCs had the 'London Transport' fleetname, reflecting the transfer of responsibility for private hire to Central Buses. LTC 14C is at Westminster in the summer of 1938. D W K Jones

Left T 150, one of General's original batch of Hoyal bodied Private Hire Regals, was withdrawn and sold when the LTCs arrived at the early age of seven years. At an early stage in their careers these coaches were fitted with standard Green Line style indicator boxes. D W K Jones

Another handsome coach pushed out by the Renowns was this Duple bodied Daimler CH6 which had been acquired from West London Coaches in January 1934. DST 6 is seen in its last season at Old Palace Yard Westminster. D W K Jones

Among single-deckers withdrawn during 1937 were the Dennis Arrows, which were numbered in the same class as the Lances. DL 37 was a Birch bodied coach which was acquired by the LGOC in November 1932 from Red Rover Saloon Coaches of Aylesbury. This photograph, taken some years before its withdrawal, shows it still at work on the Aylesbury route. J F Higham

The Weymann bodied Morris Viceroy YB6s, new to East Surrey in 1931 and latterly operated from Amersham garage, were one of the types replaced in 1937 by Cubs made redundant by the conversion of routes to large saloon. MS 5B was photographed some time earlier when working on the truncated route 369, which was withdrawn in May 1936. J F Higham

Although there were no new single-deck buses in the 1937 delivery programme, there were nevertheless a number of withdrawals as services were converted either from single-deck to double-deck or from one-man to two-man operation, using larger vehicles. The last of the Dennis Lancets (DT) and Arrows (DL) were withdrawn from Country Bus service at the beginning of November 1937, when they were replaced by spare 5Q5s. The October 1937 programme of service changes, in which twenty-seaters were replaced by

This interesting assembly at Slough GWR station contains, from the left, Q 97 on trunk route 353, TD 138 on local route 444, TR 7 on route 441 and C 1 on route 442. The Cub had been transferred to Country Buses in November 1935. D W K Jones

large saloons on the Addlestone area routes, witnessed the departure from scheduled operation of the two Dennis Aces which had come directly into the LPTB fleet in 1934, having been ordered by Gravesend and District (DC 2,3), the six remaining small Thornycrofts (NY 2-6 and 9), which had also been working at Addlestone, the Morris Viceroys (MS 1, 2 and 4-11), which were replaced at Amersham by spare Cubs, and the last of the Gilfords which had hung on in bus service at Hertford and St Albans.

Parked in descending order of age at St Albans garage on 13th February 1937 are GF 92, a former Strawhatter coach now downgraded to bus duties on route 382, DC 1, the Dennis Ace ordered by Gravesend and District but delivered to London Transport, and an unidentifiable Cub. D W K Jones

TF 1C in its original condition with a modernistic all glass cab. D W K Jones

Right **CR 1, as yet unnumbered and bearing 'WT' garage plates and a stencil for St Albans route 355, is parked in Broadway on 8th January 1938, ready for inspection by the Board. It has already caught the eye of passers-by who might be less impressed by the C accompanying it, which is presumably there for comparison. The styling is very similar to TF 1 but there is a more orthodox cab.** D W K Jones

After a quiet year for single-deckers in 1937, things began to hot up with a vengeance in the first few months of 1938. The massive programme for 1938 already mentioned in chapter two included, in its original form, forty Regals and seventy-four Cubs but when the double-deck order was reduced by seventy, the number of Regals was increased to 110, seventy-three buses and thirty-seven coaches. This programme was yet further modified in March 1938, when the seventy-four Cubs were deleted and the number of Regals increased to 150. The reason for this was one of great significance because added to the programme was one oil-engined coach and one single-deck bus. These were in fact TF 1 (DYL904), a new underfloor-engined coach developed in conjunction with Leyland Motors, and CR 1 (ELP294), another Leyland development, this time a rear-engined version of the Cub.

Before turning to the details, it is worth looking at the 1939 programme, which was provisionally approved at the same time, as the two programmes ran together into one continuous delivery. The single-deck segment of the plan called for seventy-three omo buses (the seventy-fourth being CR 1), twenty-eight 32-seat buses, eighty-eight 30-seat coaches and eighty-eight 34-seat coaches. There was a great deal of debate going on at this time about the best solution to the problem of the poor financial performance of the Green Line and there was a strong desire to have vehicles with a greater passenger capacity. The debate even got down to such details as the position of the emergency door, as an extra seat could be put into the TFs if this was on the offside at the front. Also considered was a 30ft three-axle version of the TF seating thirty-eight or a three-axle 'T' (presumably a Renown) which would seat thirty-four. Nothing came of these fascinating ideas, presumably because the Traffic Commissioner had already made it clear that he would not approve thirty-footers on the Green Line because he believed they would cause additional congestion in central London. However, the internal layout of some of the proposed thirty-seat Regals was altered to increase their capacity to thirty-four, which rather undermined the point of the TF.

The more important of the two experimental vehicles, in terms of the number ultimately likely to be needed, was the coach, which Leyland designated Tiger FEC, though it had almost nothing in common with the contemporary standard Tiger. The full potential of the Q had not been realised but the basic idea of having the whole of the floor area available for passengers was one that interested London Transport, hence its alliance with Leyland in this project. The most revolutionary feature of TF 1C was in the layout of its chassis, with its engine laid horizontally on its side under the floor, but it also introduced to London buses the air operated preselective gearbox, supplied by AEC, and air brakes. The engine was a modified version of the standard Leyland direct-injection 8.6 litre unit and was mounted flexibly.

Apart from the extreme front end, the thirty-four seat bodywork supplied by Leyland bore a strong resemblance to the 9T9s and LTCs, except that the saloon windows curved downwards at each end. The driver's cab was a remarkable attempt at something modern. The driving position was very high, which dictated a very deep windscreen starting high in the roof and finishing somewhere around the level of the driver's shins. The wheelbase was 17ft 6ins and no advantage was taken of the area beside the driver, which was simply a large curved wing, because of the need to accommodate a sliding entrance door. TF 1 was received from Leyland on 10th July 1937 but was not licensed for service until 1st December. It went to Tunbridge Wells for use on routes C1 and C2.

CR 1 and TF 1 at Chiswick Works in 1938.

Left **The interior of a CR, showing the set back driver's cab with doorless angled access to the saloon. The half bulkhead on the lower right protects the emergency exit, whose handle can be seen at the top of the window.**

Below **CR 1B in service from Windsor garage at Slough station on route 442.**
R S Turnbull collection

CR 1 was mounted on a Leyland Cub REC chassis, quite unlike the standard Cub, which had the same 4.4 litre engine as the Country Cubs but mounted longitudinally across the back, in a form now very familiar but then quite revolutionary. It had a four-speed constant mesh gearbox. The body was built at Chiswick and in layout was similar to the TF but with a more conventional driver's cab and front dome, incorporating a standard destination indicator box. Internal fixtures and fittings followed the then current bus practice and the top of the engine compartment, which was contained within the body shell, was laid out as a luggage rack. It was licensed in January 1938 and went into service at St Albans. Although considered successful enough to justify a production order, the CRs were a little troublesome and it was they, rather than the older Cubs, which were to be withdrawn and stored during the war.

The 266 single deckers of different seating capacities and planned as a mixture of buses and coaches, emerged as one basic type of vehicle known generically as the 10T10 class and numbered T453C-718C, all coaches. They were registered in two batches: T453-565 were ELP177-289; and T566-718 EYK201-353. Instead of buying new buses, the Board had decided to meet the requirements of the programme from the 9T9 and 1/4Q4/1 coaches which would be displaced from coach work by the new Regals. The 10T10s were of special significance in having composite bodywork, wood and metal framed. The first 150, constituting the 1938 programme, had thirty-seat bodies but before work started on the 116 of the 1939 order (actually in the summer of 1938) the design was modified so as to accommodate thirty-four passengers and this variant took the code T10/1. The changes made to increase the capacity to thirty-four included the removal of the bulkhead behind the door and its replacement by a low partition which projected slightly into the stairwell. This arrangement was to prove a nuisance in service and consideration was given in August 1938 to making a further modification to the sixty as yet unbuilt, which would have reduced the capacity to thirty-three, presumably by having a single seat at the front. Nothing came of this.

The bodywork followed the pattern set by the 9T9s but without the built-up bonnet, wing and bumper bar. Unlike the LTCs, however, the 10T10s did have their nearside wing built into the front bulkhead in the style tried out on STL 2434 (see chapter two). The rear mudguards were also of a different design which widened out behind the wheels and had no backsweep under the body. Finally, the passenger door opened into a recess, rather than being enclosed.

Another important difference in this model lay in its chassis, where the power unit was the A180, a pot cavity version of the 8.8 litre direct injection oil engine, built under licence from Leyland. The choice of engine had been influenced strongly by the Board's happy experience with the Leyland 8.6 litre units on the STDs and were to prove a stepping stone to the yet larger 9.6 litre version which appeared on RT 1 a year later. These engines had a combination of power and sweetness of tone which made them a unique joy to travel behind.

The first five 10T10s were licensed on 26th March 1938 and were sent to Windsor garage then still a stronghold of the TR and TD class Leylands. Further deliveries to Windsor in March and April were intermingled with others to Godstone, another Tiger garage. Their arrival came soon after the major changes to Green Line services on 9th February and they were therefore a kind of belated birth present for routes G and P in their new guises. The next route to have 10T10s was the D, which was completed during April when Staines received seven Regals and Dunton Green nine. April also saw a start on the conversion of the C1 and C2, which was completed on 1st June by which time Addlestone had received ten and Tunbridge Wells six. By now, the Tigers and Titans had been cleared out of Green Line work and substantial inroads were being made into the 7T7 coaches which had pioneered the network only eight years earlier. A temporary use was found for five Tigers (TRs 9, 12, 14, 17 and 33) and eight Regals (Ts 250, 359, 361, 362, 364, 365, 366, 367), which joined the Private Hire fleet during March and April, the Tigers at Old Kent Road and the Regals at Clay Hall and Holloway.

Only twelve 10T10s were licensed during May, all but two on the first of the month, whereas those in April had been spread through the month. This more economical arrangement was now adopted for the remaining deliveries and no fewer than forty-two took to the road on 1st June, followed by four more on 2nd, one on 3rd and two stragglers on the 15th. Attention now turned to the H1 and H2, with East Grinstead (ten), Luton (five) and St Albans (five) all being changed over on 1st June, at the same time as routes B (Amersham seven; Swanley four), and N (Epping seven; Windsor eight). Route K3 at Dorking took the five licensed on 2nd and 3rd June.

The new coaches were now pouring out of Chiswick at the rate of about ten a week and another thirty-six started work during July, twenty-nine of them at the beginning of the month. Epping took a second bite of the cherry with eighteen (two of them in June) for routes V and W. Also during July, Chelsham and Two Waters received their quotas of eight and five for routes E and F, while Tring's seven were not completed until 1st August. To improve performance on the stiff climb up Titsey Hill between Oxted and Chelsham these twenty vehicles were fitted with back axles having a ratio of 6.25:1, instead of the normal 5.2:1, and were given the chassis classification 1/10T.

Needless to say, the withdrawal of the 7T7s was not straightforward, as there was a progressive reshuffle so that twenty-seven and twenty-nine seaters were withdrawn and, where appropriate, their place taken by thirty-seaters. This was particularly marked at Grays and Romford (London Road), where nearly a hundred exchanges were made for this reason, despite the fact that they too would soon receive the new coaches.

The switch to production of the thirty-four seaters bore fruit on 1st August at the beginning of a run of deliveries to Grays for the Z1 and Z2. Inevitably, with Chiswick's quirky system of numbering, the changeover did not come neatly at a particular point in the series. The lowest numbered 10T10/1 was T 522 (which was licensed on 1st September), while the highest numbered thirty-seater was T 606 (1st July). Before Grays was completely restocked, attention switched to the other side of the river, where routes A1 and A2, operated by Northfleet and Staines, were changed over on 1st August, each garage receiving eight thirty-four seaters. This marked the start of the removal of the 4Q4s from Green Line service, a process which continued on 1st September with allocations to High Wycombe (two) and Amersham (five) for routes Q and R, which nevertheless remained predominantly 6Q6, and to Watford (Leavesden Road) who got four for the T. From then until the end of deliveries, Romford (London Road) dominated the proceedings, taking no fewer than sixty-nine, including the last to be licensed, T 691, on 25th March 1939. In just over a year, the 10T10 had established itself as the principal rolling stock for the Green Line network.

The only pre-1936 vehicles still scheduled for Green Line service, other than duplication, in March 1939 were forty-six 1/7T7/1s at Romford (London Road). They operated on routes X, which had been transferred from North Street when that garage closed on 30th November 1938, and Y2; but not for much longer. Seventy-five of the thirty-four seat coaches in this programme, materialised as TF 14C-88C, (FJJ615-618, 629-674, 761-777 and FXT41-48; coded 2TF2). The bodywork of the new TFs was built by Chiswick Works to the same general style as the 10T10s but as the saloon floor was higher and flatter, there was no step in the window line. They also had a neater front end than TF 1, similar to the arrangement pioneered by CR 1 but with a radiator grille and filler cap in the wing housing. The internal layout was similar to the Regals but with one delightful difference. There was a much prized seat for two passengers ahead of the front entrance, almost alongside the driver which, in the absence of a

Below **Considered by many to be the most handsome of the pre-war single-deckers designed by Chiswick, the 10T10 was a direct descendant of the 9T9 and LTC classes and combined the best of both designs, further enhanced by the new deeper AEC radiator shell and by the use of wheel disc trims. T 475 navigates Hyde Park Corner on its way to Windsor on route G, the first route to be graced by the class.** G H F Atkins

Bottom **The first coaches to be dislodged by the new Regals were the Tigers and Titans. TR 35C is at Eccleston Bridge with a 7T7, whose future as a coach is little longer than that of the Tiger.** D W K Jones

Above **The TFs had such a short time in service before the war that they were little photographed in service. In this case, TF 37C appears to be on a private hire job but it is dressed for route Y and is carrying a running number, so this may be a press showing.** Charles F Klapper Collection, Omnibus Society

Below **Looking forward inside a Green Line TF, the general appearance is similar to a 10T10 but with a staggered front bulkhead containing an angled door to the cab, which allows for the front seat to be placed ahead of the entrance on a raised platform. The TF was the last type to have winding handles above the windows.** L T Museum U29240

Bottom **The single-deck bus Titans were also withdrawn as a result of the arrival of the new coaches, TD 131B being delicensed in July 1938. This photograph was taken earlier at Slough.** J F Higham

conventional bonnet, gave a magnificent view ahead. Access to the driver's cab was from the passenger saloon through a communicating door in the angled section between the rear of the cab and the front nearside bulkhead, which was further forward. Because of the higher floor, there was an additional step at the entrance, making three instead of two. This was another handsome model, with a wonderful sense of power and grace and it is a great pity that further development was stopped by the war, which started just as the last ones were going into service.

The first twelve (TFs 15-26) were licensed at Romford (London Road) on 25th March but further deliveries were then stockpiled until another twenty entered service on 1st May. All but two of the remainder entered service gradually until the last (TF 88) was licensed on 5th August. Two saw no service as coaches before the outbreak of war. TF 14, whose chassis had been the first to arrive from Leyland on 31st December 1938, had been licensed as a private trainer on 2nd February and remained as such until 24th March, after which its body was removed and its chassis returned to Leyland, for reasons unknown. Its body (number 1 in the new series) was then attached to the chassis of TF 75, which went into service on 9th June. TF 14 itself received a new body numbered 50 on 4th August and had the curious privilege of being licensed for the first time on 1st September, the very day that the coaches were withdrawn for conversion to ambulances. The last to be completed was TF 76, which received its body on 21st August, but it was not licensed until 15th September, as an ambulance.

With the arrival of the Leylands, Chiswick's apparent inability to plan very far ahead was evident as the entire batch was sent to Romford to replace the older Ts and the sixty-nine 10T10s which had only just arrived there. Elsewhere, routes for which thirty-four seaters were considered necessary had already been stocked with the smaller capacity 10T10s and the allocation staff now indulged in one of their favourite pastimes: re-allocating large blocks of nearly new vehicles over huge distances. Romford's Regals went to garages already operating 10T10s, and these in turn displaced older vehicles. One of the more short-sighted decisions seems to have been to put thirty-seaters on the E and F because these specially modified vehicles were replaced in May 1939, when only ten months old, by second-hand thirty-four seaters, which had their rear axle ratios modified and therefore became 1/10T10/1s.

Other routes which switched to the larger capacity were the H1 and H2 at East Grinstead, St Albans and Luton, N (Epping and Windsor), and V (Epping). Routes which benefited from the displaced thirty-seaters were the K1 and K2, which lost their 9T9s at Dorking, Hatfield, Hitchin and Leatherhead and the I and J at Crawley, Reigate and Watford (Leavesden Road), also in place of 9T9s. The 9T9s were now relegated to bus work at Addlestone, Dartford, Dorking, Guildford, Hatfield, Hitchin, Leatherhead, Luton, Swanley, Tring, Watford (High Street) and Windsor, some of those at Watford being used for the conversion of route 309 from one-man (Cub) to two-man operation in August 1939.

Shortly after the Green Line TFs started to go into service, the first of twelve Private Hire coaches were arriving (TFs 2C-13C, FJJ603-614, coded 2TF3). Park Royal Coachworks Ltd had secured the order for these coaches against competition from Brush, Duple, Harrington and Weymann but only the latter and Park Royal offered metal framework, which was preferred by the Board and as Park Royal's price was cheaper, they won the work. Although superficially similar, these vehicles differed in a number of ways from the Green Line version and only the cab and front lower section were common to both types. The Private Hire examples had deeper side windows extending further into the roof, glass cant panels, opening roofs and a higher standard of interior finish. The rear end was completely different from the main batch, as the emergency exit door was moved to the rear bay on the offside, leaving a single window across the back which, with the absence of a rear indicator box, gave this aspect a very non-London look. They were painted in the Private Hire livery of dark and light green, with a streamlined style sweeping down at the front, which underlined the differing appearance.

All twelve were allocated, between April and June, to Old Kent Road, where they effectively replaced the eight Private Hire Ts and five TRs which had been delicensed at the end of the 1938 season and also the superb former Hillman Renown LT 1429, which was withdrawn on 1st May 1939.

Above **Private Hire TF 2 in the livery of two shades of green specially adapted to suit the contours of the design, is on duty at Westminster on 10th July 1939 during its first and only season as a touring coach. The roof has been opened and the light and spacious interior is apparent even from this angle. The projection at the front of the roof is the radio aerial.** Charles F Klapper Collection, Omnibus Society

Below **This rearward view of the saloon of a Private Hire TF shows the single piece rear window, the extensive glazing and their unusual style of moquette. Also notable for a London Transport vehicle were the Art Deco lampshades.** L T Museum U30728

Single-deck design in transition. T 682C on the far right of this group in Minories 'coach station', Aldgate represents the ultimate in vertical engined design in 1939 but is already about to be ousted from its Romford home by revolutionary underfloor engined vehicles like TF 60C on the left. The vehicle in between is T 703C from Grays garage. This and Romford were the last garages to get new coaches before the war. G H F Atkins

The arrival of the TFs ended the career of the former Hillman AEC Renown, LT 1429, which was withdrawn into store in April 1939 and later destroyed by a bomb on Bull Yard, Peckham. New in September 1932, the Harrington body made this the most truly coach-like coach in the LPTB fleet. D W K Jones

One of the original East Surrey bus Regals, T 372, circles the war memorial in Hertford, passing on the way the Northmet electricity offices, still showing signs of their Underground Group origins, and an LNER mechanical horse. This bus was withdrawn in 1939 and broken up in November. AEC

NORTHMET
ELECTRICITY
HERTFORD
350A THE HADHAMS
STANSTEAD ABBOTTS
WARE CROSSING
PG 6780
L N E R

Most of the earlier coach Regals were withdrawn and sold as the 10T10s and TFs arrived, although about eight were held at garages for weekend duplication. Thirty-two of the front entrance variety had their destination indicators modified to the larger type and survived as buses for many years while another nineteen similar ones remained in the fleet, in their coach condition, making only occasional appearances in service. These helped to cover the withdrawal of all but six of the twenty-seven bus Regals which had been acquired when the Board was formed, from the Watford Omnibus Company, Charles Russett and Sons and, by far the bulk, from London General Country Services. Also withdrawn during this run of replacements was the sole Dennis Mace (DC 3), which had been acquired from the Penn company in July 1935 and had latterly been used on route 455A from High Wycombe garage.

The most interesting survivors were thirty-one which were completely transformed. They were given new oil engines and the 1935 Weymann bodies transferred from the Reliances, which were at last withdrawn. All thirty-one, which were given the code 11T11, were painted green and sent to the Country Area at Leatherhead, Two Waters, High Wycombe, Watford (Leavesden Road), Reigate and Amersham, all garages which had operated Reliances. In some cases, there was an intermediate stage when 7T7s were used, to cover the period while the rebodying was taking place. The 4Q4s released from the Green Line also helped out in this process. The first Regal conversion emerged from the works in March 1938 and the programme was completed in December. Five of the 11T11s were soon on the move again as they were transferred to Central Buses for the conversion of route 211 from Cub (omo) to large saloon (tmo) on 31st May 1939. The buses transferred were Ts 208, 213, 215, 216 and 223.

The last single-deckers to appear were the CRs (2-49, FXT108-155; coded 2CR2). They differed from CR 1 mainly in having the larger 4.7 litre engine, although there were also detailed changes to the Chiswick bodywork. The size of the order for these had a rather chequered career. The original total of seventy-four was obviously an overestimate, given the number of small single-deckers still running, and was suspiciously identical to the original order for Cs, yet it appears to have gone unchallenged for some time. There had been a steady drip of conversions from small to large saloon over the years and there were now only twelve Bedfords and forty-one

Top **This cheeky little snub nosed creature is a Dennis Mace, the only one owned by London Transport, who acquired it with the business of the Penn Bus Company in 1935. DC 3, which was at High Wycombe and normally ran on route 455A, fell victim to the intake of new vehicles in 1939.**
D W K Jones

Centre and right **Before and after on route 427 in Reigate; these two photographs were taken at almost the same spot and show a Weymann bodied Reliance and an 11T11 bearing one of the same type of body removed from the Rs.**
R S Turnbull

Dennis Darts in the fleet. The maximum number of small buses scheduled, over both operating departments, was already down to 134 at the beginning of 1938 (when the original decisions were being taken) and still falling. The number of CRs ordered was reduced to fifty-nine (which still seems generous) before the order was placed but even this later had to be reduced to forty-nine (including CR 1). In fact, as larger buses were substituted, the small bus fleet was shrinking all the time and a further reduction of four was contemplated, but abandoned as impracticable, when the Cubs on route 309 were replaced by Ts in the summer of 1939. The displaced Cubs were transferred to Epping to replace Bedfords on route 339.

The chassis for CR 2 was received at Chiswick on 19th July and it emerged as a complete vehicle on 8th September. It and CR 3 were licensed on 9th September and the majority were licensed by 5th January 1940, principally at Kingston (routes 206 and 216), Hounslow (237) and Uxbridge (220, 223, 224) but also two at Enfield (205) and one at Harrow Weald (221). Eight more were licensed in 1940 and 1941 but four saw no service until after the war. Most were painted red, all in wartime trim with white wings and headlamp masks, and helped replace the remaining Darts but six were painted green (CR12B - 17B). They were allocated to Windsor, where they were operated mainly on routes 442 and 462, with a single Saturday turn on the 461 and were joined there by prototype CR 1 from St Albans in March. Indirectly, they replaced the last few Bedfords (BD class) at Hertford on route 333.

The CRs were the last new buses to enter service during the 1930s and as such were true war babies. Their arrival closed an exciting chapter in the history of London's buses and their subsequent history was somehow symbolic of what lay in store for the proud six year old organisation at 55 Broadway.

Top **The arrival of the 10T10s provoked the consignment of the remaining AEC Reliances to oblivion. Although designated R 39C, this former Battens Park Royal bodied thirty-seater had been demoted to bus work by the time it was photographed working from Two Waters garage towards the end of its seven year London life.** D W K Jones

Centre **Now numbered T 426B, this 9T9 has been relegated to bus work on route 412 at Dorking as a result of the arrival of the 10T10s and TFs.** W J Haynes

Left **An official photograph of CR 9 shows it to be much the same as CR 1, except that the unnecessary stepped and curved waistline has been straightened, resulting in a tidier window arrangement and a deeper roof, the sidelamps have been moved to the outside of the body, the nearside wing has a deeper curve and the fuel filler cap has been moved forward. As it entered service after the outbreak of war, CR 9 is fitted with headlamp masks of the original design, its sidelamps are masked and the wing tips are painted white.** L T Museum U30718

CHAPTER FOUR TROLLEYBUSES FOR TRAMS

At one of its preliminary meetings, on 8th June 1933, the LPTB decided, as a first step, to consolidate the smaller municipal tramway undertakings with those of the former London County Council. Because of its close relationship with Croydon Corporation the South Metropolitan system appears to have been included in this arrangement. The LCC's General Manager, T.E. Thomas, was charged with the responsibility of ensuring a smooth transition, without altering the principles on which the undertakings were operated, pending a full review by the Board. The headquarters of this combined organisation remained at the old LCC offices in Belvedere Road, Waterloo. For the time being, the company tramways, which were already controlled from 55 Broadway, continued under their old managements but T.E. Thomas became General Manager of all tram and trolleybus operations and this was all finally consolidated with the transfer of the Tram and Trolleybus department's headquarters to 55 Broadway on 20th August 1934.

On Saturday 1st July 1933, all trams and trolleybuses, of whatever former ownership, appeared with the new legal lettering:
LONDON PASSENGER TRANSPORT BOARD,
55 BROADWAY, WESTMINSTER SW1
on paper bills pasted on the rocker panels. Liveries were unchanged and no immediate attempt was made to suppress municipal crests but in most cases those cars which had carried a fleet name had it painted out in the main body colour of the former owner. At this stage fleet numbers were not altered but the smaller municipalities and the South Met company were each given a code letter to use as a suffix to their existing numbers:

C – Bexley; D – Erith; E – Croydon;
F – Ilford; G – East Ham; H – West Ham;
K – Walthamstow; S – South Met.

The LCC, LUT and MET fleets retained their existing numbers, without suffix letters, for the time being. Once the managers had had time to think about it, a system of renumbering was worked out and the following blocks were allocated:

LCC	1, 2, 101-160, 402-2003
Ilford	5- 44
East Ham	45- 100
Leyton	161- 210
West Ham	211- 344
Croydon	345- 399
Walthamstow	2004-2065
Bexley	2066-2098 (never used)
Erith	2099-2117 (never used)

It was not until the company systems were brought under the management of Belvedere Road in the spring of 1934 that a numbering scheme for their cars was promulgated, by which time it had already been decided to replace the Bexley, Erith and South Met

Above **E1 class car 795 was one of those given experimental treatment by the LCC in its dying days. It was given aluminium body panels and flush body sides but its general appearance was not otherwise altered. It is on route 54 at Catford in September 1933, still carrying the LCC coat of arms but with LPTB legal owner stickers.**
W J Haynes

systems by trolleybuses. No numbers were therefore allocated for the South Metropolitan company and those previously earmarked for the two municipalities were used instead for the LUT and MET fleet:

MET Felthams:	2066-2119
LUT Felthams:	2120-2165
MET experimental:	2166-2168, 2255
MET older cars:	2169-2254, 2256-2316, 2412-2521
LUT experimental:	2317 ('Poppy')
LUT older cars	2318-2411, 2522-2529.

The LCC already had close working relationships with Croydon Corporation and the east London municipalities but was less familiar with the operations and practices of those in south-east London. Immediately after the Board appointed him to manage the transfer of undertakings, Thomas therefore despatched an inspection team to look at the Bexley and Erith fleets to assess their condition and judge whether any action was necessary to bring them up to Belvedere Road's standards. Evidently they left a good deal to be desired, as observed by Anthony Bull, later Vice Chairman of London Transport, on a visit to the systems on the Board's first day when he was appalled by how noisy they were and concluded that they needed early replacement. Half of them were open-toppers, a feature which the Board wished to eliminate as quickly as possible, so twelve redundant LCC M-class four-wheelers were brought out of store and reconditioned at Charlton, ready for transfer to Bexley immediately after the Board assumed ownership of the undertaking. They replaced a like number of Bexley's A-class cars, which were truly venerable, having been the rolling stock used to open the system in 1903-4. The rest of Bexley's As were similarly replaced during the next couple of weeks. The rest of Bexley's fleet also comprised thirty year old cars, seventeen former LCC B-class vehicles which had been acquired during the First World War to meet the demands of the munitions factories and to replace the ill-fated Dartford council fleet. These had been fitted with covered tops, of an unusual design, in 1911 and were therefore more acceptable, but even so they also were replaced by reconditioned Ms and had all gone by the middle of October.

Erith's open-toppers, including the four bogie cars acquired some years earlier from LUT, were also replaced by M-class four wheelers, as was its one and only covered top bogie car, originally owned by Hull Corporation. One former Croydon car, a Brush four-wheeler dating from 1911 (LPTB 348) also went to Erith at this time. The covered top four wheelers continued to run until replaced by trolleybuses in November 1935 but, to keep them going for their last couple of years, their old trucks were replaced by better ones salvaged from scrapped Croydon cars.

The new Board did not wait long before beginning to rationalise its assets. The small corporation depôt in Nelson Street, East Ham was closed on 16th August and its activities transferred to the West Ham depôt in Greengate Street. The four-wheelers went to West Ham but the bogie cars went to Bow and seven former West Ham cars were transferred to Leyton. Holloway LCC depôt also became host to strangers in September, when all twenty of Walthamstow's bogie cars were exchanged for E1 class cars of the 1930 batch. The purpose of this exchange was to put the faster cars onto route 29 where they were a better match for the Felthams, so solving the problem which had faced the LCC since 1930. Another transfer, which may well have happened anyway, since it was between two of the companies, was of eight LUT U and U2 type cars to Stonebridge Park, to replace expiring MET trams.

A short extension of trolleybus route 1 from the 'Red Lion' to Warren Drive, Tolworth on 20th September 1933, although merely the completion of LUT's plans, was also a kind of harbinger of London Transport's ideas on the future of its tramways. Lord Ashfield's views on the subject had undergone a significant sea change since he announced the Underground Group's policy three years earlier. At that time, the intention was to modernise the heavily trafficked routes and to use trolleybuses on the lighter outer area services. The Board's policy was made clear in November 1933 when it announced its intention to seek statutory powers to operate trolleybuses over ninety route miles of tramway. Two things had happened in the meantime, which clearly weighted the balance against the tram. The more important were the recommendations of the Royal Commission on Transport, which applied nationally, that no new tramways should be built and that existing systems should be abandoned progressively. The other matter was the experience which the Group itself had gained with the first phase of its previous policy. Whilst the trolleybuses had proved to be an unqualified success, the benefits gained by the Felthams had been nothing like so clear-cut. Alongside this, the new generation motor buses had also attracted additional traffic to such an extent that, as early as the spring of 1930, the Board of the London and Suburban Traction Company was already questioning the desirability of spending more money on trams.

An indication of the way the wind was blowing was given in one of the Board's earliest decisions. At the end of July 1933 it informed the London County Council that it did not intend to proceed with the construction of a tramway along the South Circular Road between Grove Park and Eltham, for which it held powers inherited from the council under the LCC General Powers Acts 1928-29. T.E. Thomas, the former LCC General Manager, who is generally regarded as being a tram man through and through, recommended instead that powers should be sought for a trolleybus service between Woolwich and Catford via Westhorne Avenue, Baring Road and Downham estate.

Left **Newly drafted ex-LCC M class car 1699 and former Bexley car 20C, also an old LCC car but of class B, pass each other in early LPTB days.** K W Glazier collection

Right **Former MET A-type car, now renumbered as LPTB 2412, on route 64 in Harrow Road.** K W Glazier collection

The LPTB already had blanket powers, under Section 23 of its Act, to abandon any of its tramways, subject to three months notice being given to the Highway Authorities. The first abandonments under this provision, on 7th December 1933, were a short section in Mitcham between Fair Green and Cricket Green, which was really a terminal branch for route 6, and another between Anerley depôt and Penge. The Mitcham abandonment led to the creation of London's longest tram route, as route 30 was simultaneously extended from Tooting Junction to West Croydon to cover the withdrawn South Metropolitan route 6 and the short section of former LCC route 6, which was cut back from Cricket Green to Tooting Junction. Former Croydon Corporation tram route 4, between West Croydon and Penge, was not replaced as its route was covered almost entirely by motor bus 75.

The Wilmington line of the Dartford UDC system, latterly operated by Bexley UDC, was similarly covered entirely by a motor bus route, Country Bus 401, and was abandoned in its turn on 19th April 1934. One tram had been used to provide a fifteen minute headway but only one trip was busy enough to justify replacement by a special works journey on the bus route. This was followed on 16th May by the first true tram to motor bus conversion when the LUT's 'Cinderella', the Merton to Summerstown branch, met an end which had seemed inevitable for many years. The decision to close it now was precipitated by Wimbledon council, who were planning to rebuild the bridge across the railway. Tram route 14 was cut back to Wandsworth High Street (except for a few peak journeys to Summerstown) and its place was taken by an extension of bus route 67 from Earlsfield to South Wimbledon.

The movement of operated mileage was not always in one direction; in fact Frank Pick required that for every mile transferred from one department to another, a compensating mile should be moved back. The scheme involving the replacement of buses on route 40 by trams on the Loughborough Junction and Norwood services on 1st November 1933 is mentioned in chapter five, where other examples of such schemes can also be found. A similar scheme, introduced on 28th February 1934, involved a major shift in favour of trams on the Euston to Enfield alignment with no fewer than twenty buses being removed from the schedule of the 29 group of motor bus routes, mainly between Victoria and Wood Green.

There was one minor piece of investment in new tramway, albeit with rationalisation in mind. On 18th December 1933, a connection was made between the former LCC and Erith systems at Abbey Wood, which enabled the operation of Erith's cars to be transferred to Abbey Wood depôt. Erith depôt was closed on 28th December and eventually sold back to the council, who continued to use it for over forty years as a vehicle base. Although through running to Woolwich or beyond was now possible, tram route 98 continued to run only between Abbey Wood and Bexleyheath for the rest of its time.

A more significant amount of new tram track was brought into use at North Finchley on 20th January 1935, when a new one-way system was introduced in High Road and Ballards Lane linked by a new section of road called Kingsway. The work had been the brainchild of Middlesex County Council when it was still the tramway authority for the area and was carried out under the authority of the Middlesex Light Railways (Extension) Order, dated 30th June 1933. Included in the new layout was a terminal loop through Nether Street, which in later years effectively became a public transport station, although on the public highway. It is still in use as such at the time of writing.

The last car on the Penge route ran on 6th December 1933. This little ceremony, involving two ladies in evening dress and rather a lot of tramway staff, took place at West Croydon when car 39S, a 1906 four wheel open topper, was about to run into Anerley depôt for the last time.
J B Gent collection

The new track in Nether Street, North Finchley, which effectively annexed this stretch of road as a road transport station for all time, with LUT U2 type car 2404, MET Feltham 2090 and an LCC E1.
K W Glazier collection

Mile End change-pit on 10th May 1934, with two Leyton E3s and West Ham E1 style car 302 would have disappeared had plans to extend the overhead system to Aldgate been carried through but this programme was abandoned in favour of conversion to trolleybus. L T Museum U14495

The London Transport Act (1934), which included authority to install and work $58\frac{3}{4}$ miles of trolleybus route, received the Royal Assent on 31st July 1934. The Act was a substantial piece of legislation which also contained a considerable number of improvements to the Underground but amongst it all was a provision allowing the Board to convert its Bow Road and Whitechapel Road tramways from conduit to overhead current collection. This was intended as a first step towards converting all its expensive conduit system, this having been one of the first recommendations made to the Board by T.E. Thomas on his transfer from the LCC. It was in fact identical to a proposal which he put to the LCC Highways Committee in February 1932, in which he argued that the old antipathy of local councils to overhead equipment on æsthetic grounds could no longer be sustained because those same councils had been busily engaged for some time in erecting street lighting standards along most main roads. His proposal was that combined lighting and traction poles should be substituted for the existing lighting standards, thereby minimising the additional intrusion caused by the overhead equipment. In the event, this programme was not pursued as it was overtaken by a more vigorous programme of conversions to trolleybus. The idea of having combined standards was however carried through to the trolleybus conversion.

Typical of the operations identified as suitable for conversion to trolleybus were the old Borough of Ilford tramways. LPTB No.41 (Ilford 29) was one of the Hurst Nelson cars which opened the system in 1903. It was rebuilt with a Brush domed top cover in 1906 and later fitted with Ilford long wheelbase trucks. In this March 1937 picture, it is about to run into the depôt in Ley Street. D W K Jones

Prototype class X2 trolleybus number 62 was the winner of the trials for a standard London vehicle and set the trend for a fleet of six-wheelers. The chassis was essentially the same as Number 61 but the body was radically different and the design formed the basis of all subsequent vehicles.
L T Museum

In readiness for the impending conversion programme, London Transport took delivery of two experimental trolleybuses, one six-wheeler and one four-wheeler. Number 62 (classified X2), which was licensed in July 1934, had an AEC 663T chassis, similar to number 61 but differing in many important respects from the 'Diddlers', while 63 (X3), licensed in August, had the 661T 16ft 3in wheelbase chassis, based on the Regent motor bus. The Metropolitan Cammell Carriage and Wagon Company supplied the seventy-three seat all metal rear entrance body on number 62 and English Electric the sixty-seater on number 63. Both were full-fronted and of conventional layout, except that a longitudinal seat was fitted on the nearside of the lower deck facing the driver. A new style of indicator display, based on the layout adopted on tram number 1, was introduced on these two vehicles and was to become the standard for the Tram and Trolleybus department from then onwards. The arrangement on 63 was later altered to a shallower destination box with a smaller number blind alongside but this remained unique. There seems to be no satisfactory explanation why the trolleybuses were not equipped with the same layout as the motor buses, other than the probability that such decisions were taken in isolation by Chiswick and Charlton.

The three-axle model won the competition and was to be adopted as standard, even when a short wheelbase vehicle was required. In February 1935, the Board announced that it was placing orders for 120 trolleybuses, split between AEC, who were to build fifty-two and Leyland, sixty-eight. The AEC model was the 664T, a more accurate number for the long wheelbase version than the 663T used for earlier similar chassis. The bodywork contract was placed with the MCW sales organisation who split it between Weymann Motor Bodies Ltd (ten) and Metro-Cammell Carriage and Wagon Co Ltd. All were seventy-seaters built to a standard London Transport specification, similar in appearance to number 62. They were numbered 132-183 and classified C1. The Leylands had TTB2 chassis with a wheelbase of 16ft 6ins and an overall length of twenty-seven feet. Intended for low trafficked routes or for use on narrow and twisting roads, these sixty-eight vehicles had sixty-seat bodywork supplied by the Birmingham Railway Carriage and Wagon Company (64-93, classified B1) and Brush (94-131, B2), whose design was a shortened version of the long wheelbase type.

While these developments had been taking place, the Board had been reviewing the future of the tramcar fleet, bearing in mind that at this time there was no commitment or even plan to abandon the bulk of the most heavily used parts of the tram system. In January 1934, Frank Pick called for a report on the age and condition of the fleet and for recommendations as to whether or not London Transport should replace a number of the older trams by new cars. The review committee considered four possibilities: outright purchase of new cars; the purchase of new bodies to go onto trucks salvaged from older cars; refurbishment of lower decks and complete renewal of upper decks, as already tried by the LCC; and a programme of modernisation. The committee concentrated its thoughts on the 1,200 cars which had high speed equipment, of which 800 were considered to be in need of attention. They recommended against the purchase of new cars or the more radical refurbishment proposals and opted instead for modernisation of the existing structures.

Before these decisions had been made, Charlton had been quietly turning out a few modernised cars, based on the model of 1370. In each case the cars had been involved in heavy accidents and were in need of substantial rebuilding, those treated being 1373 (April 1934), 1103 (May 1934), 982 (May 1935) and 1260 (May 1935). Another accident damaged car which received similar treatment was 1444, one of the ME/3 rebuilds of 1932, but in this case the top deck was a wooden one built at Charlton in the same style as the aluminium domed ones. A completely new body of a similar design was also placed on the original trucks from 1370 and this combination appeared in May 1935 as number 2, London Transport's only new tramcar.

Charlton also produced a series of refurbished cars with varying degrees of improvement, starting with cars 467 (class E) and 962 (E1) in April 1934. These introduced the basic body styling which was to be adopted in the 'Rehabilitation' programme, with repanelled upper saloons and inset destination and route number blinds but the lower deck panels were unchanged and they were not given driver's screens. A more substantial job was carried out in June 1935 on E1 class 1397, which was given windscreens and flush fitting lower deck sides but it was car 1038, which was turned out in January 1935, which became the model for the main programme. There were various improvements compared with the earlier experiments, including: an improved design of spring cushion seating covered in moquette, blue and grey on the lower deck and green on the upper deck; better lighting, set in chromium plated reflectors; and more modern finishings, including the use of lighter natural grain wood panelling and chromium plating of grabrails and seat handles. Following an inspection by the Chairman, this design was approved.

This modernised body with rounded end, domed roof and flush side panelling was fitted to E1 class car 1260 in May 1935 following heavy accident damage. It ran at first in north London and is here at Stamford Hill on route 53. D W K Jones

ME/3 class car 1370 had a complicated history under LCC souzerainty, having originally been 1446 with an older style of body. Although completely remodelled by the LCC, it did not enter service until 2nd July 1933 under LPTB management, which may well be when this photograph was taken at Grove Park, judging by the car's obviously untouched newness. R Elliott

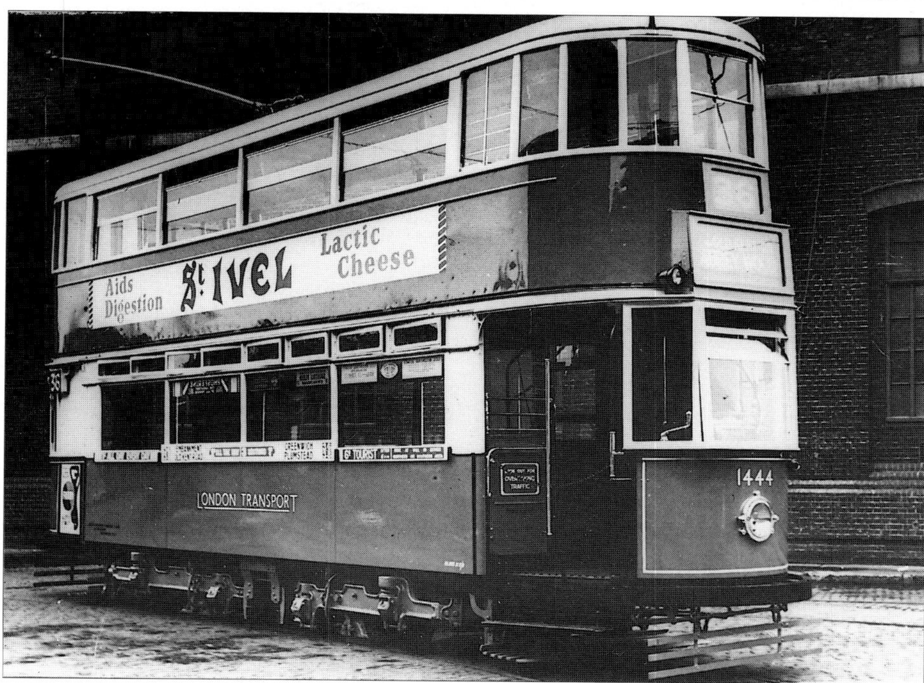

Car 1444 seems to have had a jinx as it was one of the ME/3 rebuilds of 1932 but was so badly damaged in an accident that it was given this rebuilt body and new top deck in 1934. It was eventually destroyed by bombing during the war.
B J Cross collection

The programme was ratified by the Board on 3rd June 1935 and a sum of £106,250 was requisitioned for the first phase of the programme, covering 250 cars. Work was planned to proceed at the rate of five cars a week and this first batch was due for completion within a year. Had the whole programme gone through, therefore, London would have had a modernised tram fleet by the end of 1938. In the event, the programme was stopped after the first 150, presumably because by then the Board's views on abandonment had crystallised and it was clear that the tram system would not survive for the additional ten years of life which the modernisation was intended to buy. The first 'Rehabs' (as they were always known) went into service at New Cross depôt in November 1935 and the last of the main production run also at New Cross in October 1936. At the end of the programme, however, Charlton switched from the older E1s and rehabilitated instead fifteen of the 1921-2 cars, all of which went to Wandsworth, four of the even more modern Croydon Corporation E1s (1927), which were sent to Thornton Heath and four HR2s, which stayed at their natural home, Camberwell.

The programme was completed in February 1937. Apart from two of the prototypes, all 'Rehabs' were allocated to south London depôts as these were expected to be the last to change over to trolleybuses. Attention was now switched to a programme of fitting windscreens to the remaining cars which were expected to have a long enough life to justify the expenditure but the programme was not completed during the 1930s and screenless cars could be seen as late as 1941.

The 150 standard rehabilitated cars were built to the same design as car 827, with flush metal side panels, inset roller blinds, drivers' windscreens and improved interior finishings and fittings. This photograph taken in Brockley before route 66 was diverted to Victoria, is particularly interesting because the destination display is 'Somerset House', a terminology which was never generally adopted to replace the more familiar ' Savoy St (Strand)'. Photomatic

Although one of the last of the early 'rehabs', car 1001 was an oddity in not having a driver's windscreen and retaining its old style side route boards. It ran at Stamford Hill, where this photograph was taken, until being withdrawn, long before the rest, in June 1939. W A Camwell

In this night-time view of Camberwell depôt, three of the rehabilitated HR2s can be seen in the first, second and fourth bays, surrounded by unadulterated siblings. K W Glazier collection

As the first of the reconditioned trams began to appear, the first of London Transport's tram to trolleybus conversions took place. On 27th October the former LUT routes 57, 63 and 67 and the Hammersmith to Kew Bridge section of the 26 were replaced by new trolleybus routes 657 and 667, using the new C1 class vehicles. The next stage took place on 10th November, when tram route 98 and part of route 40 were abandoned in favour of B2 class trolleybuses working on new route 698, which continued beyond Abbey Wood to Woolwich. Tram route 40 was cut back from Abbey Wood to Beresford Square. The 698 was joined two weeks later by route 696 between Dartford and Woolwich. The line beyond Dartford to Horns Cross was abandoned and no replacement service was provided, except that as a consequence of changes to the route pattern in Dartford, Country Bus route 492 provided a new link across the town from Crayford to Horns Cross. The only concession made was to reduce the standard fares and introduce Workmen's tickets on Country Bus routes between Dartford and Horns Cross. Both the 696 and 698 were operated from a new depôt in Erith Road, Bexleyheath and the old corporation premises in the Broadway were closed. A third route was added to the Bexleyheath portfolio on 16th May 1937 when Sunday only route 694 was introduced between Erith and Woolwich via Bexleyheath, supplying a link from north to west at Bexleyheath.

The opening ceremony of Bexleyheath trolleybus route 698 on 10th November 1935, with one of the B2 class Leylands waiting on the still unfinished forecourt. This depot was built in such a sensitive residential area that drivers were instructed not to switch on their generators until safely out onto the highway. L T Museum U18906

The old South Metropolitan route 7 between West Croydon and Sutton was withdrawn on 8th December 1935, from which date new trolleybus route 654 came into being. It was extended to Crystal Palace on 9th February 1936, completing the removal of the remaining South Metropolitan trams on route 5. These were London's last open toppers, having survived the last open top motor buses by fifteen months. Anerley depôt was closed and, although it was used for a time for storing and scrapping redundant cars, it was surplus to the Board's requirements and was eventually sold.

All the trams replaced by the new trolleybuses were scrapped, except for the former LCC M class cars which were sent to East London to replace older municipal cars.

The Board had obtained further powers for trolleybus operation in its 1935 Act and had included much of the suburban system in the 1935-40 New Works programme. Officially, the bulk of the LCC system was still excluded from the plans but the process of tramway abandonment now took on an inevitability which was progressively confirmed by gradual extensions of London Transport's powers until, with the final 132 route miles included in its 1937 Act, they covered the entire system. The first route to go under the fresh powers was the 89 between Hammersmith and Acton, which was converted on 5th April 1936 to trolleybus route 660, a temporary arrangement which lasted only three months. Former MET routes 66 and 68 followed suit on 5th July, when the 660 disappeared into a new major trunk route from Hammersmith to Edgware (666). The journeys between Cricklewood and Edgware on tram route 45 were also withdrawn and the 64 reduced to a Monday to Saturday peaks only operation. The track north of Edgware was abandoned and bus route 241 was left as the sole servant of the piece of road between Edgware and Canons Park.

During the rest of 1936, trolleybuses were introduced to most of the north-western system, to Forest Road Walthamstow and to what remained of the former LUT network along Uxbridge Road and through Boston Manor. The North Finchley to Cricklewood line went on 2nd August, when route 645 started (Edgware – North Finchley) and the number 660 re-appeared (Hammersmith – North Finchley). The Harrow Road route changed over on 23rd August, with the introduction of routes 662 and 664 from Paddington Green to Sudbury and Edgware respectively. The Forest Road conversion, which took place on 18th October, partially realised the link

The last open top vehicles of any kind in London were these South Metropolitan cars dating from 1906 which worked the Crystal Palace service until it closed on 8th February 1936. Car 36S is at the Crystal Palace terminus at the top of Anerley Hill. K W Glazier collection

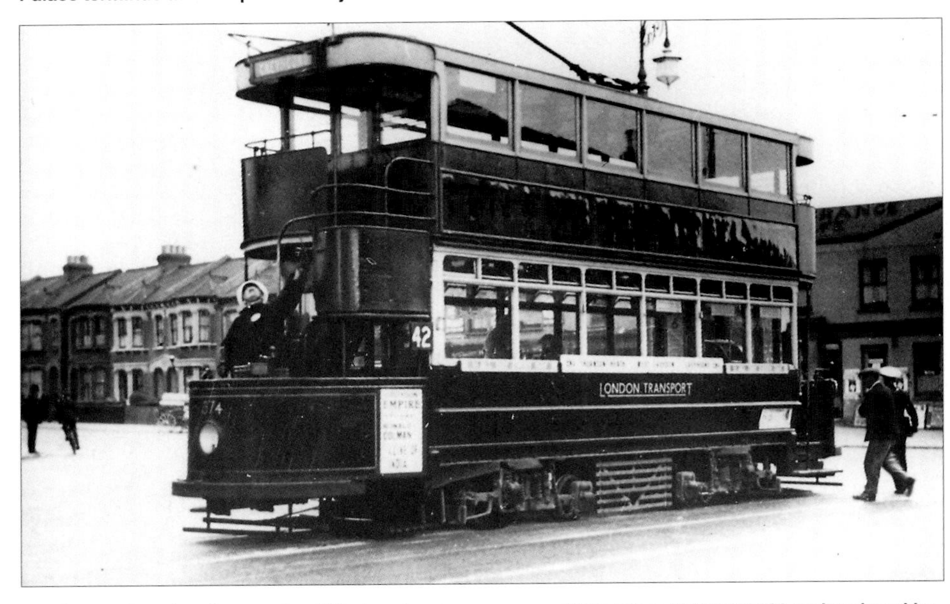

The former Croydon Corporation B/2 class bogie cars were withdrawn in October 1936 and replaced by E1 and E3 cars made spare elsewhere as a result of the trolleybus conversions. No 374 is at the Thornton Heath terminus of local route 42. J B Gent collection

One of the London tram terminals where it was found difficult to reach agreement with the authorities about trolleybus turning facilities was London Bridge (Tooley Street). This photograph was submitted in evidence to support the Board's private Bill and shows class E1 car 770 reversing at Bermondsey Street at 10.40am on 16th April 1936. The heavy commercial activity serving the riverside wharfs was one of the hazards and evidence of this can be seen here, with three horse drawn drays blocking the way for other traffic to pass trams. L T Museum U20105

LUT T type 2353 is at Shepherds Bush working a short on route 7 to Southall. All remaining cars of this type were withdrawn during 1936. M J O'Connor

across the Lea Valley for which Middlesex County Council had obtained powers many years earlier, as the new trolleybus route (623) continued beyond the isolated tram terminus at the Ferry Boat Inn, via Seven Sisters Corner to Manor House. Motor bus route 41, which had been extended to Forest Road to provide the link across the valley, was not immediately altered but was cut back to Tottenham Hale on 17th February 1937 at the same time as it was extended at the other end from Crouch End to Archway in place of route 232.

The final changeover of the year embraced the long trunk route 7 from Shepherds Bush to Uxbridge, which had so recently been categorised as ideal for fast modern trams (route 607 – 15th November) and the rather sad little line from Hanwell to Brentford (route 55 replaced by 655 – 13th December). The decision to convert route 7 is an interesting illustration of how quickly the Board's policy with regard to tramway abandonment developed and changed. Among the shoal of applications for improved or altered facilities with which the Board had been inundated in its early days was one from the Uxbridge Development Committee asking for the trams on route 7 to be replaced by trolleybuses. In his response Frank Pick said that trolleybuses were being considered for some areas but the density of traffic on route 7 made it a route 'not entirely suitable'. At that time the Board was clearly unconvinced of the ability of a rubber tyred vehicle to shift heavy passenger traffic but it soon changed its collective mind when the early conversions proved that they could. This phase of the conversion scheme was completed on 17th January 1937, when former Walthamstow Corporation route 85 was withdrawn. The replacing trolleybus route (685) continued beyond the tram terminus at Higham Hill to open up new territory through Billet Road to the 'Crooked Billet', where there was now a major junction on the new North Circular Road.

The trolleybuses for the north-western and Walthamstow routes were a further batch of two hundred AEC 664Ts, half of them with bodywork by Metro-Cammell (184-283; class C2) and the rest bodied by the Birmingham Railway Carriage and Wagon Co (284-383; class C3). Acton, Hendon, Stonebridge and Finchley depôts had both types, while Walthamstow took C3s. For the Hanwell conversions the first seventy-nine of a new batch of Leylands with Metro-Cammell bodies was used (385-483; class D2). Apart from an all-Leyland prototype (number 384; class D1), these were London Transport's first long wheelbase models from that manufacturer. Also delivered during the year was a further batch of ten short wheelbase Leyland 'LPTB60s' with BRCW bodywork (484-488, class B3; 489-493, class B1). The B1s and B3s, which were licensed in September 1936, were intended as spares for the earlier short wheelbase models but the B1s were used at first as trainers and the B3s were allocated to West Ham where they worked peak hour extras. All ten later went to Holloway.

All the remaining older LUT cars of types T, U, U2 and WT were withdrawn for scrap by the end of this programme as were the survivors of the former MET A type. Deep inroads were also made into MET type B. Some of the cars withdrawn came from Wood Green, where their place was taken by Felthams displaced from Finchley when route 45 was withdrawn. One Feltham was not transferred. The experimental central entrance car (2168) was taken out of service and later, in March 1937, sold to Sunderland Corporation. The former LUT Felthams from route 7 suffered a different fate. Immediately before the conversion, they were all in turn taken to Hampstead depôt where they were fitted with body mounted plough carriers to enable them to run on conduit track. After 15th November they were transferred to Telford Avenue and Brixton Hill depôts where, although in utterly alien territory, they were able to put their performance to good account on the long straight run along the Brighton Road to Purley. Because of the extra length and width of these cars, alterations had to be made to the stanchions in Telford Avenue depôt and a short stretch of track in Balham Hill had to be widened. The one-time Walthamstow Corporation cars withdrawn at this time were from the LPTB series 2004-2041, originally dating from 1910 or earlier.

A trolleybus on new route 607 puts its booms at full stretch to avoid work on the removal of redundant tram track at the junction of Wood Lane, Shepherds Bush Green. In the background is a 6Q6 Green Line coach on one of the Uxbridge Road routes. The Omnibus Society

West Ham 1906 vintage car 276 on route 1 at Stratford Broadway shortly before these routes changed over to the trolleybuses, whose wiring is already installed. C Carter

There had been another tramway abandonment in east London on 7th October 1936, when the erstwhile East Ham Corporation route between Royal Albert Docks and Wanstead Park (73) was withdrawn, but this did not involve trolleybuses. The 73 was covered throughout by motor bus route 101 and was deemed to be entirely surplus to requirements between the Docks and Manor Park. The only change made to the 101 was to increase the service north of Manor Park and, because the Traffic Commissioner would not approve a terminal working for buses at Wanstead Park, this had to go right through to Wanstead. Ten additional buses were needed and instead of a predominantly STL allocation, the whole service was now supplied by TD class Leylands of the former Independents.

A continuous programme of tramway abandonment started in June 1937 and was destined to continue unabated for the next three years. East London bore the brunt of the changes, principally in East Ham, West Ham and Walthamstow. Routes 69, 87, 97 and 99 disappeared on 6th June, replaced by the 669, 687, 697 and 699; and the 1, 1A and 95 went on 12th September, covered by the 689 and an extension of route 685 from Markhouse Road to Canning Town which brought a service to Church Road Leyton for the first time. The sections of routes 55 between 'Bakers Arms' and Temple Mills Lane and 57 between 'Bakers Arms' and Chingford Mount were also withdrawn as part of the June changeover. The special service 99A between Plaistow and West Ham stadium which ran in the evenings for Greyhound Race meetings, continued to be operated by trams until it was replaced by buses on 3rd August.

The September conversion took place at the same time as a further onslaught on the west London system. Route 30 was replaced completely by trolleybus 630, while routes 12, 26 and 28 were split so that trams could be withdrawn south of Wandsworth and west of Clapham Junction. They were replaced respectively by routes 612 (Battersea 'Princes Head' – Mitcham Fair Green, overlapping trams as far as Wandsworth), 626 (Acton – Clapham Junction) and 628 (Craven Park – Clapham Junction), leaving the in-town rumps to be dealt with at a later stage.

Walthamstow and Hammersmith depôts became entirely trolleybus, while Wandsworth and West Ham became joint tram and trolleybus sheds. The seven runnings supplied by Thornton Heath depôt on route 30 were transferred, with their staff, to Hammersmith on conversion to trolleybus, which avoided the need for another joint shed and enabled the closure of Purley depôt. The transfer to Hammersmith was intended to last only until Thornton Heath itself became a trolleybus depôt but this arrangement had to continue throughout the trolleybus era until 1960, when there were still staff 'temporarily' on transfer when the route closed.

Four days before the Walthamstow and Hammersmith changes, there was another case of a motor bus route taking over from trams. This coincided with the opening of the new Chelsea Bridge, which provided an opportunity for the Queenstown Road tram route to reach a better objective than the wilderness alongside Battersea Park. This was achieved by a massive diversion of bus route 137, to run via Sloane Square, Chelsea Bridge and Queenstown Road to Clapham Common Station. Although tram route 32 was withdrawn a balance of tramway mileage was maintained because changes were made to routes 34 and 66 to cover the withdrawal of the 137 in south London. The 66 was withdrawn between Camberwell Green and Savoy Street and diverted instead to Victoria at twice its former frequency, while additional shortworkings were introduced on the 34 between Camberwell and Blackfriars. Because of the strengthened cross-river service provided by route 137, the service on tram route 34 to Chelsea was simultaneously reduced. No trams were withdrawn.

A new turning circle was built for trolleybuses at the Victoria & Albert Docks terminus and work started was still going on when the trolleybuses ended. C3 class trolleybus 352 was one of the BRCW bodied AECs which helped with the Walthamstow and West Ham conversions. Charles F Klapper collection, Omnibus Society

For the 1937 conversions, 281 trolleybuses were taken into stock, comprising 100 AEC 664Ts, 160 Leyland 'LPTB70s', one AEC/LPTB chassisless vehicle and the balance of twenty D2s. The first sixty Leylands (494-553; class D3) had Birmingham Railway Carriage and Wagon Co bodies and the other hundred (654-753; class F1) were all-Leyland products. The body contract for the AECs was split between Brush (554-603; E1); Weymann (604-628; E2) and Park Royal (629-653; E3). The chassisless vehicle (numbered 754 and classified X4) was the only trolleybus built by London Transport, at Charlton Works and was to be the forerunner of a large fleet based on this construction principle. It was always immediately recognisable as it had an experimental exit door at the front of the lower deck. It was allocated to Finchley.

Most of Hanwell's virtually new fleet of D2s were delicensed and replaced by the entire batch of F1s between March and December 1937, as their more powerful motors (95 h.p. instead of 80 h.p.) made them more suitable for the long fast runs possible on the Uxbridge Road. The D3s went to Wandsworth, for the 612, and Hammersmith, for routes 626,628 and 630, where they were joined by some of the delicensed D2s from Hanwell. Other D2s displaced from Hanwell went to Walthamstow for its new routes 687, 697 and 699, the balance being made up by E1s. West Ham took the E2s and E3s for its share of those routes and for the 669, 685, 689 and 690.

The remainder of the older Walthamstow cars were withdrawn during 1937 but the twenty bogie cars dating from 1926 and 1932 (2042-2061), which had been running at Holloway since 1933, were transferred to Bow depôt, where they continued to run on the 61 and 63 until 1939, after which they moved to south London. All of the former West Ham fleet of four-wheelers, dating variously from 1905 to 1910 were withdrawn for scrap during 1937, leaving the bogie cars to maintain the main road services to London for their remaining three years. The Hammersmith and Wandsworth conversions led to the first major withdrawal of ex-LCC E class cars, while the east London abandonments included a number of M class four wheelers, which had earlier replaced more elderly municipal vehicles.

Above right **London's longest tram route (Harrow Road to West Croydon) was not long-lived as it was replaced by trolleybus route 630 in September 1937. Class E car 437 is running on temporary sleeper track during the reconstruction of Mitcham Road railway bridge.** J B Gent collection

Right **The new trolleybus turning circle at Frays River Bridge, Uxbridge, was also handy for shortworking Green Line coaches from London. The original allocation of D2 class Leylands to route 607 was replaced by the higher powered F1 class in 1937 and one of these, 678, is on the Uxbridge stand with new 10T10 coach T 641.** Charles F Klapper Collection, Omnibus Society

Former MET E type car 2303 at the western Alexandra Palace terminus, in a siding near the LNER station. All these single-deckers were withdrawn for scrap in 1938.

The biggest year for conversions from tram to trolleybus was 1938, during which the maximum number of scheduled trams dropped from 1,691 to 1,327 and the first significant inroads were made into the inner London conduit network. Bus services also became increasingly involved with the trolleybus programme, as the Board pursued its policy of optimising the use of the new overhead equipment by switching mileage between motor bus and trolleybus operations. One of the earlier conversions, on 23rd February, involved the abandonment of the two Alexandra Palace branches and the introduction of new and altered bus routes to cover them. The Turnpike Lane to Alexandra Park section of routes 39 and 51 was covered by new routes 144 (from Ilford), 144A (from Enfield 'Halfway House') and 144B (from Forty Hill), while route 37 was covered by new single-deck route 241. For the time being, the western branch, from 'The Victoria' up to the palace was closed altogether while a new road was built. This was officially opened by Frank Pick on 28th May and the service was restored on 1st June, when route 233 was extended through the palace grounds to Wood Green, linking both former tram routes and replacing the short-lived 241.

The balance of mileage between bus and tram was restored by the replacement of buses by trams along the main road from Enfield to Euston. Bus routes 124A and 238 were both withdrawn and the section between Forty Hill and Enfield and the 'shorts' between Edmonton 'Cambridge' and Turnpike Lane joined together to form new route 144B, which continued to 'The Victoria'. The sections of route down the main road were covered by a more frequent service on tram route 29 and by the introduction of additional trams on 39A between Winchmore Hill and Wood Green; this in turn was covered by an extension of tram route 41 on 6th March. The 144B brought additional buses to Great Cambridge Road between Southbury Road and 'The Cambridge', while the 144 (Ilford–Muswell Hill 'Victoria', an amalgam of shorts on route 145 with the 124) introduced buses for the first time to the section of North Circular Road between Gates Corner and the 'Crooked Billet'.

The removal of local tram services from east London was completed on 6th February, when the former Ilford system was abandoned and new trolleybus routes 691, 692 and 693 introduced. The vehicles used were E1s and these replaced all the remaining cars from the Ilford Corporation fleet. Most went for scrap but the eight cars which dated only from 1932 (33-40) were sold to Sunderland Corporation, where they saw a further sixteen years service.

More of the old Metropolitan Electric Tramways network disappeared on 6th March, with the closure of the lines from Barnet to Kentish Town via Archway and North Finchley to Wood Green. Trolleybuses came to the heart of London on new routes 517/617, 521/621 which operated in a loop via Farringdon Road and Grays Inn Road, and 609 which terminated short of the Moorgate tram terminus at Finsbury Square. A new link was also forged across North Finchley with new route 651 (Barnet–Golders Green). Tram routes withdrawn were the 9, 13, 17, 19, 21, 51 and 71 (between Wood Green and Aldersgate). The two Aldersgate services were replaced by a diversion of motor bus route 45 to run via Aldersgate and Islington to Holloway, instead of Kings Cross, over which section the new Holborn loop trolleybus routes took its place. The section of route 19 south of Archway was covered by a more frequent service on bus route 134. The withdrawal of trams south of Archway presented the Board with a dilemma as to what to do about Workmen's fares. At first the favoured solution was to introduce special 2d Workmen's Returns on the Underground but eventually the unusual decision was taken to have them on Central Bus route 27, which became the only motor bus route to have designated 'Workmen's buses' (between Archway and Warren Street). This arrangement continued until 1950.

Car No. 31, in Ley Street Ilford, had two previous owners: Ilford Council and Barking UDC from whom they bought it in 1914. It was photographed a few days before its withdrawal in February 1938. Those travelling to hear the Mills Brothers perform at the Hippodrome would in future be using a trolleybus.

Below **The desolate landscape of a redeveloping central Barking greets newly introduced E1 class AEC trolleybus 583. This class had Brush bodywork.**
Charles F Klapper Collection
Omnibus Society

Left **The Felthams, introduced with such high hopes only eight years earlier, disappeared from the streets of north London in 1938 and found themselves running in alien territory south of the river. Nearing the end of its days at Wood Green, car 2079 glides along the recently installed track in Kingsway, North Finchley, with a 645 trolleybus following.**
Photomatic

Above **Camden Town on 26th July 1938. Trolleybuses have already replaced trams on route 29 and the 27, on which ex-MET H type car 2182 is approaching, will go in November. The Wallace Heaton photographic suppliers used the backs of buses for a series of punning adverts which lasted until the company was taken over in the 1960s.** H B Priestley

The line from Wood Green to Enfield was closed on 8th May and new trolleybus routes 625, 629 and 641 replaced tram routes 39, 29 and 41 respectively. The 625 was actually an extension of some 623 'shorts' and therefore ran from Woodford ('Napier Arms'), at first to Wood Green, then to Winchmore Hill on Mondays to Saturdays from 12th October. With this conversion, the route mileage of trolleybuses exceeded that of trams, although the scheduled mileage was still heavily in favour of trams for the time being. During the rest of the year abandonments spread to the Hampstead network on 10th July (routes 3, 5, 7 and 15, replaced by 513/613, 615 and 639) and the former MET network north of Stamford Hill (routes 59 and 79 and part of route 49 from 16th October; route 27 from 6th November). The route number originally allocated to the 513 was 637.

The new trolleybus routes on the Hertford Road were the 627, 649, 659 and 679. The section along Southbury Road, Enfield was replaced by the extension of route 107 from Enfield to Durants Road. Other motor bus services were heavily cut, as the new trolleybus routes were scheduled at higher frequencies than the trams they nominally replaced. Bus route 69 was withdrawn altogether between Tottenham and Wormley, route 39 was withdrawn between Manor House and Tottenham and diverted to Turnpike Lane instead, while the service on route 42 between Finsbury Park and Stamford Hill (renumbered 42A) was halved. The other half of the 42 was diverted at Stamford Hill to run via the withdrawn 76A to Turnpike Lane.

This stage of the conversion also had the unique distinction of involving the Country Bus department whose route 310 was strengthened between Hoddesdon and Enfield to replace the extreme northern end of route 69. Earlier plans had envisaged the 69 being diverted at its northern end to Enfield Town to cover the Southbury Road tram route.

The Hampstead routes closed on 10th July 1938 and the traction poles had already been erected when E class car 581 was photographed working on route 5. A London Transport designed 'domed' Tram Stop is on the right of the picture. H B Priestley

The new vehicles for 1938 comprised 150 AEC and 150 Leylands and the first ninety-six of a further large order for 300 Leylands. The main batch of Leylands (755-904) were all bodied by Metro-Cammell and were classified H1, while the AECs were split between Weymann (905-952; J1) and the Birmingham Railway Carriage and Wagon Co (955-1029 – J2; 1030-1054 – J3). Trolleybus 953 was an experimental vehicle which employed 'unit construction', in which a lightweight chassis is built integrally with the body structure at the construction stage. AEC chassis components were used by Weymann for this vehicle. Metro-Cammell used a different approach for number 954 which was a purely chassisless vehicle, using AEC running units. These two were pre-production prototypes for the planned fleet of unit-construction and chassisless vehicles and were classified M1 and L2 respectively. The balance of ninety-six new vehicles was the first part of a repeat order for three hundred all-Leyland vehicles (1055-1354 classified K2).

The H1s were first used at Holloway for routes 517/617 and 609 and later for the Hampstead routes but by far the largest batch went to Wood Green for the 625, 629 and 641. Walthamstow's allocation for the 625 was also H1. The J1s went to Finchley, while the J2s were shared around all the depôts where conversions took place in 1938. The J3s were fitted with run-back and coasting brakes and were intended for use on Highgate Hill but as that conversion was delayed, they were used at this time on route 679. The Ks were used for the Hertford Road routes and were allocated to Edmonton for that purpose.

Trams withdrawn for scrap in 1938 included the survivors of MET type F and LCC class E, while a start was made on withdrawing the older cars from the huge E1 class. The MET Felthams which had latterly been concentrated at Wood Green were all despatched to Telford Avenue and Brixton depôts to join the LUT examples working on routes 2A/4A, 8/20, 10, 16/18 and 22/24.

Above **The MET H type ran for the last time on 15th October 1938, when routes 59 and 79 were withdrawn. In its dying days, car 2170 runs under the threatening overhead lines in Tottenham High Road, followed by a Walthamstow bogie car on route 27.** H B Priestley

Despite all this contraction, there was a small bit of investment in entirely new track during the year. On 15th May 1938, the new one-way system at Vauxhall was commissioned. This included new roads on the alignment of the old station yard, which became the eastern end of South Lambeth Road, and linking South Lambeth Road with Wandsworth Road (Parry Street).

Stamford Hill after the arrival of the first trolleybuses on route 649 but before the trams have finally been dismissed.
Charles F Klapper Collection, Omnibus Society

The conversion programme in 1939 was almost as large as for 1938. The southern end of the Hertford Road network was completed on 5th February, when trolleybuses on routes 643, 647, 649 and 683 replaced trams on routes 43, 47, 49 and 83 and tram routes 71 and 75 were withdrawn. The conversion of route 53 to trolleybus 653 on 5th March brought tramway operation at the Euston terminus to an end. At Aldgate, the 653 used the newly opened bus, trolleybus and coach station alongside the railway south of Aldgate High Street. This had started life in LGOC days as a layover point for a limited number of buses between peak hours and had later been used for Green Line coaches. It had now been extensively enlarged to provide a terminal for the trolleybuses replacing the east London trams. The plans for this station were quite elaborate and included many facilities for passengers, such as departure indicators for coaches and waiting rooms, but completion of the project was stopped by the war and the 'lay-by' as it was more commonly known, remained a bit of a dump, with very primitive facilities, for the whole of the trolleybus era. The remaining Leyton services were next to go, on 11th June (routes 31 Leyton – Hackney station Sunday only section, 55, 57 and 81 replaced by 555, 557 and 581). These routes were originally to have been numbered 671, 673 and 681. This was the last conversion completed before the outbreak of the Second World War on 3rd September but work was well advanced on preparations for the conversion of route 77, which was replaced by trolleybus route 677 on 10th September, exactly a week after the war started. Two further conversions took place before the end of the year: on 5th November, when routes 61 and 63 at Bow changed over (661 and 663); and on 10th December, when the long awaited abandonment of route 11 to Highgate Village took place (611). From this date, the isolated section of route 31 to Hackney, now with no immediate prospect of being converted to trolleybus operation, was cut back to Holborn Hall and diverted to Agricultural Hall (Islington Green). It is interesting to note in passing that route 31 had been given a unique extension from Hackney to Stamford Hill for one day only on Christmas Day 1938. Whether or not this was likely to have been continued after conversion to trolleybus operation is something which will never be known. Apart from the subway routes, only the Barking Road trams were still running in north London at the end of 1939. These were abandoned on 9th June 1940.

Above **The track round into Leyton High Road had already been cut and route 81 itself had less than a year to go when this scene at the 'Bakers Arms' attracted the photographer. E1 car 907 is on its way to Woodford, alongside a Bluebird LT on a private hire and leading an E3 on subway route 31, while further off there is another E1, a Gilford coach and an LT motor bus.** H B Priestley

Left **Tram, bus and trolleybus at work in Graham Road Hackney, presenting a microcosm of the Board's central area operations. E1 car 881 is working out the last days of route 77 and the open staircase LT on the left will soon be due for withdrawal. The new order is represented by the STL on route 22 and a trolleybus slipping across the back of the picture in Mare Street.** J B Gent collection

Apart from the balance of the K class deliveries, London Transport had ordered 315 AEC trolleybuses, which were expected to be enough for the completion of the north London conversions. However, it was later found necessary to order a further fifty and these were Leylands. The bulk of the AECs were either of chassisless or 'unit' construction, the largest group being the chassisless L classes with Metro-Cammell body structures, of which there was a continuous run of 175 vehicles. They were numbered 1355-1369 (L1), 1370-1378 (L2) and 1380-1529 (L3). The L1s had coasting and run-back brakes, for use on Highgate Hill, but were otherwise identical to the L2s, all having English Electric controllers. The L3s were also identical except that they had Metrovick controllers. Number 1379 was classified X5 and was a prototype for use through Kingsway Subway, with an offside door and loading platform at the rear.

The 'unit construction' vehicles had Weymann body structures, were numbered 1530-1554 and classified M1. The balance of 115 was on conventional AEC 664T chassis, bodied by Birmingham Railway Carriage and Wagon Co. (1555-1644; N1) and Park Royal (1645-1669); N2). The L, M and N classes all differed from earlier vehicles in having the rainshields at the front of the roof rounded into the corner pillars to give a streamlined effect. There were detailed variations in the treatment between the classes.

The fifty Leylands (which did not start to arrive until October 1940) comprised a repeat order for twenty-five all-Leyland vehicles (1672-1696; K3) and a batch of twenty-five with the later style of Metro-Cammell body (1697-1721; P1). There were also two further experimental vehicles, both variations on the chassisless principle. The first to go into service was 1671 (X7), an all-Leyland twin-steering demonstrator, which was on loan from February 1939 and then purchased outright. The other was an AEC/English Electric numbered 1670 (X6) which was allocated to West Ham in January 1940.

The K1s and K2s were used for the Hertford Road and Leyton conversions as well as route 677, while the 653 got L2s and L3s and the 611 L1s and the earlier J3s. The Bow conversion was carried out with Ms and Ns, while the remaining vehicles from these classes not required at Bow were used, together with L3s for the Barking Road routes in June 1940. Trams withdrawn comprised older members of the E1 class, the newer East Ham and West Ham Corporation cars being sent to south London for further service. There were twenty-three HR2s displaced from route 11 for which London Transport had no use which would justify their special hill climbing qualities. An approach had been received from Leeds City Transport, who were interested in buying thirty for a new tramway they were contemplating building and the Board decided that it was advisable not to wait for the south London system to be abandoned before realising the value of these quite modern assets. The sale was therefore agreed but in the event only the first three went to Leeds, who were able to acquire them at a price of only £750 each. The remainder went to Camberwell to join the rest of the class but remained effectively surplus to requirements as they appear to have replaced nothing.

At the end of 1939 the maximum number of trams scheduled for service was 1,076 and of trolleybuses 1,279.

Above **The old Aldgate tram terminus which Minories trolleybus and coach station was intended to replace was a congested spot in Whitechapel High Street opposite Aldgate East station. This photograph, taken during the evening peak on 24th May 1934, captures the atmosphere of this lively gateway to the East End as it was before bombing and later road developments changed its character irrevocably. Ex-Leyton E3 207 is loading at the island opposite Joe Lyons's tea shop with another approaching in the distance. Ahead of it is an LCC E1 on route 71, two East Ham bogie cars, a balcony car from one of the East End municipalities and in the distance two trams can be seen crossing the Gardiner's Corner junction. A former Strawhatter Gilford coach is in the foreground and other STs, LTs and Independent buses are further off, but commercial traffic comprises mainly horse drawn drays.**
Alan Nightingale collection

CHAPTER FIVE CENTRAL AREA SERVICES 1933-1939

The London Passenger Transport Board did not have the freedom of action in planning and developing its services which its progenitors had probably envisaged. It was still required to consult the London & Home Counties Traffic Advisory Committee about any increases in service levels on roads which had been subject to Restricted Streets Orders under the 1924 Act and it required route approval from the Traffic Commissioner for any new sections of route or to run buses of different dimensions or operating characteristics. The Traffic Commissioner proved to be no soft touch. Having just got a taste for regulatory power when the LPTB was formed, he was inclined to continue in the same vein and was frequently considered by the Board to have overstepped his powers. Furthermore, the Board's investment decisions were governed by the requirements of the Revenue Pool, whose interests were safeguarded by the Standing Joint Committee. Within these constraints, the Board nevertheless managed to exercise its statutory duty to 'extend and improve' transport in its area and, in doing so, was commendably willing to listen to its customers' views. One of the most important items on the agenda of each Board meeting was the Public Relations report in which all major matters raised during the month were reviewed. Any discontent which this revealed was always taken seriously and many of the Board's actions flowed directly from such discussions.

There were examples of many strands of the Board's policies during its first year and by no means all of them slavishly continued those of the Combine. However, the first changes of significance instituted by the Board may well have been planned by the LGOC, as they took place on 23rd August 1933, but as they included the introduction of four new night services, they had the authentic ring of a public service decision. The new nighters were the 184 (Southall), 611 (Barking), 613 (Leyton) and 619 (Edmonton). More conventionally, new services were introduced to Goffs Oak and Cuffley from Waltham Cross (205), using Darts and along The Drive, Ilford (148C).

Co-ordination and the avoidance of wasteful competition were two more of the Board's statutory duties and, as in all things, it very quickly showed that it took them seriously. In the Winter Programme for 1933, starting on 4th October, after only three months stewardship, the LPTB unveiled its first co-ordination scheme. Under this bus route 40 was withdrawn between Camberwell Green and West Norwood, tram 34 was switched at its London end from Southwark Bridge to Blackfriars and the 48 absorbed the 80 to become Southwark Bridge to West Norwood, at the expense of its Brixton section. The Rosendale Hotel service previously supplied by route 40 now became a spur off bus route 2 (an interesting violation of the Bassom principles). Buses were therefore withdrawn from the section of tramway between Herne Hill and Loughborough Junction via Milkwood Road and changes in

Above **The uplifted snout of Seven Kings LT 645 is the clue that it was one of the class to receive new oil engines in July 1934, two months before this photograph was taken in Grosvenor Gardens, Victoria. Continuing the theme of transition, the Bassom route numbering system was about to be abandoned and the new LONDON TRANSPORT fleet name had already been applied.** G H F Atkins

frequencies meant that there were also fewer buses running along the sections of tram route in Coldharbour Lane and Walworth Road and between Aldgate and Wanstead Flats.

As outlined in chapter one, the principle of co-ordination, as applied to operations taken over from Independents, often meant their withdrawal. It would be inappropriate to chronicle every one of these changes but a few examples will give a good illustration of the approach adopted by Pick's Traffic Committee. When Empress Motors was taken over on 1st February, the two buses which it worked on route 6A on Mondays to Saturdays were abandoned but its weekday running on route 26E and its weekend runnings on route 42 were all retained, pending a proper scheme of co-ordination. When Birch's considerable activities were absorbed on 28th February, the main operations on routes 214, 231, 526 and 536C were all retained, although with some increase on route 214 and a reduction on the 231, but all special Sunday workings on routes 42, 73A, 173D and 127B were abandoned as superfluous.

The 526 came in for special scrutiny very early in the review process and the knives remained out until the route was finally destroyed in 1938. The first proposal, however, might well have enabled it to survive the introduction of trolleybuses but unfortunately met with opposition from the Central Bus Operating Manager and was abandoned. Had the proposal gone through, the 526 would have been given a massive intermediate diversion between Harlesden and North Finchley to run via Stonebridge Park, North Circular Road and Henlys Corner, in place of the 518 which would have been withdrawn.

Quite separately from its acquisition, co-ordination and development of mainstream services, the Board was also keen to enter the excursions and tours market in a big way. In November 1933, the operators were given the task of determining the extent to which special traffic to Dog Racing, Speedway and Horse Racing could be met by adapting the existing bus and coach network or by running extra trips on existing services. Road Houses, large Public Houses on the new arterial roads with ample parking facilities, were a popular new institution and the Board was also interested in developing routes or running special trips to serve the substantial traffic which they were generating. If a satisfactory programme could be prepared and a workable agreement entered into with the Trade Union, the Board was prepared to consider establishing a separate department with a central London base for about a hundred coaches, which would also cover sightseeing tours, afternoon and evening tours to the countryside, special services for the many events in and around London and Private Hire. An embryo sightseeing operation, comprising a morning City tour and an afternoon East End tour on Mondays to Fridays, started in the summer of 1936, as a joint venture with Dean & Dawson, London Coastal Coaches and Pickfords. Inevitably, though, this process took some time and other more pressing matters took precedence, but the central London base did eventually materialise in the basement of the new Gillingham Street (Victoria) garage. Unfortunately this did not open until 20th March 1940, by which time the war had intervened, and this project never reached the planned level of activity.

London Transport coaches DL 38 and 39 and an AEC Regal coach, labelled for the Board's long-time associate in this field Dean & Dawson, are at Wembley in 1936 showing the flag in the private hire field which was dominated by independents. D W K Jones

Below **Double-deck buses were able to reach Edmonton through Silver Street for the first time in May 1934, when new route 199 was introduced. NS 1474 at the Park Road stand.** Alan B Cross

Coincidentally with the introduction of new schedules on 28th March 1934, when it would be normal to expect Sunday services to be increased for the summer, no fewer than seven routes were withdrawn on Sundays and three others had sections withdrawn. This was a reminder that amidst all the upheavals taking place, there was still a declining demand because of the Depression and that the effects of the suburban coach boom were still being felt. It was also a reminder that London Transport need have no fear that a competitor would come in to fill any gaps left by such withdrawals.

Using the largest capacity bus possible was one of the policies inherited from its predecessors and there were to be many examples of upgrading by the LPTB in the next few years. An early example came about as a result of the road improvements which were being made to create the North Circular Road. The low bridge at Silver Street station, Edmonton had been a particular nuisance over the years as it imposed the use of single-deckers on important busy routes 201, 551 and 602, all at this time operated by single-deck LTs. The road under the bridge was lowered at the beginning of 1934 and a scheme of changes was introduced as part of that year's summer programme on 16th May. The 551 could not be double-decked throughout as it was restricted to single-deck through Totteridge and by the railway bridge at Mill Hill, so it was cut back to Arnos Grove. The Edmonton end was covered by a diversion of LT-operated route 604 to run to Whetstone ('Griffin') instead of Edmonton station. The 201 was withdrawn altogether and its route covered by the extension of NS-operated 299A (renumbered 199) from what we now know as 'The Cambridge' to Edmonton (Park Road/Cooks Ferry). This particular change appears to have been a little too draconian as additional 'shorts' were introduced between Turnpike Lane and Weir Hall in July, which effectively put back the buses which had been saved.

The intention had been to convert the 602 to double-deck without change but this did not take place immediately because there were some overhead obstructions in the Borough of Wood Green, which the officers of the council were not prepared to remove because it was the council's policy to oppose double-deck buses. This was a good example of the kind of hindrance which the Board was to meet constantly when trying to introduce new routes or make other improvements. Usually they were overcome after diplomatic bargaining, as was the case here. STs replaced the single-deck LTs on 4th July. Some of the LTs were re-allocated to Romford (RD) for the G2, G6 and 187 and to Kingston for the 105, releasing Ts to replace the S-type on routes 61, 62 and 503. Not all could be found homes and this was one of the origins of the surplus of this type already discussed in chapter three.

Another policy strand apparent in the May 1934 changes was that of 'localisation', although it was not called that in those days. The irregularity of the long routes which ran far out into the suburbs from central London, particularly the City, had been worrying the operators for some time and it was now decided to embark on a policy of route shortening. The May 1934 example appears to have violated one of Frank Pick's 'rules of thumb', which was that there should be an overlap preferably equal to a twopenny fare but at least equal to a penny fare. Both routes 185 and 188 were broken more or less 'end-on' at Hanwell garage and Acton respectively to become short-workings on the 184 from London Bridge. The Wembley 'rump' of the 185 became a new 218C, while the Acton to Greenford section of the 188 was absorbed into a long extension of the 55, which already covered this road on Sundays. This was actually a reversion to an earlier arrangement.

Route 10 was diverted over the new Lambeth Bridge to Victoria on 16th May 1934, introducing new links through Lambeth Road and Horseferry Road. ST 714 rounds the corner from Greycoat Place into Horseferry Road, while a horse quietly contemplates its subservience to man between bouts of hauling its dray. Alan B Cross

A fine bustling summer's day in Northfields Avenue looking south from the railway bridge. The through bus service to Oxford Circus, on which Bluebird LT 1369 is performing, was withdrawn in May 1935 and replaced by local route 55.

ST 578 is about to leave the south side of the temporary Waterloo Bridge, on its way from Aldwych on the special service which had to be introduced when the bridge was made two-way in 1934. The heavy vehicles going onto the bridge illustrate the problems of congestion which this decision created. Stan Friedman

Route 93 was diverted to serve new housing at Priory Road North Cheam on 27th June 1934. The changing face of suburban London could hardly be better illustrated than by this picture of NS 748 overtaking a pony and trap, with evidence of suburban sprawl in the background. Malcolm E Papes

Development of a different kind affected a number of important central London routes from 22nd June 1934. The LCC had finally lost patience with the politicians across the water and had decided to demolish the old Waterloo Bridge and build a new one. The temporary bridge was not suitable to carry all the displaced traffic and was therefore restricted to southbound traffic only from 6am to 10pm Mondays to Fridays and 3pm on Saturdays. London Transport had tried to persuade the police to allow northbound traffic in the morning peak and southbound in the evening but were unsuccessful. However, they did manage to get dispensation to run a special service in both directions between Alaska Street and Aldwych. The normal routes had to be diverted or curtailed and from 22nd June routes 1, 68 and 169 were diverted via Westminster Bridge and Whitehall, at first via York Road but from 31st October this was altered to be direct via Westminster Bridge Road. The 6A and 67 were at first both diverted via Stamford Street and Blackfriars Bridge but from 31st October, the 67 did a big detour via York Road, Westminster Bridge, Victoria Embankment and Norfolk Street. Routes 33 and 166 were simply withdrawn between Waterloo and Aldwych. These special arrangements continued to a greater or lesser degree until the outbreak of war in September 1939. As a direct result of the congestion caused on and around Westminster Bridge, routes 59 and 159 were diverted via Lambeth Bridge and were destined to stay on that route (except for a Sunday variation after 1978) for good.

On 3rd October 1934 the Bassom system of route numbering was abandoned (see chapter one) and there were also a couple of interesting route extensions. In Dockland, in response to an approach from the London Waterside and General Manufacturers' Association, part of route 106 was extended from Poplar to Victoria Dock (Tidal Basin Road), using the newly built Silvertown Way Viaduct. This brought buses into an area previously unserved because of its narrow and unsuitable roads, but where 18,000 people were employed. In the northern suburbs, new development in the Southgate and Winchmore Hill area was served by an extension of route 244 (ex-603) from Southgate station to the Chase Side Tavern. It had been hoped to continue via Old Park Ridings and Old Park Avenue to Enfield but there were a number of obstructions which Enfield Council was not prepared to deal with because local residents had objected to buses. These roads had to wait nearly forty years for a service.

London Transport continued the policy of transferring routes to Country Buses if they ran outside the Metropolitan Police District and the first case occurred on 5th December when the Romford garage operations on route 370, whose new number had been allocated in anticipation of the change, were transferred to Grays. Country Buses already ran part of the service as they had taken over the Eastern National share on 1st August 1933.

Other areas served for the first time during 1934 included Grand Drive, Raynes Park (Darts on route 225), Warden Avenue, Alexandra Avenue and Rayners Lane (206 extended), Aldborough Road and Cameron Road (149 diverted), Priory Road North Cheam (93 extended and new 156A) and Sewardstone Road (205 extended).

Ex-Royal Highlander Guy OND G 4 was still working on its home ground when route 206 was extended to Rayners Lane station on 6th June 1934. The extension of the 206 was primarily intended to improve interchange with the Metropolitan Line at Rayners Lane and was the outcome of a review of such deficiencies which took place during 1934, an interesting reminder of the Met company's own concern. J F Higham

To the apparent concern of its conductor, a diversion has brought Hammersmith's LT 1272, and the NS leading it, into the unaccustomed surroundings of the East Carriage Road in Hyde Park, which they are about to leave through the Marble Arch gate. The development of the rear end design was all the more remarkable for being separated by only a matter of four or five years. Arthur Ingram

NS 1708 pulls up at one of the 'fixed stopping places' introduced by the LPTB from 1935.
Alan Duke

Route 511, on which a generation of Independents had sweat their brows, was eliminated in route changes on 17th April 1935. During the Board's short tenure, STs 478 and 714 are standing at the 'Royal Forest Hotel', Chingford.
W J Haynes

An important first step along a path which was eventually to result in the transformation of bus operating practice in London took place on 20th March 1935 when a modest scheme of fixed stopping places for buses and trams was introduced between Hampstead Road and Seven Sisters Corner. Almost everywhere, at this time, buses stopped on request at any point, a principle which was later lost, only to be rediscovered under the new name of 'Hail and Ride' for minibuses in the 1970s. There were exceptions to this rule, notably in busy town centres or at particular points where the Police considered some order necessary for safety reasons but the overwhelming mass of operation held to the 'on request' principle. This applied even on quite short sections of road between the fixed points, such as between the stops at Hyde Park Corner and those at Knightsbridge station.

The pilot scheme proved successful enough for the Board to consider extending the idea to the whole of the busy central zone. They were not keen to extend it too far out, as they thought that the loss of convenience for passengers might have a deleterious effect on income. The first plan was to cover an area over an eight mile radius from Charing Cross but this was later reduced to a zone bounded by Mile End, Hampstead, Hammersmith and West Norwood as a first tentative stage. Nevertheless, when the first scheme was introduced on 8th January 1936, it covered the whole road from Gardiner's Corner to Barking Broadway. This was followed a week later by the route from Victoria to Downham Way but there was then a lull until 21st October when fixed stops were applied to a huge length of route all the way from Seven Sisters Corner to Tooting Broadway via Dalston, Shoreditch, London Bridge, Elephant, Kennington, Clapham and Balham.

The principles followed were that there should be no fewer than six and no more than eight stops a mile, that there should be a mixture of 'Compulsory' (usually at Fare Stages) and 'Request' and that trolleybuses and buses should serve common stops. This last point soon gave rise to a problem because it was the normal policy of the Tram and Trolleybus department for all stops to be 'Request', except where safety requirements dictated otherwise. Instead of applying a standard rule, it was decided that on common sections, the Tram and Trolleybus principle should apply and that Compulsory stops would not be needed at Fare Stages, except for safety reasons.

The arrangements were gradually extended, road by road, until the first 'area' scheme was introduced on 21st July 1937. This covered all roads within the Central Division, enclosed by Edgware Road, Victoria, Pimlico, Vauxhall, Camberwell, Albany Road, Old Kent Road, Tower Bridge, Aldgate, Shoreditch, Islington, Kings Cross, Euston, Eversholt Street, Albany Street and Marylebone Road. Further similar schemes were applied segment by segment working around the area outside the central zone, starting with the portion between the river and the main road from Marble Arch to Shepherds Bush on 29th June 1938 and finishing on 12th April 1939 with the Bermondsey and Rotherhithe area. Alongside these, wherever trams were replaced by trolleybuses, fixed stops formed a part of the project and this had the effect of pushing the system well out into the suburbs. There was one particular section of suburban road which was treated, although not connected with trams or trolleybuses: St Helier Avenue, between Rose Hill and Morden Hall Road, was restricted to fixed stops from 13th January 1937.

To return to 1934, the gradual improvement of suburban roads enabled small but important improvements to be made from time to time, although their accomplishment was never straightforward. One such example was that of the routes between Chingford Mount and Chingford, where a one-way arrangement had been in operation for double-deckers for some years by which they approached Chingford via New Road and Larks Hall Road and departed via The Ridgeway and Chingford Mount. Single-deckers on route 602 had operated both ways via The Ridgeway but these had been double-deck since July 1934 and, following the removal of further obstructions, route approval was given for route 38 to operate both ways via The Ridgeway. This revision was introduced on 17th April 1935, from which date route 102 was diverted via New Road and Larks Hall Road, a pattern that was to survive for more than thirty years.

These changes coincided with a scheme of co-ordination for the Walthamstow area, the first of many subsequent 'Walthamstow schemes'. When the last London Independent of all, the Prince Omnibus Co, was taken over on 4th December 1934, its two weekday runnings on route 38E and the two on 551A had been abandoned, along with the special Sunday runnings on route 69. The only operations left untouched were those on route 511, which was being reviewed as part of the scheme. Although this did not come into operation until 17th April 1935 it would have been introduced much earlier but for the delays in taking over the Independents, notably Prince. The 511, by now renumbered 34A, did not survive the changes but was withdrawn altogether. The service up the hill to Chingford proper was not replaced but was left to route 38 alone. The section between Leyton and Chingford Mount was covered by extensions of tram route 87 from Bakers Arms to Chingford Mount and of an augmented bus route 34B from the 'Crooked Billet' to Leyton bus garage. There was also a higher frequency on bus route 34, which also covered the route down to Stratford.

The flags are flying on Ludgate Hill in celebration of George V's Silver Jubilee, which was honoured on 6th May 1935. There is a good cross-section of the Board's bus fleet here, with an STL1, an ST, an NS, a Bluebird LT and an STL3. J B Gent collection

In May 1935 the Board had its first taste of organising London's transport for a major national event when the Silver Jubilee of George V was celebrated. The Royal Procession took place on 6th May and the area around the route was closed to traffic between 8am and 1.30pm. A slightly larger area was closed after 9pm when the special illuminations were switched on. Normal Bank Holiday services were run on most routes but those serving the procession route started earlier than usual, with central London arrivals at about 6.30am. Bus and tram services which normally crossed the procession route were turned short on each side at Stamford Street, Bank, Chancery Lane, Kingsway, Charing Cross Road, Charles II Street, Bond Street, Knightsbridge, Horse Guards Avenue and Westminster Station (trams). North-south routes through Hyde Park Corner were diverted via Belgrave Square and all Park Lane routes through Hyde Park, Cheapside routes were diverted via Grays Inn Road, Old Street and Moorgate and the 76 was diverted over London Bridge. Green Line coaches were similarly diverted, except that those heading out towards Hammersmith went via Sloane Square and the I and J were cut back to Oxford Circus. The Illuminations Area was bounded by Hyde Park Corner, Victoria, Lambeth Bridge, Waterloo Bridge, Kingsway, Oxford Street and Park Lane and a similar mixture of curtailments and diversions operated.

A new route 235 which started on 5th June between South Croydon ('Swan & Sugar Loaf') and Selsdon was of interest in being the last new route to use the single-deck S-type. It also restored the service along Croham Road, lost when the 254 was diverted to avoid the low bridge, but its purpose is somewhat obscure.

A fairly common way in which the introduction of new routes was stimulated in this period was for the company building an estate to approach London Transport with an offer of subsidy. There had been a very early example in December 1933, when one Dart was operated on a route numbered 235 between Cheam Station and Banstead ('Victoria') via Upper Mulgrave Road, Sandy Lane, Cuddington Avenue and Banstead Road. This was a short-lived venture which did not result in the introduction of a permanent service and Cuddington was never again served except for a short period in 1953/4. Another such approach, which this time resulted in a permanent service being introduced, was made in 1935 jointly by John Laing & Son and the Old Lodge Estate (Purley) Ltd. The outcome was new route 203 between Old Lodge Lane, Purley and Mitchley Avenue which started on 11th September 1935. This was unusually interesting in being the only example of Gilfords being run by the Central Bus department, three (GFs 193-195) being transferred from Country Buses for the purpose. The Gilfords were replaced by Dennis Darts on 18th April 1936.

Other contemporary examples where the outcome was different were both in the north. An approach from a Mr Hicks, who was building an estate on The Ridgeway, Cuffley was turned down because the Board had recently refused local requests for such a service on the grounds that the level of demand was likely to be too low. Instead, Hicks was given consent to run his own service, on the basis that any passengers taken to Cuffley Station would add revenue to the Pool through the LNER. An application from Noel Rees for the Board to run a service between Cockfosters and Barnet via Monken Hadley was also rejected but in this case favourable Private Hire terms were offered instead. Presumably, this approach was adopted because the Board did not think such a route had a long term future, whereas they could see a future for the 203.

Other areas which got bus services for the first time during 1935 were: Barley Lane (restored) and Goodmayes Lane (new 62), Wrythe Lane (157 re-routed), Perry Vale and Woolstone Road (209 re-routed), Cambridge Road and Banstead Road South, Carshalton (213 re-routed), Tattenham Way (164A re-routed) and North Circular Road between Bowes Road and Finchley (new 112). There was one example of 'upgrading', on 17th April when Dart-operated route 206 was replaced by an extension of ST-operated route 114 from South Harrow to Rayners Lane.

Route 235, which started on 5th June 1935, was the last to do so with S-class single-deckers. This picture was taken at the Selsdon terminus. J B Gent collection

Below **Specially drafted into the Central Bus fleet to start up subsidised route 203 on 11th September 1935, GF 193 is at the Mitchley Avenue terminus, where builders' huts and materials are ready for action. The slip board in the front saloon window announces that there is a minimum fare of 2d.** D W K Jones

The 206 (see page 116) was replaced by an extension of double-deck route 114 on 17th April 1935. ST 664 is at the other end of the route, Edgware station, a few years later when the eastern side of the station colonnade had already been removed to make way for the ill-starred Aldenham extension of the Northern Line. Charles F Klapper Collection, Omnibus Society

Above left **The isolated community at Addington at last got a bus service on 4th March 1936 when route 64 was extended to Featherbed Lane from Selsdon. Its STs were simultaneously replaced by STLs, presumably to provide extra capacity for the new customers, not all of whom are likely to have trekked to Selsdon daily to take advantage of the bus service there. Tilling STL 83 is in what appears to be open country but the young cultivated tree on the near verge gives the clue that new suburban housing has arrived at Featherbed Lane.** J F Higham

Above right **Multiple boarding of buses lined up outside Morden Station helps to speed up the clearance of crowds making their way to Epsom Races. ST 701 is followed by another ST, two STLs and a 'Bluebird' LT, with another 'Bluebird' and an STL about to join on at the back, to keep a continuous flow of buses running.**

Below **The removal of an obstructing tree in West Wickham allowed the 194 to be extended to Forest Hill in place of the 78 on 29th April 1936. LT 582, which is leaving Forest Hill along Perry Vale, has now been fitted with a lamp to illuminate its route board.** J Bonell

Until 1936, when a new terminal working through Disraeli Road and Oxford Road was introduced, buses turning at Putney station on route 14 had to make this extraordinary 'U-turn' across the Upper Richmond Road junction. The Bluebird LT working on route 85 was supplied by Hammersmith garage.
Arthur Ingram

Middlesex was growing apace on all sides and the summer programme schedules on 27th May 1936 contained two examples of improvements to meet the new demand. Slightly unfashionably, the new route for Forty Lane, North Wembley, was a long trunk route running all the way from Victoria to Sudbury Town. Numbered 92, it followed the 16 as far as Cricklewood and then struck west opening up new territory through Crest Road and then on through Neasden and North Wembley. It is interesting that the original plan for the section as far as Neasden was to extend the 226, which had reached Cricklewood Broadway in January 1934.

The other changes, in west Middlesex, made possible some double-decking and saw the introduction of buses along Uxbridge Road between Feltham and Hanworth. New route 255 ran from Feltham to Teddington covering part of the 201, which was cut back to Hampton Court, leaving Bushy Park to the seasonal services. Double-deckers had been running on the 201 between Hounslow and Hanworth since 4th March 1936 and this was now turned into a wholly double-deck operation by the introduction of route 110, using STs from Hounslow garage, between Lampton and Twickenham (Hounslow–Hanworth Sundays). The 255 was short-lived; its Sunday service was covered by an extension of the 201 to Feltham on 2nd August 1936 and its Monday-Saturday service similarly absorbed on 6th October 1937. An interesting peculiarity about these changes is that they were inspired by the construction of a new bridge over the Longford River between The Mount and Hanworth village, enabling buses to run direct via Hounslow Road and it was the intention to terminate the 110 at Hanworth. It was not to be until November 1938 that this stretch of road got buses.

Two new routes which started in the Bexleyheath area on 9th September 1936 were only a partial resolution of a long running negotiation which had the aim of introducing buses into the East Wickham and Pickhurst areas and for a direct service between Sidcup and Bexleyheath via Blendon. The proposals had been approved as early as February 1935 but there was a need for road improvements in each case. The East Wickham route was held up because there were a number of gas lamps which had to be removed before double-deckers could operate. Although approval was given to the temporary use of single-deckers, this never came about, perhaps because the Board did not want to compromise its negotiations with the South Suburban Gas Co. The route eventually emerged as the 122, between Woolwich ('Earl of Chatham') and Bexleyheath on which Plumstead ran LTs. Unlike the present-day route the 122 ran via Upper Belvedere and Bedonwell Road to reach Long Lane.

The Sidcup service also ran into difficulties over the need for road improvements. These were so troublesome that a link was provided from Blendon to Bexleyheath as a temporary measure by the diversion of some 132s, renumbered 132A, via Crook Log to Bexleyheath. This proved to be as temporary as Income Tax, as when the Sidcup route finally appeared it ran only to Welling. The problem appears to have been around The Oval because the revised proposal put up for approval in May 1938 took a rather strange route through Pothkerry Avenue, Merlin Road and Wendover Way but, like its predecessor, it retained the route through Marlborough Park Avenue and Burnt Oak Lane. Although the Board was prepared to run Darts, it wanted approval for large single-deckers, which it did not get. These problems were eventually resolved and Route 241 started on 12th October 1938, running by the more familiar route through Westwood Lane, The Oval and Halfway Street and using Darts from Sidcup garage.

Another road which got a bus service on 9th September 1936 was Marlborough Lane, Blackheath but in this case its purpose was not to serve that community but to bring relief to the inadequacy then being experienced on route 21A at Blackheath station, about which the local M.P. had been complaining for some time. The means chosen was to divert route 89, which had spare capacity, to run via Marlborough Lane and Shooters Hill Road, instead of the 'Royal Standard' to strengthen the service for the heavy traffic between Blackheath station and Marlborough Lane.

Route 25 ceased to reach Victoria from 9th December 1936 when it became a short Sunday only service between Stratford and Little Heath. Seven Kings LT 511, an LT5, is seen in Victoria bus station in September 1934. G H F Atkins

A new venture for London Transport was the Inter-Station service which was taken over from P. Hearn on 7th October 1936. The changeover had been planned for 1st July but had to be delayed, awaiting the arrival of the special vehicles. Two routes were operated to and from Waterloo and Victoria: one to Kings Cross, St Pancras and Euston; and the other to Marylebone and Paddington. The service was run on behalf of the Main Line Railways and had been restricted to the carriage of holders of through railway tickets across London. The Board wanted to open it up to all-comers but an objection came from the unlikely direction of Ernest Bevin, whose Transport and General Workers' Union also represented the cabbies, who saw this as a threat to their livelihood. When it started, therefore, it remained restricted to ticket holders. As originally conceived the buses would have been one-man operated and passengers would have been looked after at the stations by staff supplied by the Main Line Railway companies. This was soon recognised as being an expensive way of doing things and conductors were carried on the vehicles instead. The service was far from a runaway success and after nine months of desultory operation, it was decided to remove the restriction on who might be carried. Various ideas were also canvassed for improving its financial performance, including one scheme which would have seen the withdrawal of route 44 (King's Cross–Victoria). By May 1938 the Board was so dissatisfied that it seriously contemplated abandoning the service. Hitler eventually made the decision for them, as this was one of the casualties of the early wartime cuts.

Other virgin operations during 1936 were: Claygate (new 206), Hinchley Wood and Hampton Court Way (152 diverted to Hampton Court); Great Cambridge Road from Southbury Road to 'Halfway House' (124 re-routed); Mollison Avenue (140 re-routed to Mill Hill; Colindale covered by new 119 from Kingsbury); and Ruislip Manor (223 extended via Pembroke Road).

Route 124 reached the 'Halfway House', a roadhouse on the new Great Cambridge Road, on 7th October 1936. ST 727 is on a journey to the new terminus at Turnpike Lane station.

This conjunction of routes at New Barnet station first came about on 24th March 1937 when route 306 lost its Enfield end and the 135 was diverted away from Arkley. ST 1128 was formerly in the fleet of East Surrey and like its counterparts has retained the original design of destination indicator, while ST 812 has been fitted with a larger display.
D W K Jones

The first direct effect on buses of the tram to trolleybus conversion began to be felt at the beginning of 1937. Now that the 623 trolleybus had started (on 18th October 1936), bus route 41, which had been extended to Forest Road (former AEC Works) in 1933 to forge the link across the Lea Valley for which the MET had tramway powers, was cut back to Tottenham Hale once more on 17th February. Then, on 24th March, the motor bus service along the Uxbridge Road was reduced in response to the introduction of route 607 on 15th November. Early plans were for bus route 17 to be withdrawn entirely west of Ealing Broadway but this was toned down in the actual changes, which had the 17 withdrawn between Hanwell garage and Southall and its frequency reduced beyond Acton. The Southall service was replaced by an extension of less frequent route 83. The frequency west of Acton was again cut in October 1937 and then, in August 1938, the Acton 'shorts' were cut back to Shepherd's Bush 'Princess Victoria'.

The various switches of mileage between bus and trolleybus and between Central and Country Buses were supposed to even themselves out. Every mile transferred from bus to trolleybus had to be matched by one going the other way and every mile outside the Metropolitan Police District taken by Country from Central had to be balanced by one within the District being moved from Country to Central. At the end of 1936, the balance was very much against Central Buses, who had lost 840 miles a day and Frank Pick issued instructions for the balance to be restored by the introduction of a new development route in the Greenford area, allocated to Hanwell garage and requiring seven or eight buses. No such service ever materialised, probably because the whole matter was to be thrown back into the pot by events in the early summer of 1937.

A transfer to Central Buses which left Country Buses slightly worse off involved route 306, which at this time was still ploughing its traditional furrow all the way to Enfield. There is some evidence to suggest that the whole of route 306 was to have been transferred, which would have made sense as the route operated within the Metropolitan Police District right out to Bushey; but this would have left too great a dent in the Country Bus mileage budget. Instead, when the changes were brought into effect on 24th March 1937, route 306 was withdrawn between New Barnet Station and Enfield Town and the rest of the route out to Watford left in the hands of Country Buses 'for the time being'. The Enfield to Barnet connection was maintained by diverting route 107 to run to Arkley on an improved frequency, via New Barnet station and Barnet Hill. The section of route abandoned by the 107 along Longmore Avenue was covered by a diversion of route 135 which now terminated at New Barnet instead of Arkley. This was a compromise arrangement as the original plan had been for the 135 to terminate at East Barnet. When no turning facilities could be obtained in that area, it was at first decided to extend the route right through to Enfield West station (Oakwood) but this was presumably too wasteful and New Barnet was chosen instead.

The inefficiencies of the Potters Bar duty schedules on routes 134 and 135 were only ever partly alleviated. Route 134 ran via North Finchley until 4th January 1938, after which it exchanged routes with the 135 and ran via Friern Barnet Lane. Photographed at North Finchley on 9th February 1936, DL 32 was removed from Potters Bar later that year.
D W K Jones

The Central Bus department had probably hoped to allocate the 306 to Potters Bar garage to try to build up its flimsy workload. As it turned out, this scheme was unpopular with them because it made the operation of route 135 by Potters Bar even less efficient than it had been for some time; the hope had been that it could be moved into Muswell Hill. In fact, the efficiency of both the 134 and the 135 had been under review ever since the routes had been transferred from Overground, as that company's conditions of service were tougher than the Board's standard and included longer spells of duty. To avoid a catastrophic loss of efficiency when the staff conditions were brought into line with general practice, serious consideration was given in the early stages to curtailing both routes at Trafalgar Square but no stand could be found there. The next idea was to divert the 134 either at Parliament Square to run to Camberwell Green via Lambeth Bridge, Vauxhall, Oval and Camberwell New Road, or extend it to Clapham Junction, though by what route and with what effect on other services is not known. In either case, the 135 would have been left unchanged but re-allocated into Muswell Hill garage. Later proposals were to include re-routeing either of them via Millbank and Grosvenor Road to Dolphin Square, Pimlico, where the residents of the flats had been pressing for the provision of a bus service.

The 135 did eventually reach Dolphin Square, in April 1938, but by a different route through Victoria and Belgrave Road, which it had been using since 23rd February when it was diverted to Pimlico 'William IV'. This coincided with the extension of shortworking buses on route 134 from Highgate Station to Victoria as a replacement for tram route 19. The extra buses for this change were made available by re-allocating part of route 135 from Potters Bar to Holloway, which avoided adding to the number of inefficient duties. The problem of efficiency was eventually solved by scheduling meal reliefs to be taken at Muswell Hill.

The big national event of 1937 was the Coronation of King George VI, which took place on 12th May. An enormous amount of time and energy was spent preparing for this major traffic event and arrangements made for vehicles to be stockpiled for use on the expected mass of Private Hire work before, during and after the great day. Up to 200 extra buses were expected to be used for official purposes and the intention was to supply these by relicensing withdrawn NSs at Chiswick Tram depôt. Additional requirements for Private Hire were to be met from engineering spares by the suspension of docking as required. On one day alone, there was one order for no fewer than 180 buses from the Rochdale Observer. Arrangements were made with the traffic authorities to allow a limited number of sightseeing tours to operate in the restricted area around the processional route during the period surrounding the Coronation and the detailed traffic arrangements for the day were also agreed well in advance.

Fate was to dictate otherwise. In the spring, the Trade Union had made an application for improved working conditions, including the introduction of a 7 hour working day (42 hour week). Although the Union reduced its main request to a 7½ hour day, negotiations broke down. After the unsuccessful intervention of the Minister of Labour, a strike was called and the buses were off the road from 1st to 27th May, throughout the Coronation period. Trams and trolleybuses were not affected as their staff were covered by a different labour agreement. The matter was referred to a Court of Inquiry, who found that some of the schedules introduced when services were speeded up in 1932 were onerous but it found against a shorter working day. Following further negotiations, a settlement was reached on 15th June which introduced revised rates of pay, with a slower progression through the scale for staff engaged after the date of the agreement, and the easement of some scheduling conditions, particularly the length and 'spreadover' of duties.

Had the strike not happened, special arrangements for Coronation Day would have been very similar to those which actually operated in 1953. The area around the processional route was closed from about 9pm on 11th May and throughout Coronation Day and buses would have terminated at special turning points on the edge of, or just inside, the banned area, each of which was allocated a special colour code, which was to have been carried on the vehicles. Green Line coaches would either have been diverted to Victoria, or, on the north side, curtailed at the Coronation terminal at Baker Street. More frequent night bus and tram services were planned; first trams and buses were to arrive at Coronation terminals at 4am and Green Line coaches at 6am. Selected suburban routes would also have had some special early starts and all routes were to have been strengthened to meet the expected extra demand.

Trams and trolleybuses did run but the only section of tram route affected by the traffic ban was along Victoria Embankment between Westminster Bridge and Waterloo Bridge. Embankment circular routes terminated for the day either at Lambeth Bridge, Westminster Bridge, Christ Church Kennington (Lambeth North) or Waterloo Bridge (Savoy Street) via Blackfriars. Kingsway Subway routes terminated at Aldwych tram station from the north.

Diversions and special services, including later facilities from suburban Underground stations, were also planned for the period of Illuminations between 13th and 17th May

The effect of the strike was an immediate reduction of about 4.5 percent in the number of passengers carried by bus and arrangements were made immediately to withdraw unremunerative buses from the busier routes, pending the introduction of new schedules under the new Agreement. By 5th January, when the first of the 'new agreement' schedules was introduced, seventy-one buses had been withdrawn. The new conditions of work created some problems with schedule efficiency and various ideas were discussed as ways of maintaining the level of efficiency. One of the more interesting notions was to exchange the southern ends of routes 53 and 36, so that the 53 would have worked West Hampstead to Hither Green and the 36 West Kilburn to Plumstead Common. This plan had to be abandoned because of the very heavy carryover traffic at New Cross and the problem had to be solved in some other way, perhaps by joint compilation of duty schedules with other routes.

North End Croydon is decorated for the Coronation in May 1937 and rehab E1 tram 1766 is at work, but there are no buses as the busmen were in the midst of a twenty-six day strike. J B Gent collection

Route 241 was double-decked on 1st September 1937 and under the new rules had to be renumbered 141. On 23rd March 1936, LT 1190 is on the stand at Elstree Way Hotel.
D W K Jones

Fortunately there was still scope for the Board to expand and many new services were introduced during the year. In Kent, the newly developing areas in Hayes were served from 4th August by single-deck route 232 from Beckenham Junction to Coney Hall, which also introduced buses to Pickhurst Lane, Station Approach and Bourne Way. The area had been served by a private service operated by the builder, Morrell, but this had been withdrawn on 29th February. It was re-instated on 16th March following a promise from London Transport that they would run an experimental service for one month.

There was a major scheme affecting services in south-east London on 8th September 1937. The embarrassment caused to the Board by the substandard fares on route 137 has already been mentioned in chapter one. The whole problem was set aside in this scheme by a drastic re-routeing, which took away the whole of the route from Hyde Park Corner to Bromley and diverted it via Sloane Square and the newly opened Chelsea Bridge to Clapham Common. In this form it bore little resemblance to the old route but it was allowed to keep its number 137. It replaced the short, unsatisfactory, tram route 32 which had terminated on the south side of Chelsea Bridge in a bit of a no-man's-land. Tramway mileage was balanced by the changes which were made to cover the loss of the 137. Route 66 was withdrawn between Camberwell Green and Embankment and diverted to Victoria and the services through Brockley were strengthened. Additionally, route 21A, whose service between New Cross and Lewisham had been under scrutiny for four years, was withdrawn between New Cross and Welling and diverted to Brockley Rise, its Welling end being covered by a new 89, which also covered the Lewisham to Bromley end of the 137. These changes were not popular and produced one of the biggest postbags which the Board had ever had.

Another casualty of the advance of trolleybuses, which must have brought a wry smile to the lips of any former Independent bus owners looking on, was route 26 (once the famous 526). Frank Pick had been trying to get something done with it for several years but it stubbornly provided a service that was too useful to be withdrawn. However, with the through service now operating on the 660, the opportunity was taken on 6th October 1937 to cut it back drastically from North Finchley to Willesden in peak hours, Harlesden at other times and to withdraw it altogether on Sundays. It survived in this form for another year but ran for the last time on 11th October 1938 when the Wandsworth Bridge end was covered by an extension of the 105 from Shepherd's Bush.

There were still many gaps in the housing around Coney Hall when new route 232 started on 4th August 1937. T 41 is on the stand in Princes Way.
Charles F Klapper Collection, Omnibus Society

Above **In the October 1938 changes the 214 lost its Weybridge to Chertsey portion. Some time before the change, LT 1126 passes one of the Board's new metal shelters in Molesey.** L T Museum U19160

Left **Tilling T 309 at the 'Dukes Head', Addlestone on the Weybridge to Woking section which was handed over to Country Buses on 12th October 1938. Under Chiswick's influence, the separate number blinds were removed from these Ts and standard width one-piece displays substituted but the wider box was always retained.** A Duke

Below left **The Addlestone area exchanges included the withdrawal of route 475. NY 9, a twenty seat Thurgood bodied Thornycroft A12 once the property of Peoples Motor Services of Ware, is at the 'Lincoln Arms' terminus** A Duke

The October changes included another stage in the transfer of mileage from Central to Country Buses. It was in fact the resurrection of the earlier LGOC plan to split the routes in the Walton and Weybridge area and comprised the withdrawal of route 214 between Weybridge and Chertsey; of 219 between Woking and Weybridge; and of the 217 altogether. Both the 214 and 219 were diverted to Weybridge station and the 214 was also strengthened between Kingston and West Molesey to serve the new housing developments in the Molesey area. In effect, the 217 was intermediately diverted between Walton and Staines to follow the 218, because the frequency of the 218 was increased from hourly to half-hourly. A new route 219A appeared, running between Weybridge station and Grotto Road, although this was really the former Country Bus route 475 in a new guise. The withdrawn sections were covered by extensions of the 461 from Walton to Hersham, simultaneously absorbing the 438, 438A and 438B; and from Addlestone to Staines; and by a new Saturday circular route 437A between Woking and Old Woking. The Cubs on route 461 were also replaced by 4Q4s. There was no direct replacement for the 219. Instead, the Cubs on routes 437 and 456, which it closely paralleled, were replaced by 4Q4s which increased their hourly carrying capacity to the same level as had been provided jointly by the three routes.

STL 11, on newly double-decked and renumbered route 124, turns off Waldram Road, Forest Hill to reach its stand, while the conductor is busy changing the destination blind. Malcolm E Papes collection

A small development route which started on 7th October 1937 was also embroiled in the Country versus Central Bus argument. Route 205A was a one-man Cub operated route between Waltham Cross and Hammond Street 'Rising Sun' which opened up new territory north-west of Cheshunt. The preferred method of serving this area would have been an extension of route 308 from Newgate Street to Waltham Cross but this whole area was within the Metropolitan Police District and the extent of Country Bus penetration south of the boundary at Wormley, to the detriment of route 69, was already a sore point. Another later idea involving the 308, to extend it to Cuffley, also had to be put on ice for the same reason, to await an appropriate opportunity. It had to wait a long time as it was not until well after the war that such an extension finally took place. Apart from those already mentioned, 1937 saw the introduction of buses to Kingston By-Pass between Robin Hood Gate and Malden (72 extended to Tolworth), Amos Estate, Rotherhithe (82 extended), Osidge Lane and Chase Side (new 125). After years of argument with the local authorities and Police, the Board at last got agreement to buses using Leigham Court Road, Streatham and a service started on 4th May 1938. Pick had approved such a service as far back as June 1934 when it was to have been part of a Clapham Common to West Wickham route via Crystal Palace and Sydenham, covering the outer end of route 78. The 78 had long since been covered by the extension of route 194 to Forest Hill (on 29th April 1936), so that scheme was no longer possible. Ironically, the route chosen was the 137, which was extended from Clapham Common to Crystal Palace, for all the world as though it was trying to get back to its own spiritual home. The delay had been caused because the Traffic Commissioner and Police were unhappy about the delays to other traffic which would be caused by the right turn from Kings Avenue into Clapham Park Road; buses crossing at Thornton Road/Sterhold Avenue; interruption of the traffic stream at Streatham Hill station; and buses crossing the centre line when turning from Leigham Court Road into Streatham Common North.

Other new territory opened up in south-east London on the same day, was in Downham, where route 209 was given double-deckers, a brand new number (124) and diverted through Hazlebank Road, Torridon Road and Sangley Road, instead of Baring Road and St Mildreds Road. In compensation, St Mildreds Road got new route 160 which went on to open up new ground along Westhorne Avenue and in Kingsground, Eltham, before picking up the Eltham to Welling part of the 227, effectively double-decking that section. Nearby, on 3rd August 1938, the new centre of Hayes at last got a direct bus service to its nearest main town at Bromley, with the diversion of route 232 via Westmoreland Road to Bromley North instead of Beckenham Junction. Beckenham Junction got an enhanced frequency on route 254, which also served Westmoreland Road whose total service was in consequence almost doubled.

One of the many south-east London improvements during 1938 was new route 160 which started on 8th May. ST 13 is on the St Dunstans stand at Catford. K W Glazier collection

In west Middlesex, Long Lane, Hillingdon had been completely reconstructed to a standard which, by spring 1937, made it suitable for buses. Uxbridge Urban District Council and the Hillingdon Ratepayers' Association pressed very hard for a bus service as the area was by now being built up very quickly. London Transport agreed to divert route 98 via Long Lane to terminate at Ickenham 'Coach and Horses', leaving the main road to Uxbridge to trolleybus route 607. When the change was introduced, on 4th May 1938, it was found possible for the same labour cost to run it on to Ruislip High Street. Another area nearby which was newly served from the same day, was Pield Heath. This was covered by an extension of 223 from Uxbridge to West Drayton via Kingston Lane, Pield Heath Road and Colham Green Road, following urgent representations from Hillingdon County Hospital which until then had been unserved. Other areas of Middlesex which got bus services during 1938 were Imperial Drive, Harrow (230 extended) and Preston Hill, Wembley (79), both in October.

Also in the October programme, West Hill Wandsworth got a bus service for the first time in an interesting group of changes which appeared to mark the Board's final abandonment of any idea of transferring the Central Bus section of route 70 to Country Buses. The 131 covered the Hammersmith to Doverhouse Road section of 72A, then continued to Wandsworth via the 'Green Man' and West Hill, the 72 was extended to East Acton, the 93 simultaneously cut back to Hammersmith and extended at the other end to Epsom and the 70 was withdrawn. The Country Bus end of the 70 was diverted at Ewell to follow route 408 to Croydon and became the 470. The changes to the 93 and 72 were partly a response to an objection from the Traffic Commissioner to any increase in the number of buses crossing Hammersmith Broadway.

Hammersmith was the centre of changes in October 1938 which removed the 93 from East Acton. The Holden-style station is about to be passed by D3 class Leyland trolleybus 529 in June of that year. L T Museum U27425

By now many changes to Central Bus routes were associated with the tram to trolleybus conversion, which reached the Hertford Road in October 1938. From the 16th of that month, in a programme which also saw the withdrawal of route 26, the famous route 69 was severely curtailed, losing all its mileage north of Tottenham to Wormley. The size of its allocation was reduced by one-third. Although there was a minor reprieve when it was re-extended to Edmonton on 16th November, this was only a temporary measure to provide a through facility while the 49/649 tram/trolleybus routes were split at Stamford Hill and the October changes really marked the beginning of the route's decline into oblivion. In fact, if the original plans for this conversion had been followed the 69 would have been withdrawn completely. In partial compensation, higher frequencies would have been scheduled on routes 35 and 76 and route 40 would have been extended from Camberwell Green to Herne Hill, which was not a million miles away from what eventually happened as part of the wartime mileage economies.

What actually happened in October 1938 was that Country Bus route 310 was substantially augmented between Hoddesdon and Enfield to cover the Wormley service and the 76A (to Wood Green) was withdrawn to enable a more frequent service to be run on the 76, which was simultaneously extended from Edmonton (Park Road) to Edmonton station. The Wood Green segment was covered by a diversion of half the service on route 42 at Stamford Hill, leaving the remainder still going to Finsbury Park but, confusingly, under the number 42A. This was, of course, yet another example of mileage being transferred from motor bus to trolleybus.

The transfer of mileage between red and green buses was again under consideration in November 1938, when route 84 was under scrutiny because it had been losing traffic as a result of the competition from trolleybuses between Golders Green and Barnet. Its survival this long was something of a miracle because it was one of the routes which Frank Pick had identified many years earlier as being a suitable candidate for being covered by a Green Line route. This was again one of the options considered in 1938, the other being the diversion of route 84 to Arnos Grove instead of Golders Green. Under either option, the section of route 313 between Potters Bar and Enfield would have been transferred to Central Buses. This proved to be yet another of life's 'might have beens', although another attempt was to be made in the turmoil of events surrounding the outbreak of the Second World War ten months later. In 1939 new suburban operations continued apace, starting with a programme on 4th January in which route 158 was given a long extension through 'Metroland', from South Harrow to Ruislip, serving Eastcote Lane and Ruislip Gardens and absorbing the short section of 223 between Ruislip Gardens and Ruislip. It was not easy to get approval from the Traffic Commissioner for this extension because it involved the use of a section of unlighted private road between Victoria Road and Field End Road. The Commissioner suggested using The Fairway instead but the objection was eventually overcome and the service was duly introduced on the planned route.

Marlpit Lane, Coulsdon was included in the same programme (new 59B) and this proved to be the prelude to a large number of new developments in south London this year. The first was an important extension of route 225 on 1st February through the new housing in Grand Drive and Hillcross Avenue to Morden Station. It was also converted to double-deck, using STLs instead of Qs from Merton garage and became route 50. Further east, Crofton Road Orpington was now physically ready for the bus service for which its inhabitants had been ready for years and for which London Transport had sought approval as far back as October 1936. It finally appeared, on 3rd May, as an extension of route 61 from Orpington to Bromley bus garage (with a Sunday extension to Bromley North).

Later in the year, on 5th July, route 130 came on the scene, serving New Addington. This was not strictly a wholly new route as the First National Housing Corporation, who were responsible for building the New Addington estate, had been running a service themselves from the estate to connect with route 64 at Addington Village, with consent from the Board, since early in 1938. At the Croydon end, the 130 used the car park at Barclay Road to stand and the use of this facility had been a condition of the Board's agreeing to run the service. Another condition had been that the road through Shirley Hills should be made suitable; had this not happened, then London Transport would have taken over the Housing Corporation's service and run it with a subsidy. The very last new route introduced before war put a stop to it all was the 119, which started on 9th August between Bromley North and Croydon, again using Barclay Road car park and at last forging the link westwards from Hayes, bringing buses to Corkscrew Hill and Addington Road.

Other areas served during the year were in east London and included Devons Road, Bow, hardly a glittering suburb but nevertheless in a large unserved area, and Elm Park Avenue. Another route which had started under the auspices of the local developer, route 229 to Claybury Broadway, was also improved on 7th June when it became 129 with an extension to Ilford and the introduction of double-deckers to replace its little Darts.

Top **STL 1597 at the 'Black Bull' Whetstone on route 84, one of the routes which London Transport would have liked to transfer to Country Buses.** A Duke

Centre **In the summer programme for 1939, new Sunday route 3A was created as an amalgamation of routes 3, 121 and 113 but it became a casualty of wartime changes. Hendon's STD 14 is in strange territory at Crystal Palace Parade, opposite the Southern Electric's High Level station and alongside the ruins of the palace itself.** Malcolm E Papes collection

Left **STL 631 at Morden station on new route 50 which served new ground in Grand Drive and Hillcross Avenue from 1st February 1939.** Charles F Klapper Collection Omnibus Society

Left **Pickup STL 553 rounds the corner from Addington Village Road into Gravel Hill surrounded by open country, shortly after the inception of new route 130 from New Addington in the summer of 1939.** E G P Masterman

Right **The new Alperton garage which opened on 7th June 1939 was built in the same simple style as all new premises in the 1930s. Inside are three of its starting fleet of STLs.** L T Museum U30543

All these developments put an immense strain on the available garage space and London Transport had been gradually improving and enlarging its existing buildings. The building of new garages had been concentrated in the Country Area for the first few years, as that was where the greatest need existed, but plans were laid for new Central Bus garages with the idea of building two or three a year from 1937 onwards. Among the sites considered were Elstree/Borehamwood (to replace Edgware), South Croydon/Caterham (to replace Croydon), Ongar, Barkingside, Mortlake (alongside the cemetery, to replace Mortlake and Twickenham), Bull Yard Peckham, Stockwell, West Wickham, Victoria, Marylebone and Pentonville, although there was no immediate need for the first three. Also, in connection with the construction of a new garage for Country Buses at Brentwood or Gidea Park, Central Buses would have taken over Romford (London Road) garage, but this arrangement depended on the provision of a new garage at Dagenham. The garages at Peckham, Marylebone and Pentonville would, between them, have added 475 bus spaces to the available garage capacity. One of the planned consequences of this was the closure of Potters Bar, which, as seen earlier, could not be operated economically. The re-allocation of work away from Potters Bar would have saved twenty crews, without altering the basic level of service.

Front runners at this stage appear to have been Peckham and Stockwell, which were vying for a position in the construction programme for 1937, although Barkingside was also being considered as a possible candidate before Peckham. There was a good deal of uncertainty about where suitable sites might be available and, if they were, whether planning permission was likely to be forthcoming. The Board therefore authorised the speculative acquisition of a large number of sites at Blendon, Hersham, Hanworth, East Barnet, Downe, Raynes Park and Richmond. In the case of East Barnet, the possibility was also considered of using some land alongside the railway at Enfield West station (Oakwood).

Apart from new garages, there was also a programme of enlargements and improvements to existing premises. These included the reconstruction of Catford, Hackney, Holloway (J) and Romford (RD). An interesting possibility, which was doomed never to see the light of day, was that Hampstead tram depôt might have been used as a temporary base for Holloway's buses during its rebuilding.

The programme authorised in 1937 was for new garages to be built at Victoria, Alperton and West Wickham and for Hackney and Holloway to be rebuilt and enlarged. Alperton was apparently imminent enough for it to be considered as the possible home for the new Leylands (STDs) due for delivery in 1937. West Wickham became a casualty of the 1937 strike but work went ahead on the rest of the programme, albeit later than originally envisaged, and the new garage at Alperton opened on 7th June 1939, taking routes from various garages and setting off a whole chain of re-allocations in north-west London. Its starting stock was entirely STL and it was allocated some of the new 15STL16s shortly afterwards. Work on Victoria garage was well advanced when war broke out and it was therefore completed and opened on 20th March 1940.

The last route to be started before Hitler intervened was the 119 which sealed the link between Hayes and West Wickham. ST 984 is at a tranquil Hayes station some time between the 9th and 31st August. Charles F Klapper Collection, Omnibus Society

Work was still in progress on building the new viaduct at Finsbury Park station for the extension of the Northern City Line to East Finchley and beyond when the war brought it to a standstill. In this view of Station Place, the area on the right is being cleared for the new roadway so that the railway can be built on the left, where an ST, an STL and an open staircase LT are standing. The joint LPTB/LNER notice above the fence announces the intended extension.
Charles F Klapper Collection, Omnibus Society

All other development came to a halt on 1st September 1939 with the German invasion of Poland which led inevitably to the declaration of war on Germany. Among the casualties were a number of plans for new services which were doomed either to be consigned to oblivion or to be delayed until much later. One of particular interest was a proposal to extend route 164A from Tattenham Corner to Surbiton via Epsom, Temple Road, Lower Court Road, Hook Road and Hook. The Traffic Commissioner considered Temple and Lower Court Roads to be unsafe and suggested instead that Chase Road and Hook Road should be used, to which London Transport had agreed. As the Epsom area had at one time been identified as ripe for transfer from Central to Country, the choice of Central Buses to run this service seems a little odd and it is no surprise that when these roads were eventually covered it was Country Buses who did so with routes 418 and 468.

Slightly longer term plans were in mind for the new LCC estate at Chingford, an interesting case which nicely illustrates the way in which co-operation between the Board and the Main Line railways worked in practice. The LCC had asked the LNER to build a station at Friday Hill so that its residents could have access to a service offering cheap fare facilities, including workmen's fares. The council were prepared to provide the land and contribute to the cost of building the station but the Board and LNER thought that the size of the planned population was not enough to support one. An alternative suggestion was that one of the trolleybus routes should be extended from Chingford Mount, bringing with it workmen's fares, but this also was considered too costly. The view of the Standing Joint Committee was that it was reasonable to expect people to make a journey of up to one mile to reach a railway facility. The Board were therefore considering instead the extension of 'shorts' on route 35 from Wood Street to Chingford via Fulbourne Road, Hale End Road, The Avenue, Chingford Lane, Friday Hill and Whitehall Road. Friday Hill itself was not yet built but was expected to be ready for use by 1941. There was also a short section of private road across Epping Forest at the northern end of The Avenue whose use would have to be negotiated. A temporary arrangement was therefore agreed by which route 35 would be extended from Highams Park to 'The Manor Hotel' (Chingford Hatch) via Larks Hall Road and Hatch Lane. Even this 'temporary' arrangement did not come into being until 20th November 1940 but, instead of the expected two years, Friday Hill had to wait a quarter of a century and the other roads over thirty years before they saw a service.

Another north-east London plan was to serve Whalebone Lane South by diverting route 149 between Goodmayes and Dagenham. Not only did this not happen but route 149 itself was withdrawn in December 1939 in the programme of fuel economy cuts. Whalebone Lane eventually got its service in 1942. In north-west London, there were plans for a service between Northwood Hills and Watford serving a rapidly developing area in Joel Street, Eastcote and Field End Road and then joining up with 'shorts' on route 158. This was dependent on the local authority's making improvements to some of the roads to make them safe for double-deckers but this was delayed and the new section had to wait until Cub route 225 was introduced in 1944. Two changes concerned with leisure activities also fell through. The lesser of these was a planned Saturday afternoon and Sunday service between Leytonstone and Barkingside via Woodford Bridge, to serve the Ashton Playing Fields. The other proposal might have had greater potential. Sound City Film Studios of Shepperton were building a new 'Sound City Amusement Park' at Littleton and the Southern Railway had suggested combined rail and entrance tickets via Staines and Shepperton stations. Discussions were in progress with Sound City for a subsidised double-deck service between Staines and Shepperton via Kingston Road, Worple Road or Ashford Road, Laleham Road, the Amusement Park and Squires Bridge Road, but the war intervened and the project collapsed.

Germany invaded Poland on 1st September and it became inevitable that the United Kingdom would be at war within days. The expectation was that there would be an immediate aerial bombardment and plans had been prepared for the evacuation of children and other vulnerable citizens from London. London Transport was heavily involved and while this was going on its normal services had to be depleted to supply the vehicles, no fewer than 1,486 of which were required on the 1st September alone. Once the evacuation was completed, on 4th September, services did not fully return to normal, as it was now necessary to economise on the use of fuel. These cuts were formally scheduled in a phased programme between 23rd September and 13th December which aimed to reduce schedules to seventy percent of their pre-war level and included the specially reduced services in the evenings, when demand had slumped because of the blackout.

As part of the cuts, the Board made another attempt to transfer routes from Central Buses to Country Buses. Another try was made for route 80, which would have been covered by a 486 (Sutton–Redhill) and for the shortened 84 which could have become Country Bus 344 between New Barnet and St Albans (Lancaster Road). Both attracted objections from the staff and neither happened, although neither did the alternative plan for route 84, which was to extend the 34 to St Albans.

Many firms moved out of London on the outbreak of war to safer premises in the Home Counties and this led to a spate of applications for Board's consent to operate special services to get staff to and from the new places of employment. For example, the National Employers' Mutual General Assurance Association sought consent for a service from Great Missenden to Frith Hill; the Vacuum Oil Company for one from Ottershaw to Addlestone station; F. Wilkinson for two to Slough from Gerrards Cross and Iver Heath; and the Sun Life Assurance Co for three to Orpington from Croydon, Surbiton and Upper Tooting. In peacetime most, if not all, of these would almost certainly have been refused on the grounds that alternative facilities were available but in the new conditions every one of them was given consent.

CHAPTER SIX RATIONALISATION IN LONDON'S COUNTRY

The Country Bus and Coach department of London Transport had a much more complicated and voluminous task on its hands than Central Buses. The large number of operators it acquired between 1933 and 1935 was more than matched by the number and variety of routes they ran and this was particularly apparent in the large urban areas of Windsor, Slough, Watford, St Albans and Grays Thurrock. In the case of Watford alone, quite apart from the services operated by LGCS and LGOC, there were five companies working on eleven unco-ordinated routes. Country Buses therefore adopted a different, more fundamental approach to the process of co-ordination which it achieved through a series of local 'schemes'.

Green Line coaches were rather different because their co-ordination was being imposed on London Transport by the Traffic Commissioner, who applied the findings of the Amulree Committee with relish. The first major programme instituted by the new department was therefore the launch of a completely re-organised coach network on 4th October 1933. At this time not all coach operations were in the hands of the Board but those that were still in private hands also had to be altered in line with Amulree's findings and were eventually blended into the Green Line network without too much upheaval. Poland Street coach station was closed and the main central London point for coaches was transferred to Eccleston Bridge, Victoria, one of the roads which formed the boundary of the banned area. Most routes now ran across London, the exceptions being the east London routes which terminated at Aldgate or Eldon Street, routes from Baldock, which turned at Kings Cross, Hemel Hempstead (Portman Square), Caterham (Horse Guards Avenue), High Wycombe and Amersham (Oxford Circus) and Aylesbury (Marble Arch). Route T survived earlier attempts to have it withdrawn and continued to feed the Underground at Golders Green.

Altogether, scheduled mileage was reduced by 10.3 per cent, fifty fewer coaches were needed and over three hundred staff were made redundant. There was an immediate loss of receipts, which went down by 19.3 per cent and the number of passengers carried fell by twenty-nine per cent. Some of these losses were attributed to the drastic reduction in picking up points now allowed within the Metropolitan Police District under the new restrictions which limited boarding to widely spaced specified points, while allowing alighting anywhere. To say that the Board was unhappy about this situation would be a grotesque understatement. It decided to apply for additional picking-up points and to attempt to get some of the more crippling routeings modified. Many letters passed between London Transport and the Traffic Commissioner and there was a remarkable series of meetings which culminated in Lord Ashfield taking Gleeson-Robinson to lunch at the Savoy on 20th November 1933. The Ministry were not too happy about this approach but gave the Commissioner permission to meet Ashfield provided he made no fresh concessions. At the lunch, Ashfield pressed for free use of the central area, freedom from restrictions on routeings in the Metropolitan Area and a free hand with regard to picking up places, as was already the case with buses. This attempt failed but Lord Ashfield took the matter up personally with the Minister and managed to get agreement to a more favourable attitude to stopping places. A fresh application for the addition of 164 stops to the network was then made and Gleeson-Robinson eventually granted 111, of which eighteen were modified.

Above **Under the new lettering scheme introduced with the 'Amulree' changes the former Queen Line route from Kings Cross to Baldock became AK. T 355, a London Lorries bodied Regal dating from 1931 and now allocated to Hitchin garage, came from the Queen Line fleet.** D W K Jones

In the Watford area scheme introduced on 31st January 1934, route 321 absorbed the Lewis workings and became the main trunk route through the town. Chiswick has yet to take control of the Country fleet and this Bluebird Regent still has no number but will eventually be ST 1033. J F Higham

The Board was not prepared to let the matter rest and a further application was made at the end of 1935 in a powerfully argued paper which reminded the Minister that since Amulree had been set up, circumstances had been changed by the formation of the LPTB which had overall responsibility for planning services. It argued that the coaches should be regarded as part of the network and that the Board should decide what that network should contain. It presented evidence which showed that the Board's activities in 'rationalising' the acquired Independent services had already reduced substantially the number of buses using the area now banned to coaches. Examples quoted were Piccadilly (down 101 buses a day), Whitehall (349) and Regent Street (301).

The application envisaged some routes being diverted via Westminster Bridge, Northumberland Avenue and Piccadilly (A/AA/C/AC/D), or via Millbank, Trafalgar Square, Regent Street, Portland Place and Marylebone Road (B/E/F/H/AH), or via Westminster Bridge and Victoria Street (K). There were also some new linkings proposed. Route BH would have been joined to the P to run Luton to Burnham Beeches, using Woburn Place, Kingsway, Strand, Trafalgar Square and Piccadilly in central London and route O would have had a double link to form new routes from Windsor to Caterham (via G) and Great Bookham (L). Finally, the application called for the east London routes to be extended at all times from Aldgate or Eldon Street to Horse Guards Avenue.

The Traffic Commissioner refused every one of the applications for additional penetration of the central area but granted the linking of G, L and O, presumably because it reduced the number of coaches turning in central London. In giving the reasons for his decision, he went well beyond the route approval powers which he was supposed to wield and repeated much of the reasoning which had started this whole process in the first place. The Board took legal opinion and Ashfield persuaded the Minister to allow the Traffic Commissioner to rehear the case. All this was still rumbling on when the coaches were abruptly withdrawn in September 1939 and the argument was never won by London Transport.

Although Poland Street coach station was closed for passenger services after 3rd October 1933, it continued to be used as a parking area for coaches laying over in central London and as the base for Green Line's Central District Control. It was also used for a time as a temporary Lost Property Office until the premises at Baker Street were ready. All use ceased on 13th February 1934, after which layover coaches were parked at Chalk Farm garage and the District Control operated from Cranbourn Chambers, above Leicester Square station.

One other change affecting Green Line took place on 3rd January 1934 when the arrangement by which coaches on the Uxbridge route were stabled at the AEC works in Southall, came to an end, presumably because there was no longer any formal link with the company. From that date coaches were garaged at Amersham, resulting in much 'dead' mileage.

The first co-ordination scheme for bus services was implemented in Watford on 31st January 1934. The former Lewis trunk operation through the town was combined with LGCS workings to form a new 321 from St Albans (Oaklands) to West Hyde ('Royal Oak'). Harebreaks, the former terminus of one of the Watford Omnibus company's routes, was served by a variety of routes coming into Watford from the north, which were diverted this way: 322 (ex 2) from Hemel Hempstead via Kings Langley and 325 (ex 15A) from Hemel via Bedmond, as well as by a new 346 (Harebreaks – Hamper Mill). At its southern end, the 346 ran via Eastbury Road, which was new to buses, to serve the rapidly expanding housing estates in Hampermill Lane and Brookdene Avenue and also covered the Watford company's Hamper Mill route. The Lewis circular route between Watford Churchyard and the Met station was replaced by the extension of 315 and diversion of 385 and his Windsor service by a remarkably long extension of the short local route 335 (Market Place – Leavesden). The two Biggerstaff routes from Buck's Hill (347) and Sarratt (344) were both extended to Leavesden. The YS route to Leggatts Rise, latterly numbered 395, was withdrawn and not replaced, although this area was served by routes 306 and 311 which were both extended to Gammons Lane. The Filkins and Ainsworth 354 between Rickmansworth and Harefield was renumbered 309 and replaced the old route of that number, except between Rickmansworth and Leavesden.

One of the incidental details of the scheme was that all buses which had previously approached Watford via Harwoods Road and Whippendell Road, from the direction of Croxley, were now diverted instead via the old Lewis route through the full length of Whippendell Road. This was to avoid what was known locally as a 'death trap', the corner of Rickmansworth and Harwoods Roads.

The 312 was officially an extension of route 311B at both ends from Watford Junction to Gammons Lane and from Little Bushey to Enfield but was surely a new route. This Strachan bodied Bristol B at East Barnet was formerly the property of the Lewis company of Watford and never received a London Transport number. D W K Jones

Vickers bodied Albion PK26 YU2974 was one of the vehicles which passed from the Metropolitan Railway to Lewis in November 1929 and was still at work on the Watford West route at Watford (Met) station on 23rd June 1934. D W K Jones

Country Buses also made a few contributions to the needs of suburban development. King Charles Road, Tolworth, became a bus route on 28th February with the extension of route 418 from Tolworth ('Red Lion') to Kingston.

The second area to have its bus services re-arranged was Gravesend and Dartford, from 16th May 1934. The changes had been deferred from the planned date of 18th April because of the takeover of Greenhithe & District on that date. Having split the system at Gravesend, London Transport restored the balance a little by including a large number of through workings across Dartford on the Denton to Dartford corridor. Routes extended to Denton included the 401, which was divided at Dartford to form two routes, the Sevenoaks end keeping the number 401 and the section from Bexleyheath being numbered 491. Other newly formed through Denton routes were the 407 from Sidcup and 477 from Chelsfield, which was part of the 497 diverted. Local routes were also relinked to provide some useful connections across the two towns and the former Enterprise service from Hartley Hill was extended from Perry Street into Gravesend. The two Swanscombe routes 487 and 488 were extended from Gravesend Clock Tower to Kings Farm Estate, covering both the former Maidstone & District and Gravesend & District routes. The two former Maidstone & District rumps to Northumberland Bottom and Singlewell were covered by extensions of 450 (from Dartford), 451 (Hartley Hill) and 489 (Ash), 490 (Longfield Hill) respectively. In Dartford, M&D's route to Hook Green ('Fox and Hounds') was linked to the 423 to give a rather odd through route to Swanley. Crayford garage probably closed with the introduction of these new schedules. It certainly did so at about this time but the exact date is not known.

As in each of the other 'area schemes', the fare structure of all local routes was brought into line with the Board's general standard and all fares with halfpenny values were abolished. Cheap returns were also withdrawn, which meant that, for example, a journey from Gravesend to Dartford and back cost a shilling (two sixpenny singles) instead of ten pence return. The only workmen's fares which survived were those between King's Farm Estate and Gravesend.

Top **UR7968, a Thornycroft A2 formerly owned by Peoples of Ware and later numbered NY 8, is at work on route 455B in Gravesend in the spring of 1934 and carries a notice announcing the forthcoming re-routeing of buses in the area on 16th May.** J F Higham

Centre **By 12th August 1933 this Maidstone & District Leyland Titan, on route 486 in Westgate Road, Dartford, had received a new 'General' fleetname but was still in Maidstone & District colours.** D W K Jones

Right **UR7353 (NY 6), another Peoples bus which has migrated from Ware to Gravesend, is at Longfield Hill ready to go to Gravesend Clock Tower, before the extension of route 490 to Singlewell in May 1934.** Alan B Cross

The first new London Transport garage opened at Epping on 5th September 1934 and it took over responsibility for all but two of the routes operated from the former Associated Coaches premises in Lower High Street Ongar and the Acme Pullman and National garages in South Street Bishops Stortford, all of which closed. Bus routes 10 and 11 moved from Bishops Stortford into Ware. Epping had space for only thirty-five vehicles, making it the smallest of the new Country Area garages. The greater part of its allocation was coaches for routes N, V and W but two single-deck buses were allocated for route 339. This was the new number for the old N9, but the section between Bishops Stortford and Ongar was withdrawn, except for a couple of school journeys to Potter Street. Penny fares were introduced on Green Line route W between Epping and Ongar but not on route V, which was now the only service over the section between Sawbridgeworth and Epping. This was not the first case of local fares being charged on the Green Line, as the same arrangement had applied on route B between Wrotham and Farningham since 16th May.

Although many Country Bus routes were already numbered in accordance with the new system introduced by Central Buses on 3rd October, there were forty-eight former LGCS routes and the whole of the Amersham & District network (forty-one routes) which had to be brought into line and this was done on 10th October. In many cases they simply had a '3' or a '4' added in front of their two-digit numbers (such as 64 to 364 and 27 to 427). In other cases this was not possible and entirely new numbers were invented (such as 12 to 342). This arrangement applied to the entire Amersham & District network, which was still at this stage managed separately but quite why the number 305 was used for A&D routes 6 and 10, rather than the 5 must remain as much a mystery as many other route numbering decisions over the years.

The important route network in St Albans was the next major re-organisation undertaken by Country Buses. The new arrangements were introduced on 5th December 1934 and again cross-town linkings were a feature. Routes joined together were: former St Albans & District 304 and 308, to form a Borehamwood to Hitchin service (304); the 321 and 321A (recently renumbered from 351) to run West Hyde to Luton; and the former National 8A and Blowers' 355, Shenley to Harpenden. The former Blowers' routes to Fleetville were covered by the extension of the 314 (from Hemel Hempstead), a service formerly associated with City Omnibus services. Townsend was served by no fewer than four routes which together formed a high frequency group along the Hatfield road: 330 and 350 from Welwyn Garden City, 340 from Bishops Stortford and 341 from Stanstead Abbots. The Welham Green section of the old 330 became part of a new 343, which continued through Potters Bar and Botany Bay to Enfield. Two new local routes were introduced, the 334 from Oaklands to St Julians, picking up the Oaklands service abandoned by routes 321 and 358; and 381 from St Albans to Batford on Saturdays and Sundays, covering route 8. The 374 was withdrawn north of Redbourn in yet another case where the Green Line route (AH) was considered adequate to look after the local traffic.

The next new garage to open was at Hertford (HG), on 2nd January 1935. The two garages in Ware, Town Hall (WR) and the ex-People's base (WE), were closed and their operations transferred to the new Fairfax Road premises. The use of garage codes had just been adopted by Country Buses and it is interesting to see how complete must have been the department's isolation from the rest of the Board's activities as it managed to duplicate three codes with the well established Central Bus ones: Amersham (AM) clashed with Plumstead; High Wycombe (HW) with Hanwell; and Watford High Street (WG) with West Green. These were later altered to the more familiar MA, HE and WA. Windsor's code also started out differently, its original being WC (for Windsor Coach) but perhaps the reason for that being changed had more to do with æsthetics. The radical decision to have garage codes at all had been prompted by the acquisition of Edward Hillman's business, which brought a second garage into Romford for the Green Line organisation (making three in all, including the Central Bus garage). To avoid possible confusion, the Hillman premises were given the code RE and the old Green Line North Street garage became RF, giving a neat alphabetical sequence with RD.

Above **The new Epping garage immediately after being commissioned. Its main business was Green Line work and four coach Regals can be seen parked inside.**
Charles F Klapper Collection, Omnibus Society

LT 1137B in use as a bus on route 330 in St Peters Street, St Albans on 20th April 1935 but before the alterations illustrated in chapter 2 had been carried out.

GF 145B is working a short to Colney Heath on new route 343, followed by an ST on the new 334. The Gilford 166SD was one of the buses acquired with the business of F. Steer (The Colne Service) who had bought it in April 1930. D W K Jones

BPF318 was one of two Dennis Aces with Waveney twenty seat bodywork ordered by Gravesend & District but delivered to the LPTB in 1934, hence its Surrey registration. It is at Guildford on route 448, the subject of a major dispute with Tillingbourne Valley which eventually led to a rare joint running agreement. J B Gent collection

A small change on 24th March 1935 concealed a major argument between the Board and another operator and revealed the LPTB's willingness to indulge in naked aggression to eliminate unwanted competition. Tillingbourne Valley had applied for consent to continue its services from Guildford to Farley, Warren Road and Peaslake but London Transport wanted to consolidate them into its own local network and was not disposed to grant consent. The dispute got to the stage where the Board was prepared to contemplate imposing setting down and picking up restrictions on Tillingbourne, while duplicating his entire network with its own stopping services. This was hardly what the authors of the 1933 Act had in mind. Common sense eventually prevailed and that rare phenomenon in the annals of London Transport, a working agreement, was signed under which Tillingbourne continued to operate but on a co-ordinated timetable and with inter-availability of Return tickets.

The complexities of the Grays area were finally tamed on 5th June 1935, when it had its own little scheme. There had been a number of earlier changes at Grays as London Transport consolidated its position in the area, gradually taking over the operations west of the town previously run by Eastern National and the many Independents. For a time the through running across the town from the Thurrock riverside communities to Tilbury had been maintained, even to the extent of route 372 being extended from Grays to Tilbury (Feenan Highway) when the businesses of F.R. Harris and R. Clark were taken over on 18th May 1934. Harris's express service from Tilbury right across to the Royal Albert Dock was also operated intact as the 372A but how long it lasted is not clear. It would certainly not have survived beyond 29th July 1934 when the Tilbury to Grays section of the 372 was handed over to Eastern National.

The principal changes in June 1935 were the withdrawal of the 371 between Baynes Garage and Romford and of the 375 between Grays and Rainham and their consolidation as a Grays to Aveley circular route, numbered 371, via Stonehouse Corner, Uplands Estate, Baynes Garage and Aveley village. The Romford section of the 371 was not replaced as it was adequately covered by Central Bus route 253, except on Saturdays when the 253 had only an irregular service of journeys; this was increased to a regular twenty to thirty minute service. The operation to Romford was taken off as part of the gradual exchange of mileage between Central and Country Buses, although it was not until 12th December 1936 that route 103 was to be withdrawn between Rainham and Aveley. To cover the withdrawn sections of route 371 east of Rainham, a new Green Line route was introduced, running via Aveley, with local fares between Stonehouse Corner and Dagenham and providing a link from Aveley to Dagenham which had been long sought after by the local community.

The White Post Corner to Rainham (Clock Tower) section of the 375 was joined onto the occasional Clock Tower to Rainham Ferry service (393A) to form a through service which also absorbed the more frequent local route 393 (King Edward Avenue – Rainham Station). The number 375 was retained for this revised operation despite the fact that it had a greater affinity with the number 393, which was now allotted to the works service between the Clock Tower and Cory and F&E Works which had previously been the 393B.

The processes of renumbering routes had so far passed the Green Line by but the first indication of the Board's chosen solution was evident in the number chosen for the new Grays route, Z2; the existing route Z was renumbered Z1 at the same time. These changes showed how the system was to be applied, with the basic lettered route having a '1' added and those with a prefix letter a '2' or '3' as appropriate. The idea of having a series numbered from G1 upwards had by now been abandoned but the logic which had been applied to the trolleybuses of having a separate numerical series was apparently not thought to be suitable for the coaches, which retained a lettered system in this modified form. There was no immediate rush to bring the rest of the network into line but there were some changes on 3rd July, when routes A and AA became A1 and A2 and the Y and AY became Y1 and Y2. Oddly, the opportunity was not taken to alter the Y and AY on 26th June, when a new timetable had been introduced under which part of the AY service terminated at Hornchurch station. This piecemeal approach came to an end on 8th January 1936, when all but one of the remainder were altered. The odd man out was the BH, which had to wait until 29th July 1936 to become H3.

One of the Titans drafted into Grays to replace the multiplicity of small buses, TD 52 came originally from the Pioneer Omnibus Company. It is at Romford on 28th March 1936 working on route 370, which was taken over from Central Buses on 5th December 1934. D W K Jones

The old Combine's first AEC Regent, UU6610 (ST 1139) had found its way to Grays by 18th February 1935 to work on the busy Thames-side route to Purfleet. D W K Jones

The biggest rationalisation scheme of all was the one for Windsor and Slough, which went into operation on 3rd July 1935. Three routes, the 41B and 42B to Burnham Beeches via Salt Hill and Stoke Green respectively and the 507B Between Egham and Staines, had already been withdrawn on 3rd October 1934 but no fewer than thirty-one routes were still involved, many of the minor variations having been inherited from Independents. On route 441, for example, there were seven variants from the main route, to Farnham Common, Slough Trading Estate, Belgrave Road Slough, Essex Avenue, Furneval Avenue, Hedgerley Village and Hedgerley Corner. These were co-ordinated into the main double-deck 441 between High Wycombe and Windsor, with shorts from Hedgerley Corner to Slough, and a single-deck 441A from the Trading Estate (Dover Road) to Slough. Hedgerley Village was left to the 442, which lost its Beaconsfield service to the 441 and in its turn covered the Stoke Common service of withdrawn route 446 and the Stoke Poges Golf Club operation of route 468.

New through routes were again an important element but in this area the boundary was a barrier to any east-west through running and the Board never did exercise its powers to run on the Maidenhead road, preferring instead to have a mileage agreement with Ledbury and Thames Valley which gave it access, among other places, to the Trading Estate. New facilities were therefore concentrated on the narrow north-south corridor and new through routes were created between Guildford and Uxbridge (436 extended over the withdrawn 458) and from Ripley to Uxbridge (437 covering the 457). These were apparently not overwhelmingly successful because they were fated to last only until 17th March 1936, after which they were again split in Windsor and the numbers 457 and 458 re-appeared.

Other changes included the extension of route 463 from Leeds Road West to Farnham Road 'George' and the diversion of route 473 to the same point via Bath Road instead of Manor Park estate. Manor Park was covered by route 444. Among the routes which disappeared were the 413 (Old Windsor), 447 (Burnham Beeches – covered by a weekend extension of Green Line route P), 467 (Egham) and 468 (Stoke Poges Golf Club). Another casualty was the service to Knowle Hill on route 469; it was outside the Board's area and the Commissioner would not allow them to run it, so the route was diverted to and curtailed at Virginia Water ('Wheatsheaf'). The 369 also lost its Great Missenden to Aylesbury section in yet another example of crude splitting at the boundary.

Top **Country Buses seemed to take some pride in moving acquired vehicles far from their old home ground. This Dennis F which came originally from the Aston fleet in Watford is now at Windsor on route 37 from Chertsey, renumbered 437 and extended to Uxbridge in July 1935.** J F Higham

Centre **The characteristic downward sweep of the canopy shows that this Dennis HV (DH 8) which was once owned by BBP, has a Birch body. It is on route 481 to Langley Village.** J F Higham

Right **Not too far from its old Woking and District homeland, this Challands Ross bodied Thornycroft BC is allocated to Windsor (WC) and operating on the 457 from Uxbridge to Staines which was replaced by the 437 on 3rd July 1935.** D W K Jones

The Ware rationalisation scheme was put into operation on 14th August. Here, the main operators had been LGCS and Peoples Motor Services and it was the co-ordination of their services and some integration with other small proprietors' routes which were its main purpose. Its principal features included a co-ordinated timetable between Enfield and Hoddesdon on three routes which then fanned out to Hertford ('George') via Ware (310, curtailed from Hertford North), Bishops Stortford via Stanstead Abbots (328, extended from Stanstead Abbots to Enfield) and Hertford North via Rye House (380, extended from Wormley to Enfield and Hertford to Hertford North). New through services were: 389 Bishops Stortford to Mardley Hill, an extension from Hertford to cover part of the 388; and 390 Coopersale Street to Hitchin (previously Epping to Hertford). The extension of the 390 from Hertford covered the withdrawal of the 333 between Hertford and Watton and the Sunday extension of 310 to Stevenage. The 333 also lost its southern end between Hertford Heath and Broxbourne and became a local route between Hertford Heath and Chapmore End, in place of one leg of route 348. To replace the Hertford to Broxbourne through service on route 333, Green Line BM was diverted via Hertford Heath and bus fares were introduced.

The area to benefit most from the changes was that served by route 354, formerly operated by R.C. Knowles, between Hertford, Little Berkhamsted and Newgate Street, which was basically a Saturday service, with a couple of Sunday journeys and one return journey on Wednesdays and Fridays. This was replaced by an entirely new daily route between Ware, Hertford and Little Berkhamsted, via Bayford (308A), with a Saturdays only branch to Newgate Street (308). The Sunday only service via Bayford station was numbered 368A. Why Country Buses saw fit to use a completely different number is not at all clear but they may have felt that the massively improved service deserved a new identity. The use of 368A for the Sunday variation is an even bigger mystery.

There were also areas which lost services, although in most cases the new pattern provided reasonable, sometimes more rational, alternatives. Examples of connections which disappeared were the Benington – Aston – Broadwater and the Graveley – Great Wymondley – Hitchin parts of the Benington to Hitchin route and the Aston – Shephall – Broadwater section of the Aston to Hertford route, all formerly operated by Rowe of Aston. A more drastic example was the Royston routes, which were split at Braughing (331A) and Buntingford (331), leaving Eastern National to take responsibility for the outer rump, which, bereft of much of its purpose, soon withered away to a few isolated journeys.

Peoples of Ware, who ran a network of services in the area, were taken over on 30th November 1933, before which this Thornycroft A12 was at work on the route to Dane End and Walkern. J F Higham

London Transport had difficulty with the Traffic Commissioner over the route of the 329 but settled on a compromise. T 384B, an ex-East Surrey/LGCS bus, is at Hertford Car Park on the compromise route. J F Higham

The changes to route 329 in the Ware scheme were an example of rationalisation plans which fell foul of the Traffic Commissioner's veto. London Transport had hoped to combine the services acquired from G.W. Currell (White Heather) between Hitchin and Datchworth and between Knebworth and Hertford with the former LGCS 329 (Woolmer Green – Hertford) into one through route. The Traffic Commissioner would not approve the use of either possible route between Datchworth and Datchworth Green and the Board had to settle for diverting the 329 to operate direct between Datchworth Green and Woolmer Green and retaining the Hitchin route as a separate operation. The preferred plan was evident in the decision to renumber the Hitchin route from 332 to 329A even though it now bore little resemblance to the 329.

The long running friction with Redcar was finally settled by Maidstone & District taking them over. Their workings in the London Transport area were handed over to the Board on 31st July, ending the competition on Green Line route C. It also left London Transport free to extend its Croydon to Sevenoaks route 403 to Tonbridge, in place of local route 402A, a move to which Redcar had objected and which was actually at the Appeal stage in the Traffic Court when the takeover took place. Maidstone & District also withdrew the Sevenoaks to Tonbridge section of the Uckfield route. Four more Leyland Titans joined the fleet (TD 192-195) and five Beadle bodied Tiger coaches (TR 36-40).

This scene was possible only for a period of six months in 1935, between the delivery of STL 1038 to Northfleet in May and the withdrawal of route 491 on 20th November. The destination contains an interesting and unusual abbreviation for 'Bexleyheath'. F G Reynolds

More changes in the Dartford area on 20th November 1935 introduced the famous number 480 to north-west Kent, as a local route between Dartford and Denton covering the curtailment of the through routes at Gravesend Clock Tower and the diversion of 401 away from this area to Bexleyheath. New single-deck route 492 struck into the heart of Central Bus territory at Lower Belvedere, serving Picardy Road and Northall Road and then providing the link across Dartford from Crayford to Horns Cross which was about to be lost on the following Sunday when the trams were replaced by trolleybuses.

St Albans and Welwyn Garden City were both towns which were spreading rapidly and a second bite was taken at that particular cherry on 27th November 1935. A wholly new one-man operated route (354) served the eastern side of the Marshalswick area of St Albans for the first time, on a circular working via Brampton Road, Woodstock Road and Sandpit Lane, which also absorbed the Sandpit Lane to St Albans town section of route 338. The 338 was diverted to serve Lancaster Road instead. The 340 was shortened to operate Hertford to Townsend and became the main local route between Fleetville and Townsend, over which section a ten to fifteen minute service of double-deckers was run. Its companion route, 341, was also withdrawn east of Hertford as well as being cut back to St Albans from Townsend. The Hatfield road was shared with the 330, which too was withdrawn between Townsend and St Albans; it was also altered to take the shorter route via Hatfield By-Pass into Welwyn Garden City. A new local 303A between Birchwood Avenue and the Garden City maintained the connection with Hatfield town. The Bishops Stortford and Stanstead Abbots ends of the 340 and 341 were covered by new routes 350 and 350A from Hertford.

Meanwhile the building programme had continued right through 1935. At Grays neither the LGOC nor LGCS had had premises and none of the local operators taken over by the Board had anything large enough to house all the buses operating in the area. For some time these were housed in a yard owned by a brewery but this was replaced by a handsome new garage, which was built at great speed and opened on 18th February 1935. In April an entirely new garage was commissioned at Two Waters, to replace a temporary shed which had been in use in Bury Road, Hemel Hempstead since 1933. It was given the code HH, despite being nearly two miles from Hemel Hempstead, presumably because Tunbridge Wells had already snaffled the more obvious 'TW'.

In August a new garage was unveiled at Amersham, alongside and replacing the former Amersham & District premises. The old buildings were retained by the Board and were used for the storage of unlicensed vehicles. The garage at Tring, which had been taken over from E. Prentice & Son (Chiltern Omnibus Service) in 1933 was also enlarged in what were virtually new premises. This brought the total of new or rebuilt garages to five, not a bad achievement only eighteen months after the Board's formation. The additional capacity in the area enabled the small premises at Harefield to be closed on 1st January 1936 and routes 309/A and 357 re-allocated to Watford High Street.

Coinciding with the main renumbering programme on 8th January 1936, already described, there were some important changes to the Green Line network. The former Redcar service, which had been running as a separate section of route C since its acquisition on 31st July 1935, was now incorporated with the C2 as a daily through route from Tunbridge Wells to Woking. Route H1, as H, had been re-routed via Elstree Village in September 1934 to restore a service to the village which had been lost when the routes had been diverted to serve the British International Film Studios at Borehamwood. Pressure for the restoration of the half-hourly service to Borehamwood was now so strong that the H1 was restored to the route through Borehamwood and Barnet By-Pass. It was also diverted at its southern extremity to serve Lingfield, from which it had been removed in April 1934. A service for Elstree village was maintained by diverting half the service on route T between Brockley Hill and Apex Corner to run via Elstree and Stirling Corner, instead of direct via Watford By-Pass. This became T2 and the original route T1.

The K group was also substantially recast and its total level of service reduced with the withdrawal of the AK. The Hitchin to Baldock section of the AK was covered by an extension of the K1, which was also diverted to follow the AK route along the main road between Welwyn and New Hatfield. A shortworking spur continued to operate to Welwyn Garden City but to Longcroft Green rather than the 'Cherry Tree', which was served instead by a new K2. South of New Hatfield the K2 followed the old line of the AK down the Barnet By-Pass to South Mimms and Barnet but instead of continuing to Archway and Kings Cross, it followed the K1 to Victoria. At this point, it picked up the stage carriage section of the Fairways Coaches Kings Cross to Worthing coach route, whose goodwill had been purchased by the Board in October 1935, and ran to Horsham via Chelsea Embankment, Walham Green, Putney, Kingston, Surbiton, Leatherhead and Dorking. The southern end of the K1 was unchanged and it continued to terminate at Dorking.

The K group of Green Line routes was restructured on 6th January 1936 and route K was redesignated K1. T 358c, which is outside the 'Two Brewers' Hadley Highstone, came to London Transport from its original owner Aston of Watford, via LGCS. D W K Jones

The 345, which was extended to Leavesden on 18th March 1936 was renumbered 346A when running via Bushey Arches on 2nd December. Bluebird ST 1077 is on the renumbered route under the mock-Tudor of Watford High Street a short time later. D W K Jones

New housing on the outskirts of Watford and expansion in Hemel Hempstead stimulated another revision of local services from 18th March 1936. In Watford the local services provided by the longer country routes were transferred to re-arranged local routes and there were some extensions and diversions to serve new areas. The various country routes which ran on to Leavesden were curtailed in the town, at Leavesden Road garage, and the routes which entered the town via the north Watford housing estates were re-routed to run more directly, finishing at a new terminus opposite the Palace Theatre in Clarendon Road. They were replaced by the extension and augmentation of local routes. The Leggatts Way routes (306 and 311) were both extended to Chilcott Road on higher frequencies, the joint twenty minute headway being enhanced to $7^{1}/_{2}$ minutes, while Leavesden and Kingswood were served by extensions from Harebreaks respectively of the 345 and 346, which were also withdrawn at their other end between Oxhey Hall Farm and Hamper Mill. In the latter case, not only was the joint service increased from every twenty to every ten minutes but extra capacity was also provided by the substitution of double-deckers for single-deckers.

The 315 was separated into two operations: a double-deck service between Garston ('Three Horseshoes') and Watford Met station; and a single-deck route between Watford High Street and Chipperfield ('Two Brewers') via Abbots Langley, from which it was extended to cover the withdrawal of route 318. Route 325 was recast as the 315A with a similar combination of double-deck and single-deck operation. The single-deck route continued to run between Hemel Hempstead and Watford High Street but was diverted to run via Garston, instead of the By-Pass and Harebreaks. The double-decker between Garston and Croxley Met station was actually part of the 315 diverted at Whippendell Road to run via Rickmansworth Road. Between them, the 315 and 315A gave a joint ten minute service over the common section and the 315A an additional three buses an hour between Watford and Croxley Green.

When the Watford services were being examined, London Transport included a review of the railway service between Watford and Rickmansworth, which was something of a poor relation in the Underground network, partly because the terminus was so remote from the centre of Watford. The efforts of the Metropolitan Railway and later London Transport to stimulate demand by improving bus connections had failed to produce the desired results and one of the choices considered by the Board was its closure and replacement by an augmented bus service. More interestingly, Frank Pick thought it worthwhile to consider converting the line into a high speed tramway, with additional halts to stimulate local travel. Neither happened but that was not because the performance of the line suddenly improved, as its financial problems continued to cause the Board and its successors a headache.

The last of the major 'schemes' covered Amersham and High Wycombe and operated from 13th May. As the area had been served fairly extensively by Amersham & District and Thames Valley, the changes were less far-reaching than in other areas and were mainly confined to minor exchanges of routeings, diversions to serve Amersham station and timetable co-ordination. The routes of the Penn Bus Company had been taken over, together with its interesting fleet of Dennis and Gilford buses, on 31st July 1935 but again its routes were fairly self-contained and required little change. Of particular interest was the joint operation of the local High Wycombe route 326 with Thames Valley, giving London Transport access to the western side of the town, just the kind of operation which could have saved many other through services had the operators been so minded. Bus fares were applied to Green Line route B to cover the final withdrawal of bus route 369 (Windsor – Great Missenden), which had lost its Aylesbury end in the Windsor scheme. Among the many minor variations was the curtailment of route 336 at Chesham, which meant that lowbridge STs no longer regularly penetrated as far north as Berkhamsted.

Country Buses continued to adjust and refine its network over the years but for the most part the basic pattern had been established by the middle of 1936. The larger towns continued to grow and there were also the suburban areas of London still served by the department's buses, which often needed changes and improvements. The growth of Beddington had an interesting effect on the services in Croydon when cross-town operation started for the first time in September 1936. Routes 403 and 415 were extended to Wallington in an arrangement whereby the vehicles actually worked through to Guildford on route 408, changing their route numbers as required on the journey. This arrangement was soon seen to be rather foolish and, from 3rd March 1937, the 403 was formally extended to Leatherhead (Woodbridge) and the 408 to Farleigh, absorbing the 415.

The driver of Dennis 4-ton PH1106 looks as though he has had enough of its charms for the day as he rests between journeys on route 359 at Chesham Broadway. The only change to the 359 in the Amersham scheme was its diversion via Copperkins Lane. D W K Jones

The Penn Bus Co. was taken over on 31st July 1935 and with it came this brand new Dennis bodied Lancet, which became DT 9B.
R S Turnbull collection

A new garage opened on 30th June 1936 at Addlestone, on the south side of Station Road, replacing the premises in Ham Moor Lane Weybridge, which had been rented from the bodybuilders Hoyal since 1932. The Weybridge premises themselves had been enlarged in 1934 to take over the operations of Woking garage when it closed. Addlestone was another garage which inexplicably took its code, WY, from the name of a nearby larger town (Weybridge), although there was no obvious reason why it could not have been AN, AS or even AT.

Another major garage project was completed in the autumn of 1936, with the opening of the new premises at St Albans. The imposing structure in St Peters Street, which included a bus station with elegant concrete Holden designed shelters, was not easy to obtain. St Albans council were not too keen on having a bus garage in such a central position in the town and there were protracted negotiations. The attractive gardens which eventually graced the main road frontage no doubt owed their origin to the deal which was eventually struck. The new garage had room for seventy buses and coaches and took over the work of Harpenden and the former St Albans & District yard, both of which closed. Another project completed during the year was the enlargement of Staines, which enabled it to take on more bus workings in the area. There was also progress on the enlargement of Windsor and it was able to take over the work of the former Premier Line garage in Bath Road, Slough (SU), which closed on 16th December 1936. The consequential new garage runs on routes O and P operated with short stage fares over bus route 443.

The splendid new garage and bus station in St Peters Street, St Albans which opened in 1936, where handsome Holden designed shelters and elegant information displays stand ready to serve the Hertfordshire people. L T Museum U21748/21750

The few changes to the Green Line which the Traffic Commissioner had approved, following the marathon application from London Transport described earlier, went into operation on 2nd May 1937. Route G was extended from Horse Guards Avenue to Windsor via Slough and simultaneously diverted via Purley Way, between Purley and Thornton Heath Pond, to serve Croydon Airport. Route O was extended from Trafalgar Square to Great Bookham via Kennington, Clapham, Morden and Leatherhead, replacing the southern end of route L. The Uxbridge service on L was covered by additional 'shorts' on route R from Oxford Circus. The terminus for route P was moved from Trafalgar Square to Horse Guards Avenue. After this there were only relatively minor changes to the Green Line up to the outbreak of war.

Work on the enlargement of Windsor was finished during the early summer of 1937 and this enabled the other Slough garage (Langley Road – SL) to close at the end of traffic on 3rd August 1937. Langley Road, which had been the LGOC base in the town until the local services were handed over to LGCS in March 1933, had been re-opened by the Board on 1st January 1934 to house vehicles taken over from local Independents. All its remaining operations were transferred to Windsor the following day, coinciding with a further revision of the local services in Slough. This saw the disappearance of routes 463 and 444 and their replacement by two new circular routes 446 and 446A between Farnham Road ('George') and Slough station via Buckingham Avenue and Manor Park respectively, giving improved links and higher frequencies for the cost of one ST. There were also substantial improvements to route 457, mainly connected with the increasing importance of Pinewood Film Studios to which a new route 457B was introduced. Other areas which got new or improved services were Upton Lea (new 457A) and Datchet (revised 473). Altogether, three double-deckers and one single-decker were added to the schedule.

Apart from its local bus and coach operations, the Country Bus department was also the provider of many special services for events of varying size and duration. These were nearly always given route numbers, which often clashed with existing routes, although they were usually in the 'wrong' series which reduced the risk of confusion. For example, for the one day Chevening Park Fête on 29th May 1935, a thirty minute service was operated by twenty-seaters on a route numbered 305 from Tubs Hill Station. The Langley Pageant, which took place at the same time of year, was a much longer affair, lasting from 27th May until 8th June with a couple of preliminary days on 20th and 25th May. For this Country Buses ran a special route 302, using two twenty-seaters, between Langley (The Harrow) and Langley Park station. Routes 457 and 458 were also both augmented to a fifteen minute headway between Uxbridge and Slough or Windsor. The Kings Walden Flower Show was a popular annual event in August, for which Country Buses laid on an hourly single-deck service from Luton (Park Square) to Great Offley ('Green Man'), numbered 326, as well as augmenting the 383 to a fifteen minute headway between Luton and Kings Walden. Such operations, large and small, were repeated all over the area through the year, year by year.

One of the biggest events for which Country Buses supplied transport was the Ascot races, served by Green Line route A1. In the early days of the Board, up to fifty vehicles were employed to give a service at five to ten minute intervals between Horse Guards Avenue and the race course car park on days when race meetings were held. As time wore on, traffic built up and the service became inadequate, so London Transport prepared plans to increase the operation for the 1938 season. The Southern Railway was not happy about the extent to which this increase was caused by traffic switching from rail because of the fare advantage enjoyed by the coaches. On Green Line there was a standard return fare of 3s 6d, whereas the rail fare was 6s 6d before 10.15am and 8s 0d afterwards. The whole matter was therefore reviewed jointly and the Board agreed not to increase the service from central London until after 10.15am but to introduce additional coaches before that time, starting at Hammersmith where they would not be in direct competition. This did not work out too well because passengers still presented themselves for the cheaper ride and many found themselves waiting in long queues for long periods. Another idea was therefore canvassed for 1939 which would have established a Green Line terminal at a west London Underground station, possibly Turnham Green, with through ticketing from the Underground network. This was considered to be an unsatisfactory compromise with no guarantee that passengers would respond in the desired way. The normal pattern was therefore repeated but with a more frequent service from Horse Guards Avenue.

The garage building programme was completed, at least for the time being, with the opening of the last entirely new structure on 7th July 1937. Although known from the start as Northfleet (NF) it was sited just outside Gravesend, on the south side of London Road in Rosherville. It had the distinction of being the first Country Area garage to have a staff canteen, a feature which was to be extended throughout the fleet in subsequent years. Northfleet, which could accommodate eighty-five buses and coaches, replaced the old Gravesend and District tram depôt in Dover Road East, which London Transport had acquired along with the local bus services of Maidstone & District in July 1933. There had also been improvements and enlargements to other garages, notably at Windsor (already mentioned), Chelsham, High Wycombe, Leatherhead and Swanley.

Above **Green Line route L disappeared in the restructuring of 2nd May 1937 when route O was extended to Great Bookham in its place. T 213C, one of the second batch of Green Line Regals, is at Eccleston Bridge, which had become the main London staging point with the 'Amulree' changes in October 1933.** D W K Jones

Plans were laid for other new garages to be built between 1937 and 1940 at Brentwood, of which more later, and at Garston, to replace the two Watfords. Land was also acquired in Hatfield for a new garage to replace the tiny ex-National premises and for others at Hitchin, Horsham and Westerham.

Plans for three more garages were put in hand during the spring of 1939, to provide accommodation for the extra buses which it was confidently expected would be needed to serve new developments in the western country area. Approval was given on 3rd May for three sites to be bought, each of two acres, at Rickmansworth, Denham and Gerrards Cross. The massive expansion which justified such an enlargement of garage capacity was presumably related to the planned extension of the Central Line to Denham but this was curtailed at West Ruislip as part of the economy drive in 1939. Post-war planning regulations prevented significant development in the areas concerned and none of these three garages was ever built. The Garston and Hatfield projects did eventually materialise in the post-war building programme.

The Board did not make improvements only for its own operational benefit; it also embarked on a big programme of investment in passenger amenities. Waiting rooms and Enquiry Offices were established, or improved, in all important town centres and handsome new shelters were placed at major stops. Frank Pick was particularly keen to improve the amenities for Green Line passengers, in the hope that increased revenue might result. Shelters were provided at all important picking up points and at all outer terminals where no satisfactory alternative existed. The principle espoused was that the shelters should be the equivalent of railway stations and should be designed to display timetables, traffic notices and any other relevant information. This principle was developed by 1938 to the stage where a kind of miniature bus station was envisaged, with illuminated stop signs, facilities for the issue of certain tickets and, in some cases, a control office linked to a synchronised clock on public display. This was yet another grand scheme of Frank Pick's to be hit on the head by the Second World War.

Provision of its own privately owned bus standing accommodation also became the policy of the Board and Frank Pick issued instructions that any new garages should be designed so that stands could be built over the top, if necessary. One of the fruits of this policy was the new bus station at Bligh's Meadow in Sevenoaks, a town where standing space for buses was at a premium. Pick had hoped that Maidstone & District and West Kent would pay their share of running the place but appears to have compromised his negotiating position by authorising its construction before any agreement had been made and the upshot was that London Transport had to bear most of the costs. The new station opened on 4th March 1936 and all terminating services used it from that date. Routes from the direction of Riverhead and River Hill were diverted away from their traditional route through Tubs Hill to run via St Botolphs Road and High Street but through buses and coaches were not diverted to pass through Bligh's Meadow until 24th June, from which date it became the main picking up point in the centre of the town.

Three examples of shelters installed for Green Line and Country Bus traffic: at Kennington Gate in Brixton Road, where one of the early style 'blank' bullseye stop signs can be seen; at Bromley Common, alongside one of the domed style of combined bus and coach stop; and a curious whirligig near Essendon, which looks as though it could give no protection from the rain. L T Museum

Above left **LS 1 was found a new rôle as a temporary waiting room in Blighs Meadow, Sevenoaks until the permanent structure was ready. It does not seem very busy on 3rd April 1937.** D W K Jones

Above **The handsome and commodious new passenger facilities at Blighs Meadow are either being ignored by passengers or are not yet open. The Holdenesque building contained a waiting room, enquiry office, refreshment room and toilets as well as an office for supervisors. A new 10T10 Regal coach, T 498, has called in on its way to Tunbridge Wells and, rather surprisingly, has the parking area to itself.** L T Museum U30440

Waiting Rooms were opened in most town centres, usually in shop premises like the mock Tudor confection in rural looking surroundings at Croxley. The more prosaic example was in Fore Street Hertford and was later replaced by a modern purpose built structure in the bus station. The bullseye and flagpole device standing proud of the building line was a good example of London Transport's flair for making its presence known. L T Museum

The coach station at Tunbridge Wells: first as inherited from Autocar, with a Green Line 7T7 almost overpowered by the huge signs advertising the 3s 10d return fare to London; and after London Transport had built a waiting room and enquiry office, tidied up the boundary and supplied lighting to the site. L T Museum

The original Aldgate lay-by as inherited from the LGOC was on this narrow strip of land alongside the District Line junction. Green Line coaches started to use it in 1933 when the 'Amulree' restructuring took place, and the petrol pump which is visible at the point where the road narrows was provided for daytime refuelling of coaches. Three 7T7s are on the stand and Central Buses have parked a couple of STLs and a TD while the crews take their meal reliefs and the work which can be seen in progress is the early stages of extending the stand over the railway in readiness for trolleybuses. L T Museum U23425

Several attempts were made to put double-deckers onto the Romford coach routes but it took a war to make it happen. T 122 is at Romford Market Place on 3rd October 1936, soon after the fleet of Gilfords inherited from Hillman had been replaced. D W K Jones

The transfer of routes between Central and Country Buses continued from time to time. On 24th March 1937, the New Barnet to Enfield part of route 306 was replaced by Central Bus route 107. Later in the year, on 6th October, the outer ends of routes 214, 217 and 219 were covered by the extension of route 461 from Walton to Hersham and from Chertsey to Staines and by a Saturday only circular route 437A between Woking and Old Woking. The Weybridge town service (475) was withdrawn and covered by new route 219A and the diversion of the other routes to the station. Fuller information about all these changes can be found in chapter five.

Three routes which the Trade Union probably thought ought to be transferred to Central Buses were the Green Line routes to Gidea Park, Brentwood and Corbets Tey and this belief was to prove a stumbling block in the attempts of the Country Bus department to replace the single-deckers by double-deckers. Consideration of this had begun at the end of 1936 when it was calculated that substantial economies could be obtained by replacing the ninety-two single-deckers by sixty-two double-deckers. The scheme was approved by Frank Pick who issued instructions for work to proceed on making Romford (London Road) garage suitable for double-decks and, most interestingly, the preparation of plans for the modification of seventy double-deck LTs to make them suitable for coach operation, presumably as a short-term measure pending the development of a purpose-built vehicle. Although Central Bus rates of pay were offered to the staff, the retention of Green Line scheduling conditions was unacceptable and the scheme eventually foundered on this rock. The development of the double-deck coach had gone ahead, but the vehicle which materialised (Q 188) was doomed by the failed negotiations never to run as a coach.

One of the other elements of the Romford proposals was the plan to build a new garage at Brentwood for seventy vehicles, which would have worked part of the Y1 and might well have been intended to absorb some of the Central Bus operations in the area. There were certainly plans to extend route 339 to Harold Wood in place of the 247, but they never came to pass. Had the garage been built, the remaining operations at Romford (RE) would have been transferred into the Central Bus garage (RD), which was more conveniently sited to operate route Y2, and Central Buses would have taken over the garage in London Road. No plans were made to house route X, as it was the intention to withdraw it when the Central Line extension along Eastern Avenue opened. Before work on Brentwood was too advanced, a site was found for a garage in Straight Road Gidea Park, by Gallows Corner and this became the favoured project for Country Buses. Planning consent was sought for the Straight Road site but in the end nothing came of any of these changes, because of the decision not to go ahead with double-decking the Y1 and Y2, and the whole project was finally abandoned.

Although the main thrust of its acquisition policy had now been satisfied, London Transport continued to buy businesses on the fringe of its area as opportunity arose and if it was likely to be to the Board's financial advantage. On 21st August 1936, it had acquired from City the Coxtie Green to Warley route formerly worked by F.H. Fuller together with two Reos and a Chevrolet which were immediately withdrawn. Unfortunately, Brentwood was another town blighted by the presence of the LPTB boundary and the Board was disqualified under section 15 of its Act from running over the section of Fuller's route to Woodman Road. This had to be withdrawn, creating an understandably outraged reaction from the local residents and was not replaced until City finally found it possible to do so on 18th April 1938. At about this time an attempt was made to rationalise operations on the Ongar road by purchasing Ongar & District and, in conjunction with Eastern National, the business of C. Simpson and Sons. Whether or not any approach was made to Ongar & District, the company continued in business until 1945 when it was sold to City. The purchase of Simpsons was not completed until 1940 and for the time being London Transport had to be content with arranging co-ordinated timetabling.

Early in 1937 a purchase was made through the good offices of the Eastern National Omnibus Co, which brought route 356A (Luton – Flamstead) into London Transport's hands. This had been operated by a local company, Union Jack (Luton) who had been looking for a buyer in the summer of 1936. The possibility that Birch Bros might be interested alarmed the Board as it would bring a stronger company into direct competition with its own routes 356 and 376. All the might of the area agreement partners was brought to bear through an agreement with Eastern National under which they were to buy Union Jack and then sell the rights to the Flamstead route on to London Transport. Luton garage started running Ts on the newly designated 356A from 15th February 1937.

T 382B at Park Square Luton on route 356A which was taken over from Union Jack on 15th February 1937. D W K Jones

T 379 on route 380, which was withdrawn from Enfield and replaced by a more frequent 310, in changes made on 16th October 1938 in connection with the replacement of the Waltham Cross trams by trolleybuses and the curtailment of route 69 away from Wormley. Behind the Regal, in Cecil Road, is an ST on route 107 which was extended to Ponders End in the same scheme and alongside that is the top of one of the new trolleybuses on route 629. D A Ruddom collection

East Surrey had scorned the possibility of taking over West Kent when the opportunity arose earlier in the decade and the LPTB was also slow to acquire the company. It finally came into the Board's hands on 3rd October 1939 but most of its buses were immediately withdrawn, including this eleven year old Thornycroft A2. D W K Jones

Another acquisition which fell foul of Section 15 was the purchase of Blue Saloon of Guildford in 1938. By agreement with the Board, it was Aldershot & District who made the purchase and then handed over the two routes from Guildford to Ripley and Woking which were mainly in the London Transport area. They became the 415 and 438 but in the case of the latter, there was a section via Woodhill and Sandhurst Grange which went more than the statutory half mile beyond the Board's limits. The route was therefore diverted via Send Road, without apparently causing too much grief. Although its fleet included some quite recent Dennis Aces and a Lancet, the time had now passed when the Board needed to hang on to such non-standard vehicles and these were sold, together with the Guys and a Star Flyer, without being operated. Both routes were allocated TR-type Tigers.

One of the last major events with which Country Buses was involved before the war was the Royal Agricultural Society's Centenary Royal Show in Windsor Great Park between 4th and 8th July 1939. Although tantalisingly close to the LPTB's operating area, the Great Park was actually forbidden territory unless an agreement could be secured under Section 18(1)(c) of the 1933 Act. By some extraordinary quirk of the licensing procedure, the South Eastern Traffic Commissioners had granted White Bus Services licences for an unlimited number of journeys between Windsor and the show ground, although the company had only one twenty-seater available. On the initiative of the Commissioner, a tripartite agreement was made between Whites, the Board and the Thames Valley Traction Company under which White was paid £25 as consideration for the two larger undertakings working most of the service. White was to operate one twenty-seater an hour and the others were to supply equal proportions of the remainder, which varied from twelve to twenty buses an hour. The Commissioner also encouraged the Board to operate a wide range of excursions to the show from all points on the compass, as far flung as Tring, St Albans, Hertford, Sevenoaks, Reigate and Dorking, as well as from suburban centres such as Enfield and Pinner.

Three more Independents were acquired in 1939. On 1st March, the route between Northchurch, Hemel Hempstead and Apsley operated by H. Aston under the Berkhamsted & District banner, was purchased and became route 332. The two Bedfords and two Dennis Lancets which came with the company were immediately withdrawn and replaced by two Ts worked from Two Waters garage. The last purchase involving vehicles in this period was the West Kent Motor Services Ltd, the option of acquiring which had been held open by London Transport ever since first granting temporary consent to its services in the LPTB area. The purchase was not completed until 4th October 1939, after the outbreak of hostilities although approval to the purchase had been granted by the Board a year earlier. The twelve month delay was imposed by the Board itself as it wished to have time to sort out what was to happen to the services operated by West Kent outside the boundary. The most controversial idea was to seek powers in its next private Bill to operate services outside its area but adjacent to the boundary. Perhaps they had learnt a lesson from the unpopularity of previous route withdrawals and curtailments but if so, they were not to avoid opprobrium in this case because the route between Bat & Ball and Edenbridge went over the boundary and had to be withdrawn beyond Ide Hill. The routes to Godden Green, Seal and Fawke Common, all outside the Board's area, were transferred to Maidstone & District, who were also given consent to continue to operate the six journeys a day from Seal to Tubs Hill Station. Unlike other recent takeovers, two of West Kent's vehicles, Dennis 30 cwts, were given numbers, D 202B and 203B and operated by London Transport for a time because the route between Otford and Kemsing was restricted to fourteen seaters. The Board's application to have the restriction lifted was soon successful and both were off the road by the end of the year.

On the same day as the West Kent takeover, the service operated between Welwyn and Hitchin by North Star Omnibus and Coach Services Ltd was acquired. During the negotiations, the Board had decided that the route should be withdrawn and covered by a few extra afternoon journeys on route 303 and the introduction of 1d fares on Green Line route K1 between Welwyn and Hitchin. Unfortunately, by the time the takeover took place the war had started, the K1 had gone and the 303 was itself inadequate, so the whole lot was replaced by the extension of shortworking 303s from Welwyn Garden City to Hitchin.

The declaration of war between Britain and Germany on 3rd September 1939 had an enormous impact on Country Buses. Green Line coach services were withdrawn abruptly on 1st September and the coaches requisitioned by the Government for use as ambulances. Where there was no comparable bus route London Transport put on a temporary replacement bus service but over the greater part of the system, the service was just lost. The new conditions also brought an immediate influx of people into the Country Bus area. Many firms moved out of London, and Home Counties hospitals received patients evacuated from London and the additional nursing and ancillary staff to go with them. Children, pregnant women and mothers of very young children were also evacuated. Country Buses were involved directly in the movement of the evacuees and were required to supply between 272 and 307 buses a day between 1st and 3rd September.

To meet all these extra requirements, starting on 1st September Central Buses lent up to 373 buses to the Country department, the maximum being reached on 7th September. The vehicles concerned introduced some novel visitors to Country Buses: forty-seven oil and thirteen petrol LTs; thirty-two STs; 262 STLs (including ten with petrol engines); thirteen STDs; and six of the Private Hire TFs. This was gradually reduced, dropping to 214 by 1st October and 194, all STLs, by the end of the year. The LTs, STs and STDs were delicensed on 30th September and stored at various Country Bus garages until being relicensed for Central Bus service: on 1st November in the case of the LTs and STDs; but not until November or December 1940 for the STs.

The private hire TFs were an interesting phenomenon because, being coaches, one might have expected them to be requisitioned as ambulances. Instead they had their glass cant panels painted over so that they could be used as service buses. All twelve were on loan to Country Buses for a time but all were returned on 29th November and then delicensed. Before they went back, consideration was given to removing the paint from the roof panels, fitting their saloon lights with special shields so that no light escaped through the glass panels and using them once again as Private Hire vehicles. A new contract with Heinemann for two coaches between London and Kingswood was one possible use for them but there really was no need for sightseeing coaches for such work and it was decided instead to use two standard coaches released from ambulance duty. The fatal decision was then taken to put them into store at Bull Yard Peckham, where all but TF 9 perished in a bombing incident on 22nd October 1940. TF 9 survived because, just three weeks earlier, it and TF 1 had been relicensed for the small amount of Private Hire work still permitted.

Although the number of borrowed buses was reduced, the Country Bus schedules were expanding in this period to meet the new demand and some routes were allocated larger vehicles. The number of double-deckers increased by almost a third in the six months after the start of the war and, although not part of this review, it is worth noting that the number of buses on loan was to start rising again in 1940 and was at one stage to go over the 400 mark.

Apart from the coach replacement services, the sort of thing for which they were needed was the increased service put onto route 341, which was also converted to double-deck, on 19th December, to cope with the extra traffic to and from de Havilland's aircraft works at Hatfield. Other examples were the need to augment route 410 to cope with the extra movement of Air Force personnel to and from Biggin Hill aerodrome, the new route 423A which started on 29th November to cater for the expansion of activities at Joyce Green Hospital and the four new works services which were introduced on 11th December to serve the Vickers Works at Weybridge. Other routes which got larger vehicles were the 332 (which became double-deck 301C on 4th October), the 339, whose Cubs were replaced by STLs on 13th December, the 431 which went from Cub to T on 4th October and the 499 which was withdrawn between Horton Kirby and Farningham, on which section there was a low bridge, so that its Ts could be replaced by STLs.

More help came in November with the re-instatement of some coach services. The loss of the very busy and important East End Green Line routes had led to considerable hardship and London Transport was allowed to re-instate the Y1, Z1 and Z2, except for the section between Grays and Tilbury, from 1st November, using STLs. In the case of route Y1, they were the front-entrance STL6s, which might well have appeared on the route when they were new had things gone right for the Board. Routes Z1 and Z2 were allocated the almost new 15STL16s. Shortly afterwards the Government released 164 vehicles, all 10T10s, from ambulance duty but this appears to have embarrassed the Board as they had staff for only thirty coaches. Twenty-one of them were used to re-instate the Y2 on 13th December but the rest were redeployed to Country Bus garages to release borrowed Central Buses and no further coach re-instatements took place until January 1940.

As with Central Buses, there were other plans which either disappeared for all time or had to wait until after the war. In May, Frank Pick approved a proposal from Country Buses for a new route 310B between Cheshunt (Old Pond) and Enfield, to ease inadequacy during peak hours and on Saturday afternoons. It would have broken new ground for Country Buses south of Waltham Cross by using the route through Bullsmoor Lane and Great Cambridge Road, an interesting development as local operation on this road had hitherto been reserved for Central Buses. A parallel proposal from Central Buses to extend route 144A from 'Halfway House' to Waltham Cross on Sundays was not approved and the 310B was to have operated daily instead. This route was eventually adopted by the 310 in 1942, to replace the Green Line.

There was also a plan to run a direct service from Halton Camp to Tring, by extending Green Line coach route B from Wendover every two hours, with 1d fares between Halton Camp and Tring. There had been a request for such a service which had encouraged Eastern National to apply for a licence to run it. This appears to have provoked the Board to produce its own proposal and to ask Eastern National to withdraw theirs. Eastern National route 105 started on 20th December 1939 and no London Transport service ever operated over these roads.

The events of the autumn of 1939 were to prove a watershed in the affairs of the Country Bus department. As in so many fields of human activity it marked the end of one phase of existence and the start of something entirely different, rather as the upheavals of new legislation had marked a similar turning point at the start of the decade.

At the end of 1939 T 286, like all other buses, has been prepared for blackout operation. The STL in the background is running on the Green Line replacement service 403D to Tunbridge Wells.
J F Parke

EPILOGUE

A stranger visiting London for the first time in 1939 could have been forgiven for thinking that London Transport had always been there, so firmly had the LPTB stamped its personality on the capital's transport system. Not that this was peculiar to London, as the workings of the 1930 Road Traffic Act had ensured that similar transformations had occurred outside London too. Despite its stormy beginnings, the Board had established a reputation for efficiency and good business management which had won most of its critics round to its support and it was also greatly respected internationally. Lord Ashfield was held in the highest esteem and the affection which he inspired was demonstrated on 12th June 1939 when journalists treated him to a celebration lunch in thanksgiving for his recovery from a serious illness.

Despite outward appearances, the Board had much still to do to achieve full co-ordination, particularly between road and rail, and it was preparing to move into a new phase when the war diverted attention to more immediate matters. In March 1939, T.E. Thomas, the former LCC Tramways Manager, was appointed as General Manager (Operations) to oversee all the Board's operational activities, both road and rail. He had already been the Road Transport General Manager since February 1936 and had done much to help knock together the disparate organisations inherited by the Undertaking. Had his new rôle been given more time, perhaps true co-ordination between road and rail might have come into being.

London Transport was also poised to do something about the unsatisfactory situation caused by its awkwardly designed boundary. There was a clause in its 1939 Bill which sought to extend the Board's powers to 'adjacent areas', the declared purpose being to avoid the kind of disruptive change which had deprived some people of bus services simply because part of a route went beyond the statutory area. The clause was withdrawn following a petition from the Thames Valley Traction Company and others, but had there been no war, it is unlikely that the Board would have allowed the matter to rest. There is evidence to support this in only partially successful efforts made by London Transport in the late 1940s to have the boundary extended. One possible course would have been some combined approach with the 'Area Agreement' companies to allow joint operating agreements in certain areas, or even the exchange of territory.

For over half its existence the Board and its managers were pre-occupied with the possibility of war. Preparations for war started early in 1937 with the formation of an Air Raid Precautions Committee which had the responsibility for ensuring that, in the event of war, staff would be as safe at work as they were at home. All new projects were designed with air raid protection in mind and a programme was undertaken to provide shelters and gas-proof accommodation. Associated with this was an instruction from Frank Pick that accommodation at new garages, works and depôts should be arranged so that provision could be made for women in time of war.

In the operational field, preparations had to be made for the blackout which would be imposed as a precaution against air attack, for the mass evacuation of the population of London and for any special jobs which the Government might require London Transport to do. One special job of great importance was the preparation of all Green Line coaches for use as ambulances, initially for the evacuation of hospital patients from the capital and later for the expected massive casualties from bombardment. The equipment for this was acquired and kept ready at garages. Blackout preparations included the purchase of the equipment necessary to shield headlamps for operation in the blackout and each vehicle was supplied with masks and fittings, which were kept in the driver's cab ready for installation.

Practice Air Raids were carried out as early as November 1937 to test the effectiveness of blackout, the one in the Grays area on 4/5th November being a good example of the sort of test which was to become a regular feature over the next two years. London Transport was asked to shield all vehicle lights between 12 midnight and 2am and the staff at Grays, Northfleet and Gravesend garages were instructed to switch off all lights not essential for safe operation. Needless to say these early efforts were far from perfect but, over the next two years as lessons were learnt, the tests gradually became more sophisticated and by the time the real thing descended on Britain on 1st September 1939 a comprehensive and efficient plan was ready.

The Second World War brutally and prematurely closed an important chapter in London's transport history. The changes wrought since 1930 had been dramatic and far-reaching but history was to show that the six years since the formation of the London Passenger Transport Board were not just its golden age, as seen by later generations, but the only period during which the aims of Herbert Morrison and his supporters could be said to have been put into practice successfully.

APPENDIX ONE **ANNUAL SUMMARY OF VEHICLES OWNED 1933-1939**

FLEET OWNED ON 31st DECEMBER 1939 (Many vehicles, including all TDs, were delicensed and in store.)

DOUBLE DECK

TD	2, 3, 5-12, 17-20, 22, 24, 25, 27-29, 32, 34, 37, 38, 43, 45-47, 50, 52-55, 57, 59, 61, 63, 65, 66, 69, 79-82, 89, 91, 94, 96, 98, 103-108, 112-130, 133-151, 154-166, 170, 171, 173, 192-195.
LT (DD)	1-999, 1137, 1204-1426
ST	1-1050, 1052-1139. (ST169 – training chassis at Chiswick.)
STL	1-130, 153-2647.
STD	1-100
Q (DD)	2-5, 188.
RT	1

SINGLE-DECK

BD	1, 3, 7-10, 15, 17, 20, 21, 23.
DA	1-22, 25-28, 30-44.
T	1-24, 26-34, 36, 37, 39-51, 56, 61, 66, 76, 85, 94, 101, 108, 109, 111, 113, 114, 116, 118, 120, 121, 124, 132, 136, 145, 156, 159*, 160, 163-165, 167, 169, 171, 172, 174-176, 178*, 180-182, 184, 199, 203, 206-209, 211-219, 223, 226, 229-237, 239, 240, 244, 248-253, 255, 261-67, 270-277, 281, 283, 285, 286, 288, 290-293, 295-298, 300, 302, 305, 306*, 307-318, 346-357, 359, 361, 362, 364, 369, 375-377, 382-385, 391, 392, 396, 403-718, 1000-1002.
LT (SD)	1001-1050, 1052-1136, 1138-1201, 1427-1429.
C	1-98, 106-113.
Q (SD)	1, 6-187, 189-238.
LTC	1-24.
TF	1-88
CR	1-46
D	202, 203; KO9092, EKP140, BKO508, CKL719, KO7272, KP2558 – all ex-West Kent, delicensed.

* Chassis only

The following table shows the number of vehicles of each type owned by the London Passenger Transport Board and allocated to Central Buses, which were licensed for service on 1st July 1933 and on 1st January each year from 1934 to 1936. As no comparable records exist for Country Buses and Coaches before 1936, it is not possible to show the whole fleet. *(SOURCE: Chiswick Works stock books.)*

CLASS	1.7.33	1.1.34	1.1.35	1.1.36
S(SD)	23	26	13	16
NS (open-top)	136	69	—	—
NS (covered)	1676	1675	1411	1184
NS (clerestory)	25	25	25	25
LS(DD)	11	11	11	11
LS(SD)	1	1	1	—
O (DD)	—	4	—	—
DH	—	18	—	—
DL	—	27	33	33
DA	40	41	43	44
DS	4	4	3	3
DE	—	5	10	10
DM	—	—	2	4
L (DD)	—	6	—	—
TDp (DD)	—	71	111	112
TDo (DD)	—	—	9	9
TC	—	—	3	3
LN(SD)	—	3	7	7

CLASS	1.7.33	1.1.34	1.1.35	1.1.36
LT(DD)p	1120	1045	782	781
LT(DD)o	106	181	444	442
LT(SD)	199	199	199	199
GF(SD)	—	—	—	3
ST	787	1014	1007	1007
DST	3	5	4	—
STLp	75	260	573	572
STLo	—	—	76	376
STF	—	—	—	1
Q(DD)	—	—	2	2
Q(SD)	1	1	—	—
T(Bus)	48	60	60	60
BN	2	2	2	2
Guy(DD)	—	1	—	—
Guy(SD)	—	5	5	5
C	—	—	1	1
TOTALS	4257	4759	4837	4912

The following table shows the number of vehicles of each type owned by the London Passenger Transport Board, which were licensed for service on 30th June in each year from 1936 to 1939. *(SOURCE: Railway Gazette.)*

	30th June 1936			30th June 1937			30th June 1938			30th June 1939		
	Central	Country	Green Line	Central	Country	Green Line	Central	Country	Green Line	Central	Country	Green Line
NS (covered)	1007*	—	—	366	—	—	—	—	—	—	—	—
NS (clerestory)	25	—	—	—	—	—	—	—	—	—	—	—
LS(DD)	11	—	—	—	—	—	—	—	—	—	—	—
TDp (DD)	112	52	—	112	25	—	111	20	—	35	14	—
TDo (DD)	9	—	—	9	—	—	9	—	—	—	—	—
TC	3	—	—	3	—	—	—	—	—	—	—	—
LT(DD)p	781	1	—	769	1	—	757	1	—	353	1	—
LT(DD)o	445	—	—	455	—	—	467	—	—	869	—	—
ST	1009	128	—	1011	126	—	1011	126	—	1011	126	—
STLp	571	—	—	572	—	—	574	—	—	424	—	—
STLo	720	101	—	1344	151	—	1760	151	—	1983	169	—
STF	1	—	—	1	—	—	—	—	—	—	—	—
STD	—	—	—	93	—	—	100	—	—	100	—	—
Q(DD)	2	2	—	—	4	—	—	5†	—	—	5†	—
DL	33	—	—	33	—	—	—	—	—	—	—	—
GF	—	53	87	—	1	14	—	—	—	—	—	—
MS	—	8	2	—	8	2	—	—	—	—	—	—
BD	—	19	—	—	19	—	—	8	—	—	8	—
R	—	39	6	—	39	6	—	33	—	—	—	—
DA	44	—	—	44	—	—	37	—	—	32	—	—
DC	—	1	—	—	3	—	—	—	—	—	—	—
DT	—	4	5	—	4	5	—	—	—	—	—	—
TDp (SD)	—	2	19	—	2	19	—	2	—	—	—	—
TRp	—	3	37	—	3	37	5‡	3	—	—	—	—
LT(SD)	199	2	1	199	2	1	191**	2	—	192	—	—
Q(SD)	53	101†	—	53	103†	77	53	103†	77	57	125†	51
Tp	60	27	293	60	39	281	58***	39	208	54	24	—
To	—	—	12	—	—	53	—	1	160	5	57	287
LTC	—	—	—	—	—	—	24‡	—	—	24‡	—	—
C	23	74	—	31§	75†	—	31§	74†	—	31§	74†	—
CR	—	—	—	—	—	—	—	1	—	—	1	—
TF	—	—	—	—	—	—	—	—	1	12‡	—	58
Misc (p)	—	9	6	—	6	6	—	—	—	—	—	—
TOTALS	5108	626	468	5155	611	501	5188	569	446	5182	604	396

* Includes 38 solid tyred.
† Includes one petrol engined.
‡ Private Hire coaches.
§ Includes 8 Inter Station (petrol engined).
** Includes 1 coach (LT 1429).
*** Includes 8 Private Hire coaches.
o Oil engined.
p Petrol engined.

APPENDIX TWO

LONDON PASSENGER TRANSPORT BOARD FLEET ON VESTING DAY 1st JULY 1933

BUSES & COACHES

London Transport adopted the fleet numbering system of the Combine companies from whom most of the buses and coaches were acquired but London General Country Services Ltd had not used fleet numbers and the Country Bus department continued this practice until responsibility for the fleet was transferred to Chiswick in 1935. Country Bus and Coach vehicles are therefore identified either by the numbers which they took in 1935 or, if they did not survive that long, by their registration numbers. Green Line had a separate numbering system which seems to have been applied somewhat haphazardly and in some cases duplicated numbers either already used by the LGOC or later allocated by London Transport. To simplify presentation, some vehicles which were withdrawn before 1935 are identified by these numbers, which are noted as such in the list. Because of this lack of official records, the information for the Country Bus and Coach fleet has been compiled from various sources and, although it is as accurate as possible, it does not have the authority of the Central Bus data which is fully confirmed by official sources.

The list is divided between double-deck and single-deck vehicles and under these headings the various types are grouped by chassis manufacturer and arranged in approximate chronological order of the oldest vehicle of each chassis make.

DOUBLE-DECK BUSES (All ex-LGOC and allocated to Central Buses unless otherwise stated.)

K class: AEC 301,302,303,304 or 305 chassis: Chiswick, Brush or Short Bros. OT44 or 46RO bodywork.
25, 194, 424, 632, 700, 719, 746, 825, 888, 897, 924, 931, 949, 969, 1121 (all delicensed).

S class: AEC 403 chassis: Short Bros OT54RO bodywork
PC9317-9322 *(ex-LGCS – allocated to Country Buses & Coaches.)*

PS class: AEC 502 chassis (PF9018 AEC 509): Ransomes Sims & Jefferies OT48RO bodywork.
PD1355, 1358, 1359, 1363, 1368; PE8309, 8310, 9754-9756, PF9018 *(ex-LGCS – allocated to Country Buses & Coaches.)*

NS class: AEC 409 chassis (NS 1-2296, 2379-2411), ADC422 chassis (NS 2297-2349, 2372-2378); mixture of solid and pneumatic tyres: mostly Chiswick bodywork but some batches by Brush, Ransomes Sims & Jefferies and Short Bros, variously 50/52 seat open-top or 52 seat covered top;
NS 1590, 2050, 2179, 2204, 2210, 2212-2214, 2216-2218, 2220-2228 and 2232-2239 were 46 seaters fitted with 'clerestory' roofs for Blackwall Tunnel operation.
1-9, 11-15, 18-22, 24-39, 41-45, 47-57, 60-64, 66-71, 73-81, 84-88, 90, 91, 93, 95-100, 103, 105-107, 109-133, 135-137, 139-142, 144-150, 153, 154, 156-159, 161-176, 178-180, 182-195, 197-207, 209, 211-218, 220-228, 230-236, 238, 239, 241-247, 249-279, 281-303, 305-330, 332, 334-351, 353-432, 434-441, 443-457, 459-468, 470-476, 478-501, 503-524, 526-560, 562-583, 585-604, 606-635, 637-639, 641-654, 657-675, 677-680, 683-704, 706-722, 724-727, 729-734, 736-742, 745-761, 763, 764, 766-776, 778-780, 782, 784-797, 799-802, 806-809, 811-814, 816, 818-823, 825, 827-830, 832-837, 839-846, 849-851, 853, 855-857, 859-862, 864, 865, 867-869, 872, 874, 876-880, 882-894, 896-898, 900, 901, 903-906, 908, 909, 911-926, 929-931, 933-936, 939, 940, 944, 946-949, 951, 954-956, 958-969, 973-976, 978-984, 986-996, 998, 1000-1002, 1004-1007, 1009-1011, 1013-1015, 1017, 1018, 1021, 1022, 1024, 1026-1029, 1031-1036, 1038, 1040-1062, 1064-1068, 1070-1072, 1076, 1078-1096, 1098-1102, 1104, 1106-1115, 1117, 1119-1130, 1132-1134, 1136, 1137, 1139, 1141, 1142, 1144-1162, 1164-1167, 1169, 1171, 1173-1175, 1177-1202, 1204-1206, 1208, 1210-1221, 1223-1253, 1255-1258, 1260-1281, 1283-1341, 1343-1405, 1407-1583, 1585-1610, 1612-1616, 1620, 1621, 1623-1627, 1629-1639, 1641, 1643, 1645-1734, 1736, 1737, 1739-1842, 1844-1876, 1878-1904, 1907-1925, 1927-1975, 1977-1988, 1990-1992, 1994-2004, 2006-2050, 2054-2070, 2072-2242, 2245-2250, 2252-2349, 2372-2411.
(NS 228, 230, 1024, 1028, 1033, 1036, 1038, 1047, 1053, 1072, 1093, 1094, 1100, 1104, 1149, 1162, 1382, 1425, 1432, 1494, 1495, 1500, 1606-1608, 1610, 1612, 1613, 1616, 1651, 1653, 1660, 1662, 1681, 1682, 1684, 1695, 1696, 1703, 1705, 1706, 1711, 1739, 1740-1743, 1747, 1750, 1752, 1753, 1756, 1757, 1758, 1761, 1764, 2284, 2285, 2378 *ex-LGCS: allocated to Country Buses;*
NS2379-2411 *ex-Tilling and British Automobile Traction (British) – allocated to Central Buses.)*

LS 1-5, 7-12: ADC 802 chassis: Chiswick H60RO bodywork (originally 64/66 or 70 seats).

PK4244: Tilling Stevens B10A2 chassis: Short Bros OT46RO bodywork *(ex-LGCS – allocated to Country Buses & Coaches.)*

D 146-148: Dennis H chassis: Chiswick OT50RO bodywork (later DH1-3) *(ex-Overground – allocated to Central Buses; not formally taken into stock until 7th July.)*

R 44: ADC 416 chassis; Chiswick OT46RO bodywork *(ex-LGCS – allocated to Country Buses & Coaches.)*

TD 133-142, 154-165: Leyland Titan TD1 chassis: Short Bros H51/48R bodywork *(ex-Maidstone & District – allocated to Country Buses & Coaches.)*

TD 143-151: Leyland Titan TD1 chassis: Short Bros OT48/51RO bodywork *(ex-Maidstone & District – allocated to Country Buses & Coaches.)*

TD 152-153: Leyland Titan TD1 chassis: Short Bros L48R *(ex-Maidstone & District – allocated to Country Buses & Coaches.)*

TD 166-173: Leyland Titan TD1 chassis: bodywork by Leyland H48R (166), L51RO (167-169), L48R (172), H51R (173) or Dodson H50/48R *(ex-Maidstone & District (166), Thames Valley (168,169) or LGCS – allocated to Country Buses & Coaches.)*

LT 1-999, 1204-1426: AEC Renown 663 chassis: Chiswick, Park Royal, Short Bros or Strachan bodywork: H54RO (LT1)/H60RO (LT2-150)/H56R (nominally LT151-740, 742-949); remainder H60R 'Bluebird' type.

LT 1000, 1051, 1202, 1203: LGOC CC chassis; Chiswick H54R bodywork.

LT 1137: AEC Renown 664 chassis; Chiswick CH50F bodywork *(ex-Green Line Coaches Ltd.)*

ST 1-836: AEC Regent 661 chassis: Chiswick, Short Bros or Strachan H48 or 49R bodywork, or (marked †) Short Bros. L48R.
(STs 107, 111, 116, 129, 132, 135, 136†, 140†, 141†, 143, 152, 157†, 159, 162†, 163†, 818-821, 833, 834, ex-LGCS – allocated to Country Buses & Coaches.)
(STs 3, 4, 6, 14, 16, 36, 343, 357, 378, 393, 397, 412, 417, 431, 447, 456, 467, 468, 510, 515, 525, 529, 531, 544, 546, 825, 826 ex-Overground – allocated to Central Buses; not formally taken into stock until 7th July.)
ST169 was a chassis housed in the Training School at Chiswick Works.

ST 1032-50, 52-88,1091-1132: AEC Regent 661 chassis: H48 or 49R bodywork by Chiswick, Ransomes Sims and Jefferies or Short Bros [STs1032-1039/1070-1084 'Bluebird' type] *(ex-LGCS – allocated to Country Buses & Coaches.)*

ST 1139: AEC Regent 661: Short Bros H51RO bodywork *(ex-LGCS – allocated to Country Buses & Coaches.)*

DL 1-25: Dennis Lance chassis: Metro-Cammell H49R bodywork *(ex-Overground – allocated to Central Buses; not formally taken into stock until 7th July.)*

DST 1-3: Daimler CH6 chassis: Chiswick H49R bodywork.

STL 1-50, 153-160, 162-177, 183: AEC Regent 661 chassis; Chiswick H60R bodywork.

SINGLE-DECK BUSES & COACHES (All allocated to Country Buses & Coaches unless otherwise stated.)

S-class: AEC 403 chassis; Chiswick or Short Bros B30R bodywork.
327, 369, 371, 377, 379, 382, 384, 386, 391, 408, 409. 417, 423-425, 433, 439, 442, 447, 458, 472, 512, 516, 524, 531, 776, 780, 822, 833, 835, 836, 841, 842, 858, 861, 866, 872, 873, 878, 881, 887, 889, 890, 892 *(ex-LGOC: allocated to Central Buses.)*
YH1101-1113. (S915-927) *(ex-LGCS)*

GD2091: W and G chassis: 26 seat bodywork§ *(ex-Watford Omnibus Co)*

DR3734, HM8507, FG4697: ADC416 chassis: Metcalfe B32R/Hall Lewis B30D/Cowieson B30R *(ex-Watford Omnibus Co)*

AD 1-53 plus 30 unnumbered: ADC416A chassis: Short Bros B29R bodywork (AD 31-35); Chiswick B30R the rest *(ex-LGCS.)*

AD 54-55: AEC 427 chassis: Chiswick B18F bodywork *(ex-LGCS.)*

PR 1 (UC2261): ADC423 chassis: Short Bros 26 seat parlour coach bodywork.

AW 9-41, PH1204-1209: AEC 419 chassis: Short Bros C28R bodywork *(ex-Green Line Coaches Ltd)*

PH8881-8883: AEC426 chassis: Short Bros(?) B30R bodywork *(ex-LGCS.)*

LS 6: ADC802 chassis: Chiswick B34R bodywork *(ex-LGOC allocated to Central Buses.)*

PE6984, 8642: Daimler CM36 chassis: B26D bodywork§ *(ex-LGCS.)*

PH1106: Dennis 4-ton chassis: Strachan B25R bodywork *(ex LGCS.)*

DS 7, 15, 34, 35: Dennis 2½-ton chassis: bodywork by Dodson B25/26R (DS 7,15), Strachan & Brown B26R (DS 34) and Dodson B20R (DS35) *(ex-LGOC: allocated to Central Buses.)*

RO7267, 7649, UR314: Dennis E chassis: B32R bodywork§ *(ex-LGCS.)*

GF6680: Dennis EV chassis: Birch C32R *(ex-Green Line Coaches Ltd D 2.)*

RO9211, 9807: Dennis F chassis B26? bodywork§ *(ex-LGCS.)*

DL 36-39: Dennis Arrow chassis: Birch C32R (36)/C28F (37)/ Thurgood C30F *(ex-Green Line Coaches Ltd D 1, 3-5.)*

DA 1-42: Dennis Dart chassis: Chiswick B18F bodywork (DA 41, 42 B17F) *(ex-LGOC: allocated to Central Buses.)*

RO6648, UR228: Albion PN26 chassis: 26 seat bodywork§ *(ex-LGCS.)*

UR3580: Albion PM28 chassis: London Lorries B32R bodywork *(ex-LGCS.)*

YW3350,3351, UU4820: Maudslay ML3/ML3B chassis: Buckingham/Vickers B32R bodywork *(ex-LGCS.)*

*M 1,3,4: Maudslay ML3B chassis: Dodson C24D *(ex-Bucks Expresses allocated to Green Line.)*

*M 2,5: Maudslay ML3 chassis: Strachan C32D bodywork *(ex-Green Line Coaches Ltd M 4, 5.)*

KM3864, 3866, KO127, 131: TSM B9A chassis: Short B31R/C31? bodywork *(ex-Maidstone & District (KM3864,3866) and Green Line.)*

KP3003, 3034: TSM B10A chassis: Short C31R/Harrington C29R bodywork *(ex-Maidstone & District)*

PG9381: TSM B10A2 chassis: Petty B32R bodywork (ex-LGCS.)

PG9385: AJS Pilot chassis: Petty B26F bodywork *(ex-LGCS.)*

G 1, 3-6: Guy OND chassis; bodywork by Duple B20F *(ex-LGOC: allocated to Central Buses.)*

G 7-8: Guy ONDF chassis; United B20F bodywork *(ex-LGOC: allocated to Central Buses.)*

UK6253, UV9120: Guy ONDF; B20F bodywork§ *(ex-LGCS.)*

UC2267-2272: Guy BA chassis: Chiswick B20F bodywork *(ex-LGCS.)*

RO4574,5301: Guy BB/FB chassis: 26 seat bodywork§ *(ex-Watford Omnibus Co)*

YH1936, 6819: Guy FBB chassis: Vickers/Hall Lewis B32R bodywork (ex-LGCS.)

*G 1-2: Guy FBB chassis: Buckingham C32D bodywork *(ex-Green Line Coaches Ltd)*

BN 1-3: Bean chassis: Birch B14F bodywork *(ex-LGOC: allocated to Central Buses)*

RF5806, GJ5077: Bean chassis: Willowbrook B20F/B14F bodywork *(ex-LGCS.)*

OT7822: Thornycroft LB chassis: B29F bodywork§ *(ex-LGCS.)*

VB4550, PG1099, 2018, 3236, 4226: Thornycroft A2L chassis: Wilton/ Challands Ross B20F bodywork *(ex-LGCS.)*

PG1757, 1758: Thornycroft BC chassis: Challands Ross FC32F bodywork *(ex-LGCS.)*

UV4086-4088: Thornycroft BC: Vickers C22R (UV4068/4087)/C32R (UV4088) bodywork *(ex-Green Line Coaches Ltd TH 1-3.)*

GM 1-2: GMC T30 chassis: C20F/B20F bodywork *(GM1 ex-LGCS; GM2 ex-Green Line Coaches Ltd)*

UR3273: Chevrolet LQ: B14F bodywork§ *(ex-LGCS.)*

*L 1-3: Leyland Lion PLSC3 chassis; C26/32R bodywork§ *(ex-Associated Coaches, Ongar.)*

CH7299, 7900, 7902, 7904, 7911, 7912, 7914: Leyland Lion PLSC3 chassis: LMS (Derby) B32F (7935 B32R; 7299 Leyland B32F bodywork) *(ex-LGCS.)*

CH7935: Albion PM28 chassis, LMS (Derby) B32F bodywork *(ex-LGCS)*

HM8661, VW5140: Leyland Lion PLSC3 chassis: Dodson B32R bodywork *(ex-Watford Omnibus Co.)*

TR 6, 11-17: Leyland Tiger TS2 chassis: Short Bros C31C bodywork *(ex-Maidstone & District.)*

TR 8-10: Leyland Tiger TS1(TR 9,10)/TS4 (TR 8): Thurgood C32? bodywork (TR 8 London Lorries C32?) *(ex-Green Line Coaches Ltd L 4-6)*

†GF 1-14, 29-30: Gilford 166SD chassis Duple C26D bodywork (1-14), Wycombe C26F (29-30) *(ex-Skylark Motor Coach Co (1-14), Associated Coaches, Ongar (29-30)*

†GF 15-19, 50: Gilford 168SD chassis: Duple C26D/C26F/Wycombe C28D bodywork *(ex-Skylark Motor Coach Co (15-18), Regent Motor Services (19) and Cream Line Coaches (50).)*

†GF 20-25, 33-40: Gilford 1660T chassis: Duple C30/32F (GF20/22), C28D (GF23), Wilton C28D (GF21) or Wycombe C26/29F (GF24, 25, 33-35) *(ex-Regent Motor Services (20-23), Bucks Expresses (24,25), Associated Coaches, Ongar (33-35) and Acme Pullman Services (36-40)*

†GF 26-28, 41-49, 51: Gilford 1680T chassis: bodywork by London Lorries C26F (26-28)/Petty C31F (41-49)/Duple C26F (51) (ex-Bucks Expresses (26-28), Acme Pullman Services (41-49) or Cream Line Coaches (51)

†GF 31-32: Gilford CP6 chassis: Duple C20F bodywork *(ex-Associated Coaches, Ongar.)*

GF 156-158, KP1487: Gilford 1660T chassis: Wycombe B26F bodywork *(ex-Maidstone & District.)*

GF 159-160: Gilford 1680T chassis: Strachan C26F bodywork *(ex-Maidstone & District.)*

KR6744: Gilford AS6 chassis: Strachan C20F bodywork *(ex-Maidstone & District.)*

R 1-34. 45-49: AEC Reliance 660 chassis: Chiswick C28D (1-5), C31D (6-25), C28D (26-34), B29R (45-49) *(ex-LGCS.)*

T 1-267, 269-306, 319-324, 346-358, 369, 371-402: AEC Regal 662: bodywork as follows:
T 1-37, 39-50, 156: Chiswick B29R (T 27 B30F) (programme of conversion to B30F in progress). *(Ts 1-14, 16-20, 22-24, 27-34, 36, 37, 39-50, 156 ex-LGOC: allocated to Central Buses.)*

T 38, 51-68, 70, 72-88, 90-95, 97-103, 105-149, 155, 157-206: Chiswick, Hall Lewis or Short Bros C27R *(ex-Green Line Coaches Ltd)*

T 150-154: Hoyal C32R *(Private Hire coaches ex-Green Line Coaches Ltd)*

T 207-267, 269-306: Duple, Ransomes Sims and Jefferies or Weymann C30F. *(ex-Green Line Coaches Ltd)*

T 319-324, 346-358, 391-402#: Hall Lewis/Park Royal, London Lorries, Strachan C29/30/31R or C29/30F *(ex-Green Line Coaches Ltd, except T 352-357 ex-Queen Line, Baldock; T 358 ex-Aston, Watford.)*

T 369, 371-390: Hall Lewis/Park Royal B30R, Short Bros B32R, Weymann B30R *(ex-LGCS, except T 369, 371 ex-Watford Omnibus Co)*

T 1000-1002: LGOC CB chassis: Chiswick B29F bodywork *(ex-LGOC: allocated to Central Buses.)*

LT 1001-1050, 1052-1136, 1138-1201, 1427, 1428: AEC Renown 664 chassis: Chiswick B35F bodywork *(LT 1427, 1428 ex-LGCS; remainder ex-LGOC and allocated to Central Buses.)*

GN4790-4795: Commer Invader chassis: Weymann B18F bodywork *(ex-LGCS.)*

MS 2, 4-11: Morris YB6 chassis: Holbrook B20? (MS 2)/Weymann B20F (MS 4-9)/Harrington C20F bodywork (MS 10/11). *(ex-LGCS except MS 10,11 ex-Green Line Coaches Ltd)*

UU5009: Morris R chassis: Buckingham B14F bodywork *(ex-LGCS.)*

Q 1: AEC 'Q' 761 chassis: Chiswick B37C bodywork *(ex-LGOC: allocated to Central Buses.)*

* Green Line numbering.

† In view of the complexities of the renumberings which took place in this class, the original Green Line fleet numbers are given for these.

‡ T 391-402 were still numbered 307-318 on 1.7.33.

§ Bodywork manufacturer unknown.

TRAMS

The following list shows all tramcars whose ownership was transferred to London Transport on 1st July 1933. The Board based its numbering on the LCC system and, except in the case of former LCC vehicles, the fleet numbers shown were not carried on the cars until sometime later. Some cars never did carry their allocated numbers and many of the older cars were never operated by London Transport and did not receive their allocated numbers either. Some of these had already been withdrawn before the Board took control. All cars listed are bogie cars (eight wheelers) unless otherwise stated. Many cars had started life with other concerns and the original owner is shown in the 'Date New' column

FLEET NOs.	LPTB CLASS	TRUCKS	BODYWORK	SEATS	DATE NEW	FORMER OWNER
1C-16C		Peckham P22 4-wheel	ER&TC	52	1903-1904	Bexley
17C-33C		Brill 21E 4-wheel	ER&TC	60	1903 (LCC B class)	Bexley
1D-6D/9D		Mountain & Gibson 21EM 4-wheel	Brush	52	1905	Erith
7D/8D/10D-14D		Mountain & Gibson 21EM 4-wheel	Brush	52	1905 (later rebuilt)	Erith
15D-18D		Brill 22E	Milnes (170 BEC)	74	1902 (LUT)	Erith
19D		Mountain & Gibson	Milnes	76	1901 (Hull)	Erith
1S-16S	J	Brush 4-wheel	Brush	55	1906	South Met
17S-26S	K	Milnes 4-wheel	Milnes	55	1902 (CCT)	South Met
27S-29S/31S/35S	L	Brush BB	Brush	69	1902 (CCT)	South Met
30S/32S-34S	O	Brill 22E	ER&TC	68	1902 (Gravesend & N'fleet)	South Met
36S-51S	M	Brush 21E 4-wheel	Brush	50	1906	South Met
1	Exptl	EMB	LCC	66	1932	LCC
5-27		Peckham 4-wheel	Brush	64	1920-1930	Ilford
28-30/32		Brush 4-wheel	Brush	54	1909	Ilford
31		Brush 4-wheel	Brush	54	1912 (Barking)	Ilford
33-40		Peckham 4-wheel	Brush	68	1932	Ilford
41-44		Ilford 4-wheel	Hurst Nelson (Brush tops)	57	1903 (later rebuilt)	Ilford
45-64‡		Brill 21E 4-wheel	Dick Kerr	56	1901-1903	East Ham
65-69‡		Brill 21E 4-wheel	UEC	56	1910	East Ham
70		Peckham R7A 4-wheel	Brush	54	1911 (Barking)	East Ham
71-80		Brush 21E 4-wheel	Brush	58	1921-1922	East Ham
81-100	EH	Brush	Brush	71	1927-1928	East Ham
101-159	HR2	EMB	Hurst Nelson	74	1931	LCC
160	E3	EMB	Hurst Nelson	74	1931	LCC
161-210	E3	EMB	English Electric	74	1931	Leyton
211-258		Brush 4-wheel	Milnes	56	1904 (rebuilt 1922-3)	West Ham
259-267		Mountain & Gibson 4-wheel	Brush	60	1905	West Ham
268-273		Peckham 4-wheel (EMB exptl on two, inc 268)	West Ham	60	1923-1924	West Ham
274-281		Mountain & Gibson 4-wheel	Milnes-Voss	58	1906 (later rebuilt)	West Ham
282-288		Mountain & Gibson 4-wheel	Milnes-Voss	62	1906 (later rebuilt)	West Ham
289-294		Peckham R7 4-wheel	UEC	54	1910 (later rebuilt)	West Ham
295	WH	Hurst Nelson	West Ham	69	1931	West Ham
296-312	WH	Hurst Nelson	Brush (302: West Ham)	69	1929-1930	West Ham
313-324		Hurst Nelson	Hurst Nelson	73	1911 (rebuilt 1922-3)	West Ham
325-330		Hurst Nelson	English Electric	78	1925	West Ham
331-333		Hurst Nelson	West Ham	69	1925	West Ham
334-343		Hurst Nelson	Brush	69	1926	West Ham
344		Hurst Nelson	West Ham	69	1928	West Ham
345-349‡	W1	Brush 21E 4-wheel	Brush	54	1911	Croydon
(350-364)§	W1	Brush 21E 4-wheel	Brush	54	1906-1907	Croydon
365-374	B2	Brill 22E	G.F. Milnes	69	1902	Croydon
375-399	E1	Hurst Nelson	Hurst Nelson	69	1927-1928	Croydon
402-551	E	Mountain & Gibson	Hurst Nelson	76	1906	LCC
552-601	E1	Mountain & Gibson	English Electric	74	1930	LCC
602-751	E	Mountain & Gibson	Hurst Nelson	76	1907	LCC
752-1001	E1	Mountain & Gibson	Hurst Nelson	76	1907	LCC
1001-1051	E1	Hurst Nelson	LCC	78	1907-1908	LCC
1052-1226	E1	Hurst Nelson	Hurst Nelson	78	1908-1909	LCC
1227-1369/ 1371-1426	E1	Heenon & Froude	Hurst Nelson	78	1910	LCC
1427-1476*	M	Hurst Nelson 4-wheel	Hurst Nelson	62	1910	LCC
1477-1676	E1	Heenon & Froude	Brush	78	1911-1912	LCC
1677-1726	M	Heenon & Froude 4-wheel	Brush	62	1912	LCC
1727-1851	E1	Hurst Nelson	H.N (1777-1851: Brush)	78	1922	LCC
1852-1853	HR1/HR2	Hurst Nelson	LCC	74	1929	LCC
1854-1903	HR2	EMB	English Electric	74	1930	LCC
1904-2003	E3	EMB	Hurst Nelson	74	1930	LCC
2004-24/31-41		Brush 4-wheel (2040/1:Peckham)	Brush	52	1905	Walthamstow
2025-2030		Hurst Nelson (Brill 21E pattern) 4-wheel	Hurst Nelson	54	1910	Walthamstow
2042-2053	K	Hurst Nelson	Hurst Nelson	69	1927	Walthamstow
2054-2061	K	Brush	Brush	69	1932	Walthamstow
(2062-2065)†		Brill 27G	ERTCW	38;s/d	1901 (Rotherham, ex Oldham)	Walthamstow

FLEET NOs.	LPTB CLASS	TRUCKS	BODYWORK	SEATS	DATE NEW	FORMER OWNER
2066-2165	UCC	EMB (2165:Eng.Elec.)	UCC	64	1930/1931	2066-2119 MET 2120-2165 LUT
2166-2168	UCC exptl	MV/Brush/UCC	UCC	64/62/70	1929/1930	MET
2169-2173	H	Mountain & Gibson	Brush	74	1909	MET
2174-2254	H	Brush (M&G)	Brush	74	1910-12 (rebuilt 1929/30) (2248-53:1926)	MET
2255 'Bluebell'	Exptl	Brush (M&G)	MET	71	1927	MET
2256-2260	F	Mountain & Gibson	MET	74	1908	MET
2261	G	Brush (M&G)	MET	74	1902 (LUT; extensively rebuilt)	MET
2262-2281	G	Mountain & Gibson	MET	74	1909 (rebuilt 1929/30)	MET
2282-2301	C1	Mountain & Gibson	MET	74	1908 (rebuilt 1929/30)	MET
2302-2316	E	Brush 4-wheel	Brush	36 s/d	1905	MET
2317 'Poppy'	Exptl	Brush (M&G)	LGOC (Chiswick)	64	1927 (MET)	LUT
2318-2357	T	Brill 22E	UEC	74	1906	LUT
2358-2402	U	Brill 22E	Milnes (2364-67:BEC)	70	1902 (rebuilt 1910-11)	LUT
2403-2405	U2	Brill 22E	Milnes	70	1902-4 (rebuilt 1928)	LUT
2406-2410	WT	Brill 22E	Milnes	70	1902-4 (rebuilt 1928)	LUT
2411	XU	Brill 22E	Milnes (rebuilt LUT)	70	1902-4 (rebuilt 1928)	LUT
2412-2466	A	Brush BB	Brush	62/68	1904-5 (rebuilt 1928-30)	MET
2467-2482‡	B2	Brush BB	Brush	68/62	1904 (rebuilt 1914-15)	MET
2483-2497	C2	Brush BB	Brush	70	1906 (rebuilt 1912-6)	MET
2498-2521	B	Brush BB	Brush	68	1904	MET
2522-2529	W	Brill	Milnes	70	1902	LUT

* 1441, 1444, 1446 (renumbered 1370) were bogie cars classified ME3 (see text).
† These numbers were never carried.
§ These numbers were never used; the cars retained their Croydon numbers 6-20 with a suffix 'E'.
‡ Not all cars in this batch had the new numbers applied to them.

WORKS CARS

(i) Acquired from the LCC.

Number	Trucks	Function	Formerly
01-04	Mountain & Gibson	Railgrinders	class H
05-010	Brill 21E 4-wheel	Stores cars	class J (05-06)/K (07-010)
011-012	Peckham 4-wheel	Wheel carrying trucks	class L
013-014	Brill 21E 4-wheel	Railgrinders	class L/1
015	Brill 21E 4-wheel	Stores and sand carrier	class C
016-036	Brill 21E 4-wheel	Snowbrooms	class B
037-054	Brill 21E 4-wheel	Snowploughs	class C

(ii) Acquired from Metropolitan Electric Tramways
(NOTE: these were not renumbered by LT, hence some numbers conflict with those above)

Number	Trucks	Function	Formerly
02	Mountain & Gibson	Crane/wheel carrier	
04	Brill 21E 4-wheel	Railgrinder	D-type
05	Brill 21E 4-wheel	Sand carrier	Probably D-type
07	Mountain & Gibson 4-wheel	Breakdown van	S. Met (ex-Croydon Corp)
08	Brush BB	Stores van	B-type
013-014	Brill 21E 4-wheel	Breakdown vans	D-type

(iii) Acquired from LUT (Not renumbered by LT)

Number	Trucks	Function	Formerly
001/003	Brill 21E 4-wheel	Railgrinders	
005	Brill 21E	Crane/wheel carrier	
006	Brill 21E 4-wheel	Railgrinder	SMET (ex- Croydon Corp)
148	Brill 22E	Vacuum cleaner	X-type

(iv) Other acquisitions renumbered by LT

Number	Trucks	Function	Formerly
055	Mountain & Gibson 4-wheel	Railgrinder/Water car	West Ham 2A
056	Brill 21E 4-wheel	Mobile welding unit	Croydon (unnumbered)
057	Ilford 4-wheel	Railgrinder/snow plough	Ilford

(v) Other acquisitions not renumbered by LT

Number	Trucks	Function	Formerly
20D	Mountain & Gibson 4-wheel	Water car	Erith 20
63K	Brush AA 4-wheel	Railgrinder/water tank	Walthamstow 63
(1A)	Mountain & Gibson 4-wheel	Water car	West Ham 1A

TROLLEYBUSES

Fleet Numbers	Class	Chassis/Electrical Equipment	Body	Seats	Date New	Former Owner
1 – 35	A1	AEC663T-English Electric	UCC	H56R	1931	LUT
36 – 60	A2	AEC663T-B.T-H	UCC	H56R	1931	LUT
61	X1	AEC691T-English Electric	Chiswick	H74C	1933	LUT